*Learning To
Manage Our Futures*

LEARNING TO MANAGE OUR FUTURES

The Participative Redesign of Societies in Turbulent Transition

TREVOR A. WILLIAMS
The University of Western Australia

with an afterword by
FRED E. EMERY

A Wiley-Interscience Publication
JOHN WILEY & SONS
New York   Chichester   Brisbane   Toronto   Singapore

Library of Congress Cataloging in Publication Data

Williams, Trevor A. (Trevor Andrew), 1944-
  Learning to manage our futures.

  "A Wiley-Interscience publication."
  Bibliography: p.
  Includes index.
  1. Social prediction.   2. Social change.
3. Occidental studies. I. Title.
HM24.W543   303.4   81-16019
ISBN 0-471-08135-3   AACR2

Printed in the United States of America

10 9 8 7 6 5 4 3 2 1

To
Eric Trist, founder of a new social science generation,
Tom Alford, who made so much possible,
and
Sally Williams, for everything

Preface

Doubts about the future prospects of western societies—societies that have reached the end of the industrial era and are in a period of major historic transition—have become increasingly widespread since the 1960s. Existing institutions and organizations cannot cope with mounting change, complexity, and uncertainty in their environments. They are founded on bureaucratic hierarchical principles which assume much simpler and more stable environments than those that have evolved rapidly since the 1950s. If societies persist with the structures and strategies of bureaucratic industrialism, their transition to whatever lies beyond the industrial age will become more and more turbulent. The possibility of massive breakdown they face now will become a strong possibility and eventually a certainty.

At the same time, societies have the potential for creating alternative future prospects by developing new social designs and strategies which increase their ability to reduce uncertainty and pursue desirable directions. Already there is considerable knowledge of alternatives, not only in abstract theories but in practical demonstration. They have emerged most clearly in the basic redesign of work organization and, more recently, in innovations at the level of communities and regions. These initiatives are founded on the values and social principles of participative democracy. They enable the members of organizations, communities, and other social systems to play much more active and effective roles in determining the valued ends to be served by their efforts, the appropriate means for attempting to achieve such ends, and in managing the trends affecting their futures.

Despite the emergence of such alternatives, bureaucracy remains the dominant organizational pattern of western industrial societies. In work and community life, the great majority of people have little or no effective control over even those matters for decisions which immediately concern them. Decisions are made for them and they are directed and controlled in the implementation of those decisions. If the deciders in bureaucratic organizations possessed sufficient knowledge, skills, and motivation to make wise choices in the best interests of all, there might be less reason to worry, but clearly they do not. Societies will not be able to plan and administer their way out of present and emerging crises through established bureaucratic structures using only their existing stocks of "expert knowledge." Bureaucratic organization and planning assume that there is a large measure of agreement about the desired ends to be achieved, that the most efficient and effective means of achieving them are already known, and that people will be willing to cooperate in implementing decisions and plans they had no hand in making. The increasing challenge to these assumptions since the 1960s is central to the crises now confronting western industrial societies.

However, reactions against bureaucratic industrialism so far have done more to reveal its basic failings than to propose constructive alternatives. Societies' members may know that existing institutions and organizations are getting them more deeply into trouble about their futures, but the majority of people remain dependent on and seemingly unable or unwilling to change them. This is not surprising given that, beginning with long exposure to bureaucratic education and subsequently to bureaucratized work and government, bureaucracy is virtually the only form of social design they know. It is understandable that, in such circumstances, many will pin their last hopes on the capacity of industrial systems to survive or on intellectual and scientific elites to chart new courses. Their hopes have little if any prospect of being realized. It is far more likely that the means of reducing uncertainty about the future, and pursuing paths that are adaptive for human survival and development, lie with societies' members themselves determining and acting upon the directions which *they* desire in cooperation with each other.

There is an apparent paradox in western societies which, if left unresolved, could have fatal consequences. How can ordinary people act upon uncertain societal trends and pursue desirable directions while the dominant bureaucratic institutions and organizations render them powerless to understand and influence the forces that shape their lives? The answer is that they can acquire the necessary understanding and use this to exert greater control over their affairs, through their own shared learning about their changing social environments and the possibilities for pursuing desirable futures in those environments. Because bureaucratic social designs prevent learning and active adaptation, it is necessary to create the conditions in which people can discover through their collaborative inquiry how to meet the challenges of their times.

This book is about designing for active adaptive learning so that societies' institutions and organizations can be redesigned by those who participate in them. Chapter 1 develops the central theme of learning and active adaptation in turbulent environments. Chapter 2 examines the implications of turbulent transition for education and, based on experience with democratizing students' learning, explores the prospects for educational designs which enable them to prepare for continuing learning and participation in the transformation of their society. Chapters 3 to 5 draw upon experience with work organizations to examine how they can be democratized into vehicles for active human adaptation through the learning of their members. Chapter 6 takes up the issue that the changing forces affecting societies' futures cannot be managed solely by organizations acting independently, yet the bureaucratic governmental systems of industrial societies are inadequate. New social designs must be developed to make possible participative collaborative planning among stakeholders in the futures of larger social systems, and experiences with searching for such designs in communities and regions are reported as a basis for exploring these larger possibilities.

The experiences were gained through sustained collaboration with organizations, communities, and educational institutes over the past decade, working in Australia, Britain, the United States, and Canada. They are reported, evaluated, and generalized with as much objectivity as I could manage, giving due weight to the obstacles and limitations as well as the hopes for human futures which they raise. In sharing the experiences with you, my intention is to go beyond existing knowledge of societies' predicaments and requirements for overcoming them. That knowledge is already abundant. The de-bureaucratization and democratization of societies in all sectors is vital to their future prospects, but a viable democratic society must also be a learning society, not one in which the knowledge and authority necessary for making future choices is presumed to be possessed by only a few. I have been persuaded by the experiences reported here that such knowledge resides also in children, housewives, factory and office workers—in people in their ordinary worlds. This is the greatest uptapped resource for securing our futures, and mobilizing it in the service of shared human desires is a major task of our age. My own relationship with these people has not been one of researcher to subject or expert to client, but one of collaboration between people who can be co-architects of their futures. Ultimately, only your own experience in similar endeavors can provide you with the necessary evidence for or against the proposition that people can and must make their futures and those of their societies. Nevertheless, this attempt to share my experiences with you may be of some help and encouragement.

My learning experiences could not have commenced or been sustained without the help and guidance of many others. The experiences started with the inspiration and intellectual leadership of Fred Emery. My regard for him as a mentor and friend is expressed by asking him to provide reflective commentary in the Afterword. Whatever has been achieved through the endeavors reported in this work, it would have been much less without Merrelyn Emery's guidance and support. She is a true colleague as well as friend. At a time when her own contributions are being undervalued, she is still prepared to assist others in their work. Eric Trist visited the University of Western Australia in 1976 and, characteristically, took a deep personal interest in local efforts to influence future directions. His pioneering work for more than forty years has done an enormous amount to reveal the possibilities for democratizing work and community life and stimulate others to explore them. Russell Ackoff and Eric Trist collaborated to create a highly productive appointment in the Social Systems Sciences Department of the Wharton School, University of Pennsylvania, during 1978 and 1979 which provided ample opportunity to build on my prior work in the different conditions of North America. Tom Alford made possible much of the work on which Chapters 3 to 5 is based, and we accomplished that work together. Without Glenn Watkins of the University of Western Australia, much of the collaboration with schools and communities could not have been attempted, and the continuing association with him is greatly valued. Early in 1978, Steve Burgess introduced me to the Craigmillar Festival Society in Edinburgh and took me beyond images of desirable future communities to see what one looked like in practice. During that period, Professor Norman Hunt at the University of Edinburgh and Professor David Weir at the University of Glasgow provided essential support in the form of teaching appointments. In the United States, many people helped me. Cal Pava read earlier drafts and his comments led to several important revisions. Bill and Donna Jo Henderson confirmed my belief in the prospects for a ''barefoot social science.'' Tom Gilmore was a valuable colleague, as were others who know who they are. My late father-in-law, Ken Black, knew well the stress of industrial-age managerial work, which killed him. With the shock of his premature death the attempt to humanize organizations took on deeper personal significance. Professors Roy Lorens and Andre Morkel at the University of Western Australia provided encouragement throughout. Beulah Trist made much of the learning journey logistically possible. As so often before, Jean Turnbull took on the task of typing the manuscript with her customary standard of excellence. The role played by Sally Williams is summed up, as much as it can be, in the dedication of this work. I hope that my mother, whose courage led our family out of postwar despair, is content with how I have used the opportunity she gave me.

TREVOR A. WILLIAMS

Nedlands, Western Australia
December 1981

Contents

Change, Learning, and Active Adaptation

The change that is occurring within and around western societies and the mounting uncertainty about their future signify that the industrial age has reached its limits. These societies are in a transitional phase leading to a new, and as yet unknown, major stage in their evolution. In the history of western civilization, transitions from one era to the next have been marked by breaks with accepted social values, by challenges to established knowledge and intellectual frameworks, and by reactions against dominant institutional and organizational structures. Such transitions are brought on by crises that arise from the workings of the existing society but that cannot be contained or resolved by that society. The emergence of each crisis comes as a surprise that cannot readily be understood and that throws into question established assumptions, values, and beliefs. The new knowledge and understanding necessary for responding to novel events and situations is not well developed, or it departs radically from familiar ways of looking at the world. Existing institutions and organizations are not designed to cope with the changes that engulf them.

These transitional periods can also present new opportunities by revealing alternatives to established structures and strategies that offer better prospects for responding adaptively to change and actively pursuing desirable future directions. As Ackoff (1974) puts it:

> Like Rome most earlier societies that rose subsequently fell, at least part way. . . . Survival—let alone "thrival"—of a society is not assured by any historical law. If anything, history seems to indicate that the fall of an elevated society is inevitable. But the future is not completely contained in the past; much of it has yet to be written. (p.3)

Successful adaptation by western industrial societies to the emerging trends that threaten them depends, first, on better understanding of the forces that give rise to these trends. Second, it requires critical assessment of the existing institutional and organizational arrangements through which societies attempt to regulate their affairs, and identification of the basic reasons why they are no longer working effectively. Third, management of uncertain transition entails active, continuous searching for alternatives that offer more promising future prospects and for ways of transforming societies in the direction of these alternatives.

The purpose of this chapter is to provide an overview of (1) the forces and trends affecting western societies' future prospects, (2) the dominant structures and strategies through which those societies are attempting to cope with change, and the maladaptive consequences of persisting with them, and (3) the emergence of potentially adaptive alternatives. However, although abstract rational analysis of the problems confronting societies and practical demonstration of alternatives can inform the human imagination and guide future choices, they are not enough. Established institutions and organizations are highly resistant to fundamental innovation even when their survival depends on it. Transforming societies' institutions and organizations requires that those who participate in the societies acquire, through their own active and continuous learning, the necessary understanding and commitment. Therefore, the fourth and ultimate concern of this chapter is with the kind of learning that produces active and adaptive responses that will enable societies to manage uncertain historic transition.

THE LIMITS OF INDUSTRIALISM AND TURBULENT TRANSITION

In western societies the industrial age has been approaching its limits since the late nineteenth century. The buildup to full industrialism is the result of several interwoven forces. Technological revolutions in energy, transport, and communications have greatly increased the range, number, and complexity of interactions within and between societies. These revolutions have stimulated the growth of large powerful corporations, which emerged in response to the breakthroughs in energy that made mass production possible and the developments in transport and communications that created the mass markets necessary for realizing the economies of large-scale production. Corporations grew also to meet the problems of coordinating and controlling large concentrations of human and material resources.

The problem of coordination was made all the greater by the effects the new industrial technologies had on the work performed by employees. Mass production depended on increasing division of labor and on standardization of parts and processes, with the consequence that finished products were produced by large numbers of people assigned exclusively to separate but interrelated tasks. The historian Samuel Hays (1957) has described succinctly the emergence of this organizational phenomenon in the United States:

> Relatively independent Jacks-of-all-trades (village blacksmiths, for example) gave way to many interdependent individuals skilled in particular economic activities. Most striking was the separation of labor and management functions, which arose slowly in agriculture but rapidly in industry. Specialized managers and specialized wage earners replaced semi-independent artisans; manual laborers no longer organized production or sold finished products. (p. 11)

It was necessary to ensure reliability of work performance in order to realize the economic potential of the new technologies but also to meet the competitive challenge of other enterprises pursuing similar objectives in the same markets. In the rush to exploit unprecedented opportunities to create economic wealth, corporations pursued growth strategies to increase their control over the factors affecting their survival and prosperity (Emery, 1977).

However, beginning in the economic sector, the power thus acquired has become so great that decisions and actions taken by corporations in their own interest increasingly generate consequences beyond the outcomes that are intended and are controllable. The impact is felt, often in unexpected and undesirable ways, throughout all sectors of industrial societies and across their boundaries to such an extent that the activities of corporations are no longer regarded as their own business but as the concern of society as a whole. State intervention has increased, and the growth of corporate power has met with reactions that limit and control its effect through the unionization of labor, government legislation, and the countermeasures of proliferating interest and issue groups such as those concerned with consumer and environmental protection. Moreover, the public sector has grown enormously in response to mounting demands for services and benefits that private enterprise does not or cannot provide. As Sir Geoffrey Vickers (1973) puts it, in the last 100 years an "institutional explosion" has occurred in western society. Massive institutional structures have arisen in all spheres of life that make increasingly complex and often conflicting demands on one another as well as on the individuals who participate in and are sustained by them. Growth in organizational size and power, in both the public and private sectors, now generates greater rather than less uncertainty. It is becoming more difficult to predict the ultimate consequences of decisions and actions, problems are so intermeshed that they cannot be separated out for discrete analysis and independent solution, and societies' institutions and organizations are confronted with uncertainty on a greater scale than they have had to cope with before (Emery, 1977; Emery & Trist, 1973; Schon, 1971).

Such has been the contribution of science and technology to the development of industrial societies that continued scientific and technological advancement is widely regarded as the main source of solutions to the problems these societies now face. Certainly science and technology have advanced well beyond the initial breakthroughs that made posible the industrial revolution to produce a second industrial (or postindustrial) revolution. This revolution is based on the mechanization of mental work, as distinct from physical work (or automation). The result has been an enormous increase in capacity to generate, store, transmit, and manipulate information (Ackoff, 1974). For a time it seemed that the revolution in information technology was providing the capability for analyzing and solving any problem, however large and complex, but during the 1970s that hope became questionable. In fact, the growth of information technology has generated still greater change and complexity. The increasing volume and speed of communication creates problems of information overload, leads to futher intensification of interdependencies within and among societies, and heightens the sensitivity of parts of the social environment to one another. Decisions and actions generate complex chains of reactions so quickly that it becomes difficult if not impossible to understand what is producing what. *Information* is not the same as *control*. Without adequate means of explaining or understanding the information that is received, the information explosion is drastically reducing the time available in which to adapt to new events. This forces organizations to respond with insufficient understanding of what is happening, and it is leading to actual loss of control (Ackoff, 1974; Emery, 1977; Schon, 1971).

These conditions signify the emergence of a new type of social environment that Emery and Trist (1973) aptly call "turbulent." The distinctive character of turbulence does not lie merely in the rate at which change is increasing nor in the complexity of contemporary western society. The social environment has become increasingly dynamic and complex since the beginning of the industrial age. When change is generated by large powerful organizations linked in increasingly complex ways through all sectors of society and among societies, however, it acquires its own momentum and direction and moves beyond the power of individual or collective actors to predict or control it. The condition that marks the turbulent transition from the industrial age to whatever lies beyond is the amount of uncertainty that confronts western societies and that they are not, as yet, able to reduce to manageable levels (Emery & Trist, 1973; Emery, 1977).

It is not difficult to identify major sources of uncertainty and the present inability of societies to cope with them. The prospect that vital natural resources could become depleted, exhausted, or prohibitively expensive was suddenly thrown into sharp focus when the Organization of Petroleum Exporting Countries (OPEC) quadrupled oil prices in 1973. So far, the reactions of governments, the oil companies, and other vested interests have created conflict and the threat of domestic and international disorder. More political, organizational, and emotional energy is consumed by these conflicts than is directed toward finding new strategies for managing societies' interdependence on a diminishing resource and toward developing alternatives. As parties press their own particular interests and claims, they compound the difficulty of finding adaptive solutions and, instead, generate further uncertainty for one another. This carries over into efforts to find alternative sources of energy. The development of alternatives generally requires high capital investment. In consequence, governments and corporations have been reluctant to begin developing them on a significant scale while conventional sources are still available. Ironically, in regard to nuclear energy, the heavy investment that has already been committed is seen as a compelling reason why, despite disasters such as Three Mile Island and the growing cost of nuclear energy, production should continue to be expanded. Each response to crisis or the threat of crisis seems to achieve no more than to create further uncertainty.

Similarly, crises are endemic in virtually all of societies' institutions. The international monetary system is no longer reliable, causing countries to lose confidence in other countries' currencies and generating mutual distrust. The British pound almost collapsed in 1976, and in 1978 the United States dollar was in serious trouble. There are fundamental weaknesses in many national economies that are producing the widespread condition of *stagflation*—that is, simultaneous increases in both unemployment and inflation. Existing economic theories and government policies have no viable answer, but again more effort is put into trying to make them work than is directed to the search for adaptive alternatives. The direction of technological innovation in the immediate future is likely to displace increasing numbers from the workforce, the "market mechanism" cannot be relied on to maintain employment and price stability within conventionally accepted limits, and societies may well have to change their basic assumptions about how to create and distribute the fruits of economic production (Trist, 1978d; Robertson, 1978; Vickers, 1973).

At the same time, public confidence in elected governments is declining, and the governments are encountering increasing difficulty in gaining acceptance of, much less support for, their policies. Organizations in the private and public sectors are having trouble with employees who demand that their real incomes be maintained and increased but who are less willing to contribute their productive effort to the dominant hierarchical organizations in which they are required to work. Moreover, while the bases of cohesion within societies are being eroded, global trends are posing still more fundamental challenges. An industry such as British shipbuilding cannot survive, except perhaps at drastically reduced levels, if other countries do not want its products. The governmental policies that stimulated the development of young manufacturing industries such as those of Australia are impotent in the face of saturated domestic markets and inability to compete internationally. The economics of industrial-age production are such that Third World countries are beginning to acquire considerable competitive advantages over the industrial west. Western societies are critically dependent on those countries for resources, which strengthens Third World demands for a new international economic and political order. The impact of these trends will vary, but it is difficult to see how the economic, social, and political structures of western societies can withstand mounting pressures much longer without major transformation.

In sum, several major forces have emerged and interacted to bring the industrial age to its limits in those societies that have attained high levels of technological advancement and industrial density. The need for active adaptation to halt the drift into turbulence and to discover and pursue new directions is undeniable, but the dominant institutions and organizations of western societies prevent such adaptation from occurring. So long as western societies remain basically unchanged, active adaptation to reduce uncertainty and shape future directions is not feasible. Conversely, transforming the societies into vehicles for active adaptation offers a powerful point of intervention to improve the human prospect. The crises of western societies are largely a conseqence of their dominant organizational forms. Given the central importance of institutions and organizations in obstructing or facilitating active adaptation, it is appropriate to examine their present structure and functioning as a prelude to considering alternatives.

BUREAUCRACY AND ITS CONSEQUENCES

Most collective activity in western society is organized in one basic way. It tends to be broken down into its most elementary components, individuals are assigned more or less exclusively to each component, and their performance is coordinated and controlled through hierarchical structures. The two essential characteristics of this organizational structure are division of functions and separation of decision making from task performance. Following Emery and Emery (1975), this pattern of organization will be referred to here as *bureaucracy*. In general, bureaucracy is most clearly evident in the organization of the military, economic production, and government administration, but hospitals, educational institutions, unions, voluntary organizations, and service agencies all also tend to have these same basic organizational characteristics. Moreover, bureaucracy is not only the typical pattern in single organizations such as corporations. The division of functions between sectors of society and among their component organizations, and the structures through which they are regulated, also reflect the same bureaucratic pattern.

The typical arrangement for a single organization is represented diagrammatically in Figure 1. The extent to which the division of functions is carried, the number of control levels, and the manner in which control is exercised will vary among organizations depending on several factors (Burns & Stalker, 1961; Woodward, 1965; Lorsch & Lawrence, 1970; Thompson, 1967). Nevertheless, the general tendency is for organizational functions and their component activities to be subdivided to a point at which persons performing them cannot control and

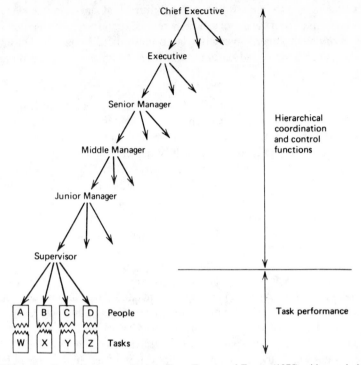

Figure 1. Bureaucratic organization. From Emery and Emery (1975) with permission.

coordinate their own efforts. Therefore, control and coordination are superimposed on task performance, but a single control level usually cannot encompass the full range of tasks. The first control level is segmented into units ("supervisors"), which must then be controlled by a second level, and so on. Generally, rules and procedures are established to make the controls more precise and to standardize performance (Emery, 1977; Emery & Emery, 1975; Herbst, 1976).

Bureaucratic organization probably has been taken to its extremes in assembly line production. The following account by Cummings and Srivastva (1977) presents a familiar picture:

> Through a method of scientific analysis, work was decomposed into its simplest units which became the building blocks for a predictable production process. . . . The requirements of each task were specified in detail so that a particular result could be obtained from a standard set of operating procedures. The basis of this form of work was a belief that maximum efficiency would result from a maximally specified task. If each worker behaved according to the one-best-method of production, predictable and

efficient outcomes would follow. Variabilities that arose in the work-place—whether from the actions of the workers, or the production process, or the work environment—were displaced upwards to a control level that absorbed uncertainties and ensured compliance with the designed order. (p.9)

The general logic is first to design the production process and physical layout, specify the tasks and methods of performing them, and then train and assign individuals to perform them. Because the operating requirements of machines are considered to be invariant, it is a matter of establishing work procedures to ensure that people behave consistently with the physical production process. In effect, production employees become extensions of, or appendages to, the machines.

This bureaucratization of work did not follow as a necessary consequence of mechanizing production. As is shown in the next section, technically and economically feasible organizational alternatives were available throughout the industrial era. Rather, bureaucratization of organizations reflected the mechanical world view that came to dominate human thought during the eighteenth and nineteenth centuries. It became fashionable to break down almost anything, inanimate or animate, into its most elementary components and the relations between the components. For employers, organizing their enterprises in this way had certain apparent advantages. By reducing production to its basic operations and maximizing the number of times each operation was repeated in a given period, the cost of capital equipment and labor per unit of output was reduced. In the case of labor, because the skills required to perform most operations were very simple, employers could keep wages at low levels. Moreover, the division of work into fractionated tasks not only made external control of employees necessary but placed the control firmly in the hands of employers and subsequently in a new class of professional managers (Susman, 1976).

Just as individual craftsman were replaced by armies of semiskilled operatives performing standardized component tasks of industrial production, traditional forms of work gave way to bureaucracy in virtually every area. In mining, mechanization made possible the destruction of cohesive self-regulating teams whose members could perform all tasks, and it led to the organization of shifts based on individuals assigned to separate tasks and under the control of supervisors (Trist, Higgin, Murray, & Pollock, 1963.) The same logic was applied to clerical work even though such work was not highly mechanized. In road transport, truck drivers working for employers generally planned their own schedules. Many drivers were minor entrepreneurs in their own right. For example, they negotiated loads for return journeys and shared the profits with their employers. Today, they are more likely to be controlled by fixed delivery schedules determined at central locations where computer systems are used.

Bureaucracy does, of course, have roots in certain ancient civilizations but with industrialization it became the organizational model for western societies. The regulatory, administrative, and service functions of governments became increasingly divided among a rapidly growing number of departments and agencies. None has sufficient scope to discharge its responsibilities without impinging on those of the others, making necessary hierarchical control of relations among as well as within them. Similarly, the mechanical world view of medical science is manifest in the organization of health care. Medical science advanced on the basis of increasing knowledge of the parts of the human body, and it progressively became divided into specialties. The proliferation of paramedical occupations and careers has followed the same pattern. Most hospitals have no less than three hierarchies—medical, nursing, and administrative—with large arrays of specialized staff within each. When one observes the daily routine of a hospital treating its patients or of a school where students move through fixed periods spent on each subject and where all are required to perform tasks in the same way, the resemblance to an assembly line is more striking than any differences. Bureaucracy is the fundamental organizational pattern in western societies. It is also basic to the crises that confront them and to their inability to deal effectively with these crises.

Bureaucratically designed organizations require a high degree of stability and predictability in their environments and inexpensive, easily replaceable or interchangeable physical and human parts (Emery, 1977). During prolonged periods of stability, organizational functioning can be made highly routine. Provided that there is sufficient warning of any significant external change, internal adjustments can be planned and orderly. So long as employees can be acquired, trained, and retrained or dispensed with cheaply and quickly, the organization can adapt to change at relatively little cost. In such conditions, those in the top organizational echelons can reserve the great majority of decisions for themselves and exercise detailed surveillance over subordinate levels. Because the amount of uncertainty in the environment is low and can be controlled, they have the time and resources to occupy themselves with internal affairs. Even in large complex organizations, the chain of command, supported by technical staff groups, is adequate for downward flow of direction and upward flow of information to monitor and control performance. These conditions existed until the late 1950s, but since then they have rapidly disappeared.

The amount of change, complexity, and uncertainty in the environment now greatly exceeds what bureaucratic organizational structures can cope with. The time available for adapting to change is drastically reduced, forcing decision makers to respond with much less knowledge of the relevant variables. More factors must be taken into account and they are intermeshed in much more complex ways, the presence or importance of factors increasingly eludes decision makers and their advisers, and the unprecedented nature of many situations lessens the value of past experience and previously acquired knowledge as guides to choice and action. The sources of uncertainty that are most important to organizations are moving beyond the organizations' spheres of influence and are becoming difficult or impossible for the organizations to control by their own efforts. The resources they require are no longer inexpensive or as easily replaced, and the need for frequent adaptation greatly increases the cost of internal adjustment. The bureaucratic organization is unable to learn and adapt sufficiently quickly and correctly, and in important areas adequate means of controlling change do not exist (Ackoff, 1974; Emery, 1977; Friedman, 1973; Schon, 1971; Trist, 1977). As this happens, the costs inherent in bureaucracy begin to soar. Organizations generally react to the turbulence that engulfs them by attempting to strengthen and expand existing controls, but the increased cost of doing so is not compensated for by any significant improvement in efficiency or effectiveness. In many instances the reverse seems to happening. The cost of maintaining organizations rises while their performance continues to decline because the inadequacies of bureaucratic organizations cannot be overcome by strengthening hierarchical controls.

At the basic operating level of the bureaucratic organization, individuals have little control over their work situations. They have neither the discretion nor the means necessary for exercising control. Control is the function of supervisors and staff groups. Individuals at the basic operating level can make no greater contribution than to carry out instructions. When the work is disrupted, for example by equipment breakdowns or interruptions to the flow of materials, they can only wait for others to solve the problem. At the supervisory level as depicted in Figure 1, the control usually is also insufficient. The more frequent and unanticipated the disruptions, the more supervisors are forced to intervene at the basic operating level to try to correct deviations from performance requirements. However, usually they will not be able to exert sufficient influence over the external conditions hampering their subordinates' performance. As a result, their interventions are likely to be ineffectual and to cause frustration and conflict. Often, in their struggles to keep their own units functioning, supervisors put pressure on one another, which further increases their difficulties. Because they do not possess the means of resolving these difficulties themselves, the interdependence among organizational units can become a source of conflict and disorder neccessitating intervention by still higher levels. In this way bureaucratic organizations both import change and uncertainty and magnify it in their internal operations. Even at the highest organizational levels, managerial attention turns further inward to attempt to resolve problems within the organization. The preoccupation with maintaining internal control distracts the organization's leadership from its most important function of attempting to find new strategies for reducing and controlling uncertainty in the environment itself (Emery, 1977; Susman, 1976).

The external strategies that bureaucratic organizations typically pursue do not succeed in a turbulent environment. Such organizations tend to be concerned exclusively with their own goals and objectives and with those parts of the environment where their immediate interests are perceived to lie. They take little account of external factors except those that directly affect them. These factors and the relationships between them comprise what is variously referred to as the *task environment* or the *transactional environment* of an organization (Thompson, 1967; Trist, 1977). They may include clients, suppliers, employees' representatives, relevant regulatory agencies, and other elements with which the organization deals in the course of conducting its affairs. Since the 1960s, even this level of external interaction has become increasingly complex, but there is a much larger environment that Emery and Trist (1973) call the *contextual environment.* The contextual environment contains interacting societal and global forces that affect entire societies and their component sectors and organizations. Trends in the contextual environment have become increasingly interconnected and are having much greater impact on organizations and their transactional environments. The trends include environmental deterioration, energy crises, stagflation, and regional and urban decline. The emergence and pervasive impact of these trends amounts to a contextual invasion of the more limited transactional environments, with which organizations are used to dealing as if the larger environment did not exist. These trends emerge and change in unpredictable ways and with consequences that are difficult, if not impossible, to anticipate and prepare for—much less control. Certainly they are unlikely to be controlled by organizations acting independently and competitively in pursuit of their own interests. Neither can existing regulatory structures and mechanisms deal with them effectively. Regulatory and administrative agencies also compete with one another, and the hierarchical structures through which governments attempt to coordinate them are too fragmented and encumbered with piecemeal legislation. Thus, the competitive pursuit of private interests and attempts by governments to legislate and administrate their way out of societal crises compound the conflicts between diverse demands and create further uncertainty (Ackoff, 1974; Trist, 1977).

Such considerations provide reason enough to regard the search for alternatives to bureaucratic organization as an urgent undertaking, but the damage bureaucracy has done goes deeper, penetrating and eroding the value foundations essential for the continued viability of societies. Bureaucratic organizations cannot cope with present and emerging sources of uncertainty, but they have also engendered among the majority of persons who participate in them a sense of powerlessness to understand and act on the forces affecting their future.

The vigorous and sometimes violent assaults against societies' institutions that were mounted during the 1960s and early 1970s reflected growing awareness of the failure of those institutions and a widespread desire to reform them. To many persons, that period heralded a societal transformation. William Irwin Thompson (1973) expressed this optimism about the implications and outcomes of the social protest movements when he wrote:

Now that the industrial revolution has reached its limits to growth, a new cultural revolution is taking place. . . . This revolution is one in which the energy of culture shifts from institutions to the whole environment. Religion moves out of churches, education moves out of schools, business moves out of factories, and politics moves out of the party system. . . . Naturally this release of energy from institutions to the entire environment seems like an explosion to those on the inside. Failing to understand these positive releases of human potential, they try to block them. (pp. 25–26)

Although the social protest movements had considerable impact, they have largely died out, whereas the institutions that were the targets of their attacks remain basically unchanged, if weakened. The "cultural revolution" appears to have lost much of its energy, but the commitment and conformity on which the institutions and organizations of industrial societies depend have not returned. In fact, many more people have become cynical and disaffected than were engaged in active revolt in the 1970s. They include not only the young whose hopes for societal transformation were frustrated. Disillusionment with industrial society appears to have spread to the older age groups as well and to a wide range of social groups.

The dominant trends in social values and behavior that now pose the major threat to the institutions and organizations of western industrial societies are hardly positive releases of human energy. They look more like attempts by people to reduce or escape from the pressures and anxieties to which they are subjected. According to Emery (1977) these reactions include the following:

1 The polarization of relations within society which is occurring because, confronted with complex issues in which many different and conflicting interests are involved while the prospects for satisfying those interests are diminishing, individuals and groups become so preoccupied with their own interests that they are unable or unwilling to recognize the legitimacy of any claims which others might have.

2 Retreating from cooperative involvement with others and becoming indifferent to what is happening to them, disclaiming one's responsibility to the wider community and society.

3 Becoming exclusively concerned with getting as much gratification as one can in the immediate present and not wanting to think about the future or about the deeper human implications and consequences of one's choices and actions.

Like the social protest movements, these are reactions against the increasing failure of industrial-age institutions and organizations, but they are maladaptive in that they actually reduce the prospects for active intervention to transform societies and pursue desired new directions.

Certainly these reactions may contribute to the eventual collapse of industrial societies' institutions and organizations, and the leaders of these societies are beginning to display some awareness of and alarm at this prospect. The central theme of President Carter's State of the Nation address on July 16, 1979 was the "crisis of the American spirit" and, in other societies such as Australia, the established leadership has found it necessary to make a concerted appeal to the people to become more actively involved in helping to overcome the nation's present and worsening plight. Such exhortations appear to have had no positive effect and are not likely to. Feeling unable to do anything themselves about the present and emerging crises, and remaining mistrustful of the bureaucratic institutions and organizations that got them into the present predicament, people are more likely to involve themselves less and less in the affairs of the society outside of their immediate concerns, which increasingly will be their own survival.

The established authorities within societies are unable through emotional appeals to inspire new public confidence in and commitment to their objectives, policies, and programs, but there are two other alternatives available and familiar within the existing institutional and organizational framework. The established authorities can try to crack down on the populace through increased control over and regimentation of individual and collective behavior. For example, as conflict between polarized groups and disobedience toward government policies increase,they may be met with reactions to strengthen and expand the mechanisms of "law and order"—that is, further bureaucratization. The authorities may also try to plan much more comprehensively for the society, relying to an even greater extent on scientifically and technically trained elites to produce "solutions" that as closely as possible approximate totally designed and planned societies (Emery, 1977). Clearly these alternatives are not mutually exclusive. Indeed, if pursued, they would depend on each other. It seems equally clear that, not only would such alternatives be unacceptable to the majority of societies' members, but they would fail.

The continued growth of scientific and technological knowledge and its application to planning, leaving the underlying bureaucratic structure of society unchanged, will not ensure that the crises and uncertainty generated by turbulent environments will be reduced and managed. It has already been argued that the information revolution, although increasing the potential for analyzing and solving societies' problems, is actually intensifying and amplifying interdependence and uncertainty. Bureaucratic organizations are not designed to adapt to large-scale systems of interrelated and rapidly changing problems, but prevalent approaches to planning are based on the same bureaucratic logic of social design. Tocher (1977, p. 425) has described the characteristics of the dominant planning model in the following way:

1 The area of study is delimited and defined.
2 The impact of the environment on that delimited area is described.

3   A model of the system so described is built.
4   A set of possible actions and procedures are invented and described.
5   The model is used to predict the behavior of the system for each member of the
    set.
6   Criteria for choosing the "best" member of the set are invented and applied.
7   The selected member of the set is implemented.

Attempting to plan in this way in turbulent environments cannot work. The problems of societies are too interrelated to be separated out for discrete analysis, there are too many unknown variables to be confident about either the definition of the problem area or the adequacy of the array of alternatives, and frequent change is likely to render the chosen alternative obsolete or inappropriate even before it is implemented. In consequence, this kind of planning typically falls behind the march of events. As Friedman (1973) puts it, western societies are confronted with a "crisis of knowing," or the dilemma of attempting to plan with decreasing knowledge of the relevant environment and the complex changes occurring within it (Ackoff, 1974; Emery, 1977; Friedman, 1973; Schon, 1971).

Even if the narrow, fragmented, problem-solving orientation of present planning approaches is replaced by much more holistic, integrated systems perspectives, as it must be if science and technology are to have a positive role in managing turbulent transition, there is a second dilemma: the question of whose criteria shall determine the choice of future directions.

The technocratic approach to planning became dominant when those persons with the power to command resources could specify a limited number of objectives to be achieved by a given project and when alternative means of achieving them could be measured and compared for cost and effectiveness. So long as there was a large measure of agreement about desired ends, or so long as those who determined the ends to be achieved had sufficient power, the approach was politically feasible. From the beginnings of industrialization, the rational values of science and the drive for material prosperity in the wider society were mutually reinforcing. This alliance was so successful that by the 1950s science and technology appeared to offer the means of achieving anything, including the resolution of social issues and conflicts. However, since the 1960s the consensual foundations of western society have been fragmented. As a result, the large measure of agreement about desired ends and concentration of effective power on which technocratic planning depends has also been seriously reduced. The implications for planning are well stated by Emery (1977) as follows:

It is not enough to have one of the optimiser's *feasible* plans. We need planning which will probably come to pass because the people involved in or served by their implementation want them to succeed. The hard won agreements that the optimiser has for the initial, hard-nosed definition of objectives are no guarantee of active support when it comes to implementation. On the contrary, I think that these agreements carry within them the needs of subsequent subversion. . . .Nor can the optimiser carry the day with his array of facts, statistical forecasts and impartial, objective calculations of the cost-effectiveness of alternative paths. These things do carry weight, but, when there is a feeling that justice is not being done facts will not convince otherwise. . . .The apparent dilemma in "modern" planning is "how does the expert make his contribution to planning without alienating people?" (p. 124)

President Johnson's advisers in his wars against the Vietnamese and against poverty encountered this dilemma, as did the advisers to President Carter on his policy for energy conservation.

Bureaucracy and technocratic planning depend on each other but are unable to avert the crises that confront them. In Friedman's (1973) terms, western industrial societies are faced not only with a "crisis of knowing" but also with a "crisis of valuing." Even if the first could be overcome by the expansion of rational planning capacity achieved through scientific and technological advancement, persisting with bureaucratic–technocratic strategies will only make the second crisis worse, for it is largely because of these strategies that the values crisis has occurred. The bureaucratic logic of social design has reached and is going beyond the limits of human and societal endurance.

ACTIVE ADAPTATION TO TURBULENT SOCIAL TRANSITION

Active human intervention to transform the present condition of western societies is critical both for their future and the future of other societies. According to Emery (1977), three essential requirements for active adaptation are the following:

1   New shared understanding of how present and emerging trends are affecting future prospects and the ability to develop this understanding continuously as conditions change.
2   The emergence of values based on awareness of increasing change, interdependence, and uncertainty that are sufficiently widely shared that viable choices can be made about future directions.
3   New forms of social organization that embody active adaptive values, make continuous learning and adaptation possible, and enable those who participate in them to take a much more active part in managing their futures.

It needs to be recognized, first, that western societies are in a genuinely new environment, that the premises of industrialism cannot provide a basis for developing effective alternatives in this environment, and that new understanding and strategies of adaptation must be sought. Second, the values of industrialism are no longer relevant or viable, and new core values must emerge. Third, it follows from the foregoing analysis of bureaucratic institutions and organizations that the development of new understanding and the emergence of active adaptive values are not possible unless these institutions and organizations are transformed.

Understanding is regarded here as a product of learning, by which individuals discover how changes in their environments are affecting the prospects for attaining desired outcomes by familiar means and as an outcome seek new courses of action that are more effective in the changed conditions. It is likely that, when fundamental change occurs in the environment, the ends to be served by human action as well as the means for pursuing them will require reconsideration. Understanding, then, is acquired as individuals gain knowledge of the environment and the changes occurring in it, and then reassess their choices about desired outcomes and the means of attaining them (Ackoff & Emery, 1972; Vickers, 1965). This does not mean that human beings must passively accept the changes occurring in their environment and merely adjust their behavior accordingly. In the present and emerging conditions of western industrial society, such reactions only increase the likelihood of crisis and collapse. However, as Emery (1977) says:

> Insofar as they understand the laws governing their environment they can modify the conditions producing their subsequent environments and hence radically change the definition of "an adaptive response." (p. 67)

Given that individuals are able to learn about their environments, they also have the potential for attempting to change them. For members of western society, this difference between passive and active adaptation is the difference between concern with immediate survival in the social environment and pursuing radically different directions to transform the environment.

In turbulent environments, learning and adaptation must occur more or less continuously. Turbulence undermines the belief that successive stable states can be reached which, once attained, will persist long enough for experience with the environment to be accumulated and used to guide future decisions and actions (Schon, 1971). This was possible in the stable environments of preindustrial societies, and even during the industrial era the means of obtaining and using information about the environment were adequate to cope with the changes that were occurring. The problems generated in turbulent environments are quite different. Active adaptive learning in such environments requires continuous searching for new directions in conditions that constantly produce novelty and surprises (Ackoff, 1974; Emery, 1977).

Even assuming that societies' members are willing to attempt to learn and adapt in this way, they are confronted with the problem of knowing whether the courses of action they choose to pursue in the environment are likely to have adaptive or maladaptive consequences. The level of complexity and uncertainty in turbulent environments precludes familiar methods of predicting and evaluating the probable outcomes of alternative courses as the basis for choice. If the environment is too unstable and unpredictable to plan in this way, then the members of societies must look beyond the accumulation and analysis of information about their world to find another source of the relative constancy and certainty they need. This source consists of the basic values and ideals they hold, according to Emery and Trist (1972):

> Values have always arisen as the human response to persisting areas of relevant uncertainty. Because we have not been able to trace out the consequences of our actions as they are amplified and resonated through our extended social fields, we have sought to agree upon rules such as the Ten Commandments that will provide each of us with a guide and a ready calculus. Because we have been continually confronted with conflicting possibilities for goal pursuit, we have tended to identify hierarchies of valued ends. Typically these are not just goals or even the more important goals. They are ideals like health and happiness that, at best, one can approach stochastically. (p. 68)

When human beings reach a point where they are unable to explain what is happening around them, or to predict what is going to happen, they must once again try to become certain, or at least clearer, about what *ought* to happen.

Values and ideals can endow human choice and action with meaning and coherence that transcend particular choices and acts and the situations in which they are taken. Values are guides to behavior. One does not attempt to pursue values but rather to observe or behave consistently with them. Ideals are conceptions of ultimate outcomes that can never be obtained but are endlessly approachable. Ideals make it possible to exercise choices between alternatives in the present by reference to criteria that are limitless in time. When consciously and widely held, ideals enable human beings to maintain continuity of direction and social cohesion so that they can agree as to which choices are consistent with desirable future directions and which goals and objectives to pursue. Moreover, as one goal or objective proves to be unattainable, others can be chosen that are still consistent with the observance of values and the pursuit of ideals. In conditions of great change and uncertainty, when people must try to plan with insufficient knowledge as to the likely consequences of their actions, ideals and values can provide guidance by indicating the future states that are desirable and giving general criteria by which to judge whether present paths are leading toward or away from desirable future states. Frequent changes in limited goals and objectives are possible without losing sight of the fundamental purposes and more distant ends to be served by human activity. When goals or objectives that are contradictory emerge, these may be reconciled more easily in the larger context of seeking paths that lead toward mutually desired future states. In a conventional scientific sense, the future is not predictable beyond a very limited extent (Bell, 1973), but emerging directions can be influenced by the continuous willed intervention of human beings in their changing environments. Ideals, then, are necessary for a degree of controlled intervention in the changing social environment so that what happens is at least in part conducive to the pursuit of desirable futures (Ackoff, 1974; Emery, 1977).

This leads to the question of which values and ideals can guide active adaptive, rather than maladaptive, choices in the present turbulent environment. The values and ideals that give any culture or society its character emerge slowly and are slow to change, yet in western industrial societies the values and ideals of their members are deeply eroded. Their values and ideals have become self-defeating and do not provide the shared sense of purpose essential for the coherent and cooperative pursuit of mutually desired future directions (Slater, 1970). Therefore, a critical issue in the future of these societies is whether new values and ideals will emerge quickly enough to enable human beings to identify alternatives that are potentially adaptive in the search for paths out of turbulence to a desirable new society.

These new, or rediscovered, ideals and values must express human awareness of, and determination to overcome, turbulence itself. In this vein Trist in Emery and Trist (1973) states:

> If I ask what kind of new values can be regarded as appropriate, my answer can only be in terms of the following criterion: that they must be values which enhance our capability to cope with the increased levels of complexity, interdependence and uncertainty that characterise the contemporary turbulent environment. (p. 172)

The self-moving dynamic of turbulence makes it impossible for single systems—be they individuals, groups, organizations, communities, or societies—to adapt successfully by their own efforts. In fact, because of the growing interdependence among these systems, they create further uncertainty for one another. The values and ideals appropriate for active adaptation to turbulent environments, therefore, would be based on awareness of this interdependence among systems and of the way their actions affect one another's prospects for pursuing desirable future directions.

The changes in values and ideals entailed by active adaptation, Emery (1977) says are the following:

1 From pursuing self-interest independently of others toward recognizing that one is interdependent with others, and seeking to establish collaborative relations based on the wish to pursue mutually desired futures.

2 From attempting to increase one's competitive power at the expense of others toward seeking paths that improve their capabilities for survival and development as well as one's own.

3 From regarding individuals as subordinate to institutions and organizations toward insisting that the latter be judged according to how they affect human well-being and development in all of its dimensions, not merely material standards of living.

4 From treating the social and physical environments as objects to be used in the pursuit of material growth, regardless of how degraded and deformed they become, toward wishing to develop them to progressively more desirable states.

The values of industrialism emphasize autonomous individual self-aggrandizement, competition, economic and scientific rationality, and exploitation of physical and human resources. Such values must give way to values that emphasize interdependence within and among societies, cooperative discovery and pursuit of mutually desired future directions, the primacy of human well-being and development over narrow economic and scientific criteria, and the progressive enhancement rather than degradation of the social and physical world.

The prospect that significant changes in the dominant values and ideals of western industrial societies will occur may not at first look very promising. Indeed, it may be difficult to envisage what changes in these societies would follow if they did occur. Fortunately, there are signs of such changes emerging in western society, and sufficient experience with them has been gained to develop a general picture of the basic departures from the ideals, organizational frameworks, and behavioral patterns of bureaucratic industrialism that they imply.

From Independence to Interdependence

The Jamestown Area Labor–Management Committee and a number of other labor–management committees in the United States illustrate the possibility of shifting from a value system that emphasizes independent pursuit of self-interest toward recognition of interdependence and identification of a mutually desired future. Jamestown is a manufacturing town in western New York state. It had a bad record of industrial disputes and poor labor–management relations that resulted in a high incidence of strikes. The community was experiencing serious economic decline, and when a major employer closed its plant in 1972, unemployment approached 10 percent. However, a new mayor, elected with bipartisan support and assisted by influential individuals, brought managers and union leaders from the main local plants together in a meeting that led to the establishment of the Area Labor–Management Committee. Recognizing that the deteriorating economic situation was adversely affecting all interests, the aim of the committee was to stimulate industrial development on the basis of labor–management cooperation.

Over several years, numerous important gains were made. The new cooperative spirit and willingness to find innovative solutions to problems attracted in a major company, which opened a new plant in Jamestown. Several in-plant labor–management committees were established. An interplant program for skills development helped to overcome a lack of key skills among younger workers. Plant employees are involved in performance development schemes and share in the gains from cost savings on terms agreed to by both union and management. A plan for the redesign of the layout in one plant was developed by the plant labor–management committee, with active involvement of foremen and operatives as well as management and engineers, and resulted in the plant being reconditioned instead of closed. Widespread employee participation in product development has achieved significant growth in new business for some companies. The adversarial relation between unions and company managements remains, but cooperation on matters affecting mutual survival and development has reversed Jamestown's economic decline (Jamestown Area Labor–Management Committee, 1977; Trist, 1977, 1978a,b).

As with the other examples of possible value shifts that will be cited, it is too early to be confident that the emergence of this potentially adaptive new direction in Jamestown will continue to grow, but the case illustrates the first basic change from maladaptive toward active adaptive values and ideals. In order to break out of a situation that was becoming increasingly threatening, diverse and conflicting interests had to recognize that their future prospects were bound up with the future of the larger system of the community and surrounding region. It is important to note that this did not require the numerous local stakeholders to surrender their freedom of decision and action to the arbitration and dictates of a higher planning authority. It did require that they acknowledge a larger set of interdependent ends beyond the immediate interests of each particular group of stakeholders and that they be willing to cooperate at that level.

From Competition to Cooperation

Given this recognition of a larger socal entity that one is and wishes to be a part of, the second value change entails seeking paths and strategies to increase the capabilities of others for enhancing their future prospects as well as pursuing a desirable future for oneself. It is a shift from a more or less exclusive preoccupation with getting as much as one can toward attempting to identify and pursue courses of action to increase the active adaptive potential of all concerned. Jamestown ap-

pears to have moved in this direction. The community of Craigmillar in Edinburgh, Scotland, is another example. Craigmillar is a public housing estate of some 25,000 people situated on the outskirts of Edinburgh. Residents generally suffer severe economic disadvantages. Average incomes are low, unemployment is 30 percent or higher, and the area has poor amenities. The industries that traditionally provided employment have largely disappeared. Only 15 percent of the people possess automobiles, and public transport is inadequate. Since 1963, however, a remarkable voluntary organization called the Craigmillar Festival Society has played an increasingly important role in building the foundations of a future for the community that could be much brighter than its past.

Beginning with a very modest festival in a local church hall, the annual Craigmillar Festival has become one of the best known in Britain and attracts large numbers of visitors. As the Society became respected for its work, it obtained successive financial grants, first from local and national government and eventually from the European Economic Community. The grants enabled the Society to develop programs of neighborhood activities to improve the physical environment, to help residents to help themselves and one another in overcoming the sense of helplessness and depression endemic in impoverished public housing estates, and to make small but significant advances in stimulating employment through job creation and vocational training schemes. In order to pursue its objectives and programs, the Society initially depended on government financial assistance, but in 1978 Craigmillar Festival Enterprises Limited was formed as a commercial enterprise to develop local economic activity in light manufacturing and service areas. All residents of Craigmillar are shareholders in the company. A Scottish bank provided a loan to enable the company to start operations, and the board includes senior executives of corporations as well as residents to ensure that the company has access to business experience at the strategy and policy levels while remaining firmly in the control of the residents.

The Craigmillar Festival Society has evolved from a small group concerned with encouraging local artistic talent to a community development organization that is mobilizing and nurturing local creative ability to tackle a wide range of problems and issues in the community's future. Government programs to alleviate poverty and its consequences in areas such as Craigmillar have been largely unsuccessful. The Festival Society, on the other hand, has demonstrated that people are capable of doing a great deal for themselves. It does not deny a role for government in local affairs, but it is trying to develop a new relationship of "shared government." This concept is seen as a partnership in which government assists the people with financial and professional resources they cannot otherwise obtain while local initiative and leadership assist people to accomplish for themselves what public authorities have been unable to achieve for them (Craigmillar Festival Society, 1978; Trist & Burgess, 1978). That such initiatives can be taken in Craigmillar and elsewhere depends not only on the identification of individuals

with the larger community but also on an awareness that one's own aspirations for the future have little hope of being realized if others' prospects are getting worse, and on a commitment to strategies that enhance the future prospects of all.

From Dehumanization to Humanization of Organizations

The third change in ideals and values concerns the basic relationship between people and organizations. In western industrial societies, the great majority of people are instruments serving organizational purposes. The impact of organizations on people is seldom regarded as a major consideration in the conduct of organizational affairs. This is clearly evident in the way in which most productive work is organized. The bureaucratic approach to organizing work is based on criteria of supposed economic efficiency, and the rewards employees obtain from working are conceived of almost entirely in economic terms. This same limited concern for the way organizations affect people is also apparent in the dehumanized treatment of the public by government agencies, of students by educational systems, of patients by hospitals, of union members by unions, and of consumers by corporations. The required change is toward asserting the primacy of human beings over organizations—that is, a change from regarding people as servants of organizational purposes to organizations as vehicles for the enhancement of human well-being in all its dimensions. When decisions must be made by relatively few on behalf of the many, such as decisions of national policy or corporate strategy, the overriding concern must be with the way persons are affected in all aspects of their lives. When the persons most affected by the outcomes can take decision and action, they must be free to do so.

The attempt by Shell (U.K.) Limited to develop a new philosophy of the company's relationship both to the wider society and to employees illustrates the change in criteria for evaluating organizations in terms of their impact on people. The Draft Statement of Philosophy produced by the company's management reaffirmed that management was responsible to the Shell Group of Companies for performing certain business functions. However, the conception of the company's overall social responsibility was broadened considerably in several important respects. The fundamental departure from conventional corporate philosophy was the recognition that the company had privileged access to, not rights of ownership over, the resources of the society and that the company was responsible to the society for the way those resources were used. This kind of social responsibility is similar to that of someone who borrows an object such as a lawnmower from his neighbor. In each case there is an implicit or explicit commitment by the borrower to return the object to its owner in the same state of repair and, perhaps, to perform a reciprocal favor. To take an example, Shell management acknowledged the company's responsibility to help employees acquire any training necessary to obtain new employment in the event Shell found it necessary to lay them off and they

could not find employment elsewhere that required the skills they had used at Shell. In other words, the company was responsible for its effects on its employees' future. Elements of Shell's new philosophy can be found in the policies and practices of many other organizations, but taken as a whole the Draft Statement of Philosophy is an attempt to establish a set of human values on which to base the company's objectives and judgments abouts its performance (Hill, 1972).

When decisions must be made at a level that precludes the direct involvement of the many affected by them, those who do make the decisions have the responsibility to ensure that consideration of human consequences takes priority over mere organizational convenience. However, it is necessary to go much further in humanizing organizations by creating conditions under which people have far greater ability to control continuously their own situations and the factors immediately affecting them. When they have this control, it is possible for them to arrange their activities in a way to satisfy simultaneously the demands of the tasks and their own needs. Beyond the income and associated benefits that people derive from work, they have certain psychological and social requirements that in varying degrees they seek to satisfy in work as well as in other life areas. Emery and Emery (1975) say that in work the following needs are basic:

1 Freedom to make decisions about their own work activities rather than having these made for them.

2 Sufficient variety to avoid boredom and fatigue while being able to spend enough time on any particular activity to settle into a satisfying pattern of work.

3 Opportunities to learn by developing new skills and knowledge and by getting feedback about performance.

4 Receiving support from others and gaining respect for support given to others.

5 Knowledge that the work being performed is valued in the society and that it requires the development and exercise of distinctively human skills.

6 Reason to expect a desirable future in work and a sense of work contributing to a desirable future in life.

People are not likely to value these attributes of work equally, and individuals will attach varying importance to them at different times and in different circumstances. Nevertheless, creating the conditions under which they can be satisfied is central to the humanization of work just as denial of such opportunities has been central to the dehumanization of work in the industrial age.

Over the past 30 years, considerable progress has been made in redesigning work organizations to make possible the joint satisfaction of organizational and human requirements. Beginning with the pioneering efforts of Trist and his colleagues in the British coal mines, it was discovered that alternative forms of work organization were feasible within the limits set by a given technology. Mechanization of the coal mines in the 1940s had led to the form of work organization, based on fractionation of tasks and hierarchical control, discussed in the previous section. The destruction of the traditional work teams, loss of control over their work, and the establishment of an incentive payment system based on individual output generated serious conflict between workers and management and among the miners themselves. The expected economic gains from mechanized production were not realized, and industrial unrest, labor turnover, absenteeism, and accident rates increased. In certain mines, however, the workers found ways of reestablishing traditional forms of cooperative teamwork compatible with the demands of the mechanized technology. Further investigation and experimentation by Trist and his associates demonstrated that these alternative arrangements, which returned control over the work to the miners through a remarkable system of cooperation extending across three shifts, not only were technically feasible but, in terms of satisfying both economic demands and the miners' own requirements in their work, were superior to the organizational design that had been introduced along with mechanization. (Trist, Higgin, Murray, & Pollock, 1963).

Since those studies and experiments, interest in alternatives to the bureaucratic organization of work has grown and diffused throughout western industrial societies to an impressive extent. Some attempts at democratization of the workplace followed from Shell's search for a new philosophy of management (Hill, 1972). In Norway during the 1960s a national program of democratizing work was carried out with the support of employers, unions, and government. The program was based on major experimental redesigns in several organizations (Emery & Thorsrud, 1969, 1976). In the late 1960s and 1970s, further initiatives were taken in Sweden, again being based on cooperation between management and the unions and supported by the resources of the Swedish Employers' Confederation (Jenkins, 1974; Lindestad & Kvist, 1975; Lindholm & Norstedt, 1975; Noren & Norstedt, 1975; Norstedt & Aguren, 1973; Torner, 1975). In the United States, concern wth the quality of working life emerged against the background of the more individual-oriented human relations tradition and the work on job redesign of Davis and others since the 1960s (Davis & Cherns, 1975; Davis & Taylor, 1972; Walton, 1972). In Europe, Australia, and Canada, interest in exploring alternatives to the bureaucratic organizational forms that were neither working nor enabling human beings to fulfill more than their material needs increased considerably during the 1970s.

The move toward these forms has demonstrated that the work people perform does not have to be degraded to a point at which they function as subhumans. First, even where industrial technologies were designed in accordance with technical and economic criteria, in many cases it was possible for employees to exercise significantly greater control over their own work than had been supposed. Insofar as people have this control, they also have the opportunity to ensure that their work remains truly human, as measured against the kinds of psychological and social requirements listed on page 23. A second breakthrough came with the realization that it was possible to adapt technologies to human requirements. In the early stages of production design, alternative technological solutions could be examined and evaluated in terms of their human implications, and choices that offered the best match between technical and human requirements could be made (Herbst, 1974). The design of Volvo's plant at Kalmar and Saab Scania's engine factory at Södertalje are two important demonstrations that such possibilities exist even within the seemingly inflexible technology of automobile production (Lindholm & Norstedt, 1975; Norstedt & Aguren, 1973). Shell Canada has taken a similar approach to the design of a new refinery, with important implications for highly automated continuous-process manufacturing. The range of technological alternatives usually available is by no means yet so great that constraints imposed by the requirements of technical functioning can be ignored. These constraints are being pushed back sufficiently, however, to allow for the development of fundamentally new forms of work organization that are more adaptive to complex changing conditions and that enable employees to satisfy their psychological and social requirements to a much higher degree.

From Deformation to the Pursuit of Beauty

These first three changes could lead societies' members to seek relations with one another and with their institutions and organizations, which are very different from the self-seeking, competitive, and dehumanized relations that currently dominate life in western industrial society. As a result, societies' members may also become aware of their potential for creating and recreating their environments in their images of the desirable. They can attempt to reverse the process of deforming and degrading their social and physical worlds and, instead, seek to enhance them and reach progressively higher states of harmony and satisfaction. This is the fourth change in values and ideals that is both necessary and possible.

Some insight into this potential was gained through an opportunity to work with young children on the design of a new playground for their school. White Gum Valley elementary school is located in Fremantle, the major port city of Western Australia. An inquiry into the condition of schools, which was instigated by the Australian government, found White Gum Valley to be severely disadvantaged in several respects, one of which was the lack of recreational facilities. Accordingly, the school authorities were asked to develop proposals for new facilities and to submit them to the government for approving of funding. Rather than having a conventional assessment of needs made by external consultants, it was decided to involve the children in determing their own recreational requirements and translating these into specific proposals. The children as the major clients were to take a central role in the planning process. From the University of Western Australia, Glen Watkins, Hilary Shilkin, three architecture students, and I acted as resources to the children and the school.

Initially, teachers in the school were asked to identify children in the age range from 8 to 12 years who had demonstrated themselves to be "leaders at play." These were children whose ideas about games during recreational periods tended to attract other children as well. From the names provided by the teachers, 30 children were chosen to participate in the planning. Their participation consisted, first, of touring the metropolitan area of Fremantle and Perth, the nearby state capital, to become familiar with as wide a variety of play facilities as possible. When the children visited each facility, they were invited to use the equipment. Following the visits, the children fed back their reactions to members of the resource team. Subsequently, the children participated in planning meetings to share and develop their values about play and to translate their values into ideas for the design of their playground. In so doing, it was necessary for them to confront several major choices and decisions. Having identified what they considered to be desirable attributes of a playground (several of which were revelations to the adults working with them), they had to address questions such as where the playground was to be located, who would be allowed to use it, how it was to be supervised, and so on. In the process, they progressively enlarged their images of the part the playground would have not only in the life of the school but in that of the surrounding community.

One group of children had considerable difficulty with the question of where the playground should be situated. They could identify only two possible locations, both of which were already being used—one by the boys for scratch football and the other by the girls for net ball. They did not want the children who played either game to lose their space. Therefore, instead of forcing a conflict, the group decided to wait to hear from the other groups in case there were alternatives they had overlooked. This proved to be the case, and the site chosen could be developed with little disruption to established activities. More important, when confronted with a situation of potential conflict, the children had resisted the temptation to polarize and fight, preferring to find out first whether there really was a conflict of interests. Their patience was rewarded, and the siting of the playground expressed a harmony of interests instead of becoming a monument to conflict and power struggles, as has happened so often in planning.

This wisdom was also evident in the manner in which the children dealt with the questions of use and supervision. When asked who should be allowed to use the playground, their first reaction was that only the children in the school should use it. Then some of the older children realized that they would soon be going to the local high school but might still want to use the playground. Eventually it was agreed that the high school students could use the playground, too, but that the younger children should have areas in which they could play safely. This lead to the question of supervision, which was important because if the playground was used without supervision, then the use of certain equipment was prohibited by law and the practical utility of the playground would be restricted, particularly on weekends. There was clearly a limit to the extra time the staff could be expected to put in. The children's solution was to ask residents in the immediate area to help; they suggested people who were retired or who spent most of the day at home. They went further and decided that the playground should have amenities for these extra helpers, such as pleasant, comfortable seating areas and interesting things for them to look at. From there, it was a short step for the children to decide that the playground should be for families as well. Their plans included a picnic area, a children's art gallery, and other facilities that could be shared by all.

Following the planning meetings, the three architecture students produced a design and model of the playground based on the children's plans. The model was displayed in the school, and all students were asked to evaluate the design and suggest changes. When the suggested changes had been incorporated into the plans, cost estimates were obtained and the proposed design was submitted to the government. The design was approved, and the playground stands as a product of a planning process in which the children discovered one opportunity after another to enlarge and pursue their conceptions of socially as well as physically desirable characteristics. It is also used extensively and enjoyed by all the groups for which it was planned.

The responses to change in Jamestown, Craigmillar, the numerous attempts to democratize work, and many other innovative initiatives grew out of increasing shared understanding of how present trends in the environment are affecting future prospects and a determination to pursue new, more desirable directions. The responses provide evidence that the futures many people would invent if they could are not those that might be expected to result from the blind pursuit of self-interest, competition with others, subservience to organization, and abandonment of the social and physical environment to the ravages of unchecked industrialism. The children of White Gum Valley and many adults who have engaged in similar planning processes during the 1970s have demonstrated the continuous nature of pursuing the new directions. As people identify and begin to pursue directions they find more desirable than the course they are presently on, they can also discover the possibilities for progressively enlarging their aspirations for the future.

Active adaptation to turbulent environments depends on discovery of how change is affecting future prospects, realization that persisting with established strategies based on industrial values and beliefs is self-defeating, and the emergence of new core values to guide choices about future directions. The basic required changes in choice behavior are summarized in Table 1.

Each example of active adaptive initiatives has been cited to illustrate change with respect to a particular dimension of human choice. However, the choice dimensions and their associated values and ideals are interrelated, and successful

TABLE 1.　Required Changes in Values and Ideals for Active Adaptation to Turbulent Environments.

Choice Parameter	Change Required for Active Adaptation	
	From	To
Concept of self in relation to others	Independent	Interdependent
Beliefs about more effective strategies for pursuing goals	Competition	Cooperation
Probable outcome of choice	Dehumanization	Humanization
Consequences for the social environment	Deformation	Pursuit of beauty

Adapted from Ackoff & Emery (1972) and Emery (1977).

strategies of active adaptation such as those that have been discussed must incorporate all of them.

It is clear that these adaptive innovations required fundamental changes in the organizational frameworks, which were exerting a restrictive influence on the choices of available futures. In Jamestown the change from independent to interdependent strategies required that a new organization be created through which mutually desired future directions could be identified and pursued in common. The revival of community spirit in Craigmillar and the enhancement of its inhabitants' future prospects would not have occurred through continued reliance on the existing governmental system. New collaborative relationships had to be developed within the community and between Craigmillar and the outside world. As an organization with roots in the community itself (and outside of yet able to establish links with the governmental system as well as with the private sector and other communities), the Craigmillar Festival Society has moved toward filling a critical vacuum by developing the internal and external relations necessary for the pursuit of new directions. The redesign of organizations to give employees sufficient control over their work to satisfy their own needs, as well as the demands of the task, required that the tendency toward maximum division of labor and regulation through hierarchy be reversed, at least partially. The release of creativity that produced the White Gum Valley playground would not have been possible through conventional planning approaches, which emphasize the role of experts and deny active participation by those being planned for. It required, instead, a new relationship in which clients assumed much greater responsibility for doing their own planning, with planning specialists providing technical service, assistance with the formation of shared images of what was desired, and translation of the images into reality.

A common theme runs through the adaptive innovations that have been described: All have involved widespread active participation in determining the ends to be pursued by those persons affected by the proposed innovation. These persons have chosen the means by which to pursue their chosen ends and have learned from the experience of acting on their environments in their search for new directions. The conditions required to allow such participation are clearly not present in bureaucratic organizations. Transforming bureaucratic organizations and creating new mechanisms for participation and collaboration are central to developing within societies the potential for the continuous active adaptation necessary to reduce turbulence and manage uncertain transition.

BEYOND BUREAUCRACY: CHARACTERISTICS OF ORGANIZATIONAL DEMOCRACY

The challenge is to create an organizational climate in which active adaptation to turbulent environments can occur. In bureaucratic organizations, the great majority of people are excluded from the process of determining the ends to be served by their efforts. They generally have little scope to experiment with alternative methods of achieving those ends and to adapt to changing conditions. Whatever information about performance they receive is usually fragmented, providing little opportunity for individuals to see how their roles relate to those of others or what contribution they make to larger outcomes. Bureaucratic organizations generally also deny individuals the opportunity to fulfill more than basic material human needs. As a result, not only are individuals unable to concern themselves seriously with the question of whether organizational objectives are being achieved, but there is little reason why they should wish to be concerned. Indeed, their personal aims may well be at odds with the requirements of organizational effectiveness. In this case, any attempts the organization makes to increase external control over individuals are likely to be met with subversive countermeasures.

The Democratization of Work

Alternatives to bureaucratic structures are being sought in many spheres, but the clearest picture of what the transformation of organizations entails has emerged from cumulative experience with redesigning the organization of tasks. The studies and experiments of Trist and his associates in the British coal industry demonstrated that industrial technology can be applied to economic production without destroying the conditions under which people are able to satisfy their own needs (Trist, Higgin, Murray, & Pollock, 1963). During the 30 years since that discovery, research and experience with redesigning the organization of work in many different countries and a wide variety of industries has revealed a basic alternative

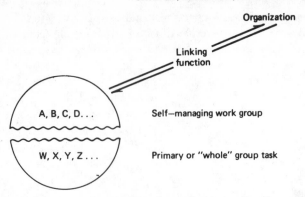

Figure 2.   Democratized work organization. From Emery and Emery (1975) with permission.

to bureaucracy. The essential characteristics of the alternative organizational form are shown in Figure 2 (compare Figure 1 with Figure 2 to see the striking differences).

The basic change is from individuals working on highly subdivided tasks to groups of employees responsible for sets of interdependent tasks comprising wholes that can be identified readily by members of the group and by the organization as the group's distinctive collective output. The members of the group work at much the same tasks that they did as individuals. Within the group, however, its members have the prerogative to arrange all the tasks to achieve simultaneously accomplishment of the overall job and satisfaction of their own needs. They often become competent to perform most or all tasks within the group, depending on the nature of the work. Decisions about the organization of work are made by the group's members within limits set by the larger organization's requirements. In other words, members are free to organize and reorganize themselves in whatever way suits them best, provided agreed-on objectives are met in terms of output quantity and quality. Once the resources necessary for performing the group task are determined and arrangements are made to supply them, it is unnecessary for management to specify the work organization of the group in any greater detail. It would incur unnecessary costs to do so and would defeat the purpose of organizing work in this way, which is to create conditions under which employees can meet the company's objectives and their own requirements under changing circumstances (Cummings & Srivastva, 1978; Emery & Emery, 1975; Emery & Thorsrud, 1976; Herbst, 1974, 1976; Susman, 1976).

Several features of this organizational alternative warrant belief elaboration. Whereas the bureaucratic strategy of organizational design seeks to optimize the performance of the technical system and then requires individuals to adjust themselves to that system, the alternative approach focuses on the interface between technology and people to achieve the best possible match between both. Susman (1976) has summarized the aims of this approach very well, stating:

It is fundamental to sociotechnical analysis to recognize that a schism exists between the technical "world" organized around rational principles of efficiency and the phenomenal world within which humans live their daily lives. The principles by which one world is organized are not necessarily or even likely to be the same as those by which the other is organized. . . . Although these two systems are different from each other they operate in parallel in any concrete work setting. The objective of sociotechnical analysis is to establish conditions allowing these two systems to operate in complementary fashion. [This is achieved] when workgroup members can effectively use elements of the technical system as objects towards which directed action can be taken to produce desired outcomes—notably, acceptable products and member self-enhancement. (161)

Achieving a best match between the technical and social systems entails consideration of the psychological and social requirements individuals have in their working lives. The more common needs have been referred to in the previous section, but they are too general to provide sufficient guidance in the design of particular jobs and work settings. Therefore, we must translate them into terms that are meaningful in specific work contexts. Also, we must recognize that the requirements vary in importance between different jobs and the individuals performing them (Trist, 1977).

In most cases there is little scope for improving work from the standpoint of both personal satisfaction and productive achievement so long as the focus remains on individual tasks. At this level, individuals in most occupations do not have sufficient control over the factors affecting their work situations. Many individual tasks are so small and fragmented that performing them does not produce a meaningful end product, and individuals responsible for separate tasks often have neither the ability nor the incentive for coordinating their efforts with one another except, perhaps, to defeat external supervision. The possibilities for innovative restructuring of tasks and task relationships generally are much greater at the level of the work group than at the individual task level. The work group as an organizational unit is large enough to encompass tasks that contribute to the production of complete products or services that are valued by group members and the organization. The work group is large enough so that group members can make significant decisions about the allocation and coordination of work activities, including developing the necessary skills for solving problems, resolving conflicts, establishing consensus, and engaging in planning. The group is also sufficiently large to provide several alternative ways of structuring and restructuring task relationships to achieve given outcomes, thereby enabling members to experiment and to adapt to change.

At the same time, the group is small enough to be managed by the members themselves. It is small enough to allow members to see the relationship between the decisions they make and the achievement of their goals. Another extremely important benefit is that the group is on a human scale so that the individual can experience a genuine sense of membership regardless of how large the whole enterprise may be. Rather than just doing a job, members can redefine themselves and one another in terms of the value of their contribution to the group's overall task. Moreover, the group is sufficiently small for there to be effective communication among its members, enabling them to increase their adaptive potential through sharing of learning and knowledge. The group's effectiveness is thereby increased even in constantly changing conditions (Emery & Emery, 1975; Susman, 1976).

Much depends, however, on the amount and type of autonomy and the scope for self-regulation that work groups are permitted. The groups are still part of a larger organizational entity, and therefore, they are constrained by the wider requirements of that entity. In the case of private corporations, for example, Emery and Emery (1975) state:

> These groups can only be semi-autonomous, not fully autonomous. . . .
> They are working with materials and equipment for which the company is responsible for getting an adequate return. They are working in conditions where the company, not they, are responsible for observing the mass of legislation laid down for basic pay rates, safety, product quality, etc. (p. 35)

In dealing with the questions of how much and what kind of autonomy work groups should have, a constraining factor is the requirement that the organization be able to meet its responsibilities to the wider set of internal and external stakeholders and to the society as a whole. For this reason, work groups can be conditionally autonomous insofar as they have freedom to arrange and rearrange their internal affairs, yet they acknowledge and accept their responsiblity to the larger organization.

To be autonomous, a work group must have at the minimum the freedom to determine working methods and the allocation of tasks among its members. The group must have as well the right to decide who among them shall make which decisions about these matters and by what processes. Their freedom consists of a relative separateness from organizational and technological constraints so that work group members have the autonomy that enables them to govern themselves in their own way. Susman (1976) suggests that the exercise of autonomy involves making decisions of "independence" and "self-governance," meaning that the members of the group have the capability for managing their internal arrangements to satisfy their own preferred ways of working. At the same time, they are able to make decisions about how they will attempt to relate their own performance to the demands and exigencies of the production process itself. Susman refers to these decisions as "self-regulation." In other words, given that work groups accept their autonomy as conditional on meeting larger organizational requirements, they must have the scope to make decisions for themselves about how to reorganize internally to meet the work-related demands that are made on them. There are, therefore, two dimensions, or areas, of autonomy. One allows work group members the room to make decisions that have no direct bearing on production but that meet their own requirements. An example is the scheduling of rest periods, which can be arranged to reduce feelings of being tied to the job but that have no adverse effects on output. The other dimension allows them to regulate their own performance as a group in relation to the functioning of the production system, deciding for themselves how best to make their contribution to productive output under both stable and changing conditions.

In many circumstances, the control over their work that the work groups have may be extended to incorporate maintenance of equipment, selection and recruitment of new members, and acceptance or rejection of inputs from previous stages of the production process (Emery & Emery, 1975. The opportunity to create all the necessary conditions for autonomy and self-regulation depends on the nature of the work being performed. The products or services the organization produces, the inputs it receives from the environment, and the methods it employs for converting inputs into outputs have an overriding influence on the work activities that must be performed, the interdependencies among them, and the nature of the coordination problems that must be solved.

There are two critical problems concerning the interdependent activities that should comprise group tasks and the required transactions between work groups and higher decision-making levels. In combining productive activities into group tasks, the first main problem is to include sufficient interdependent activities to comprise meaningful wholes from the standpoint of group members and the organization. Within a work system points can usually be identified at which each major phase commences and is completed. These points provide a basis for determining which linked activities should be merged into group tasks. Miller (1959), for example, proposes three ways in which activities can be grouped: (1) on the basis of the technology that makes certain activities more closely interdependent and related to one another than to the rest of the production system; (2) on the basis of time, as in the case of work organized into shifts; and (3) on the basis of territory, where activities are performed in a common geographic space such as branch operation. Whichever basis is adopted (and different ones may be used in combination), the purpose is to define the boundaries of work groups as organizational units responsible for performing whole tasks, or functions.

Given the definition of the boundaries of the basic work groups, the second problem concerns the relationships of the groups to one another and to managerial and staff functions. In many cases, the task each group performs affects and is affected by the task performances of other groups. In Thompson's (1967) classification, the lowest degree of interdependence occurs when each group makes a discrete contribution to total output and groups are linked only indirectly through

their effects on the overall outcome. Work groups are more directly interdependent when the tasks of certain groups cannot begin until other groups have completed theirs. Finally, the interdependence among groups is most complex when
their task performances affect one another in a reciprocal manner. These different
kinds of interdependence are shown in Figure 3.

The way in which groups are interdependent affects their exercise of autonomy
and self-regulation. Groups linked only through their separate contributions to total output are largely independent and usually can organize their activities with little or no effect on one another. Their primary transactions with the wider organization concern ensuring adequate supplies of resources necessary for task
performance, meeting objectives, and adapting to changes in organizational requirements. Sequentially interdependent groups must coordinate their task performances so that each is able to operate with minimal disruption by groups working on preceding tasks. This requirement can be achieved in two ways: (1) through
scheduling, when groups plan their activities to take account of the whole productive sequence, and (2) through buffering, when each group is protected from disruption to the flow of its inputs. When groups are reciprocally interdependent, de-

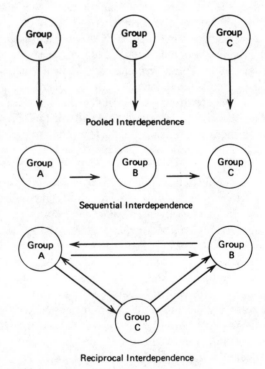

Figure 3.   Types of interdependence among group tasks.

veloping and maintaining coordination requires that they adjust to one another more or less continuously by exchanging information about changes in the requirements of task performance (Thompson, 1967).

So far as is possible, work groups should be able to coordinate for themselves not only their internal activities but also their external interdependencies. Under the conditions of turbulence in organizational environments that have been previously discussed, planners must deal with more uncertainty at the level of the work group. This uncertainty cannot, or does not have to be, reduced for the groups by higher levels of management. Indeed, the more these management levels become involved in detailed surveillance of task performance, the less able they are to deal effectively with the larger change forces affecting the organization as a whole. Conversely, as work groups become responsible for their own internal management and for coordinating with other groups, supervisory personnel are released to concentrate on relationships the groups cannot manage themselves, to engage in more long-term planning, and to assume other responsibilities which, in bureaucratically designed organizations, would be prerogatives of higher management. The main function of supervision becomes that of mediating between the work groups and the organization.

The first aspect of the supervisory role is to regulate the amount and types of change and uncertainty flowing to the work groups. Supervisors must allow the groups to assume responsibility for any boundary transactions appropriate for them to control. At the same time, supervisors must protect the groups' boundary conditions by attempting to reduce the disruptive effects of change arising in the wider organization—such as variations in quality, quantity, rate of inputs, or sudden changes in demand. The supervisory levels must engage more frequently and actively with organizational units other than the work groups—such as technical staff units, other departments, and management—to create, maintain, and modify the conditions that enable the groups to accomplish their tasks and to ensure the groups' freedom to establish their own working arrangements.

The second aspect of the supervisory role involves helping groups to develop and maintain the internal ability and willingness necessary for effective autonomous functioning. In order to be self-managing, groups must possess technical and organizational knowledge and skills not ordinarily exercised by employees when they are organized bureaucratically. These skills include the ability to formulate objectives, to develop plans for achieving objectives, to find solutions to problems, to resolve conflicts, and to use the group structure to accomplish the overall task. Particularly during the initial phase of redesigning work on the basis of conditionally autonomous groups, an important part of the supervisory role is to help to provide the training necessary for group members to acquire the relevant knowledge and skills and to facilitate the process of developing effective group organization. As groups become competent at self-management, the involvement of supervision in their internal affairs declines significantly, with more time and ef-

fort being devoted to external matters (Susman, 1976). As with the determination
of group tasks and boundaries, the nature of the supervisory role depends on the
kind of work performed and the means by which it is carried out. Depending on
these and other factors, the supervisory role in a particular group may be assigned
to a single individual and treated as distinct from the roles within the group, or it
may be established as an integral part of the group and shared among members.
Often the formal position of supervisor is abolished, and group members assume
responsibility for internal and external co-ordination (Emery & Emery, 1975).

The Democratization of Management

Given the conditionally autonomous work group as the basic unit of the organization and the function of supervision as mediating between the work group and the
larger organization, we can view the nature and arrangement of managerial functions from a different perspective. We no longer see their primary concern as one
of exercising detailed surveillance over the implementation of managerial decisions. Several writers have suggested that three levels of functions can be
identified within organizations: institutional, managerial, and technical. The *institutional level* is concerned with relationships between the whole organization
and its environment or with creating, maintaining, and modifying the external
transactions essential to the organization's survival and development. The main
function of the institutional level is to define the organization's mission and to
make judgments about the significance for that mission of changes occurring in
the environment (Selznick, 1957). Beyond merely observing what is happening in
the environment, providing leadership at this level entails making and remaking
value judgments about what ought to be done in response. Such judgments express the values on which organizational policies are based. The *managerial level*
is concerned with translating these values into objectives and the strategies for
achieving them within particular time periods, subject to limitations imposed by
economic, political, social, and technological conditions. Decision making at the
managerial level involves the development of strategic plans, attempting to incorporate and reconcile the objectives and operations of the various divisions and departments within the organization, and adjusting overall organizational plans as
conditions or objectives change. The *technical level* is concerned with the implementation of managerial decisions. This level may include specialist functions
such as production control and general regulation of work performance (Emery,
1976; Parsons, 1960; Selznick, 1957; Susman, 1976; Thompson, 1967).

Obviously the three-level scheme of management implies some form of hierarchical ordering within organizations, but it is a hierarchical ordering of functions and not necessarily of offices. In bureaucratically designed organizations,
each level of function tends to be equated with levels of authority and status vested
in particular offices. Typically, institutional level functions are the exclusive

province of the governing body and of the president or managing director. Managerial decisions are the responsibility of divisional and department heads. Maintaining control over the technical level is the responsibility of junior management, staff specialists, and supervisors. Within each level, the overall function is typically broken down into subfunctions assigned to particular offices. These vertical and lateral divisions then become the basis for detailed surveillance by one functional level of the next lower level (see Figure 1). In democratically designed organizations it is recognized that the three levels of function—institutional, managerial, and technical—are qualitatively different and that different kinds of knowledge, experience, and skills are required to perform them. However, the differences are not used to justify the unilateral and detailed domination of persons in lower level functions. The differentiation of roles within each level is not taken to extremes, as tends to happen in bureaucratic organizations. And the capabilities required to perform effectively at higher levels are not considered to be so unusual as to exclude persons working at lower levels from participation in higher-level decision making.

Consensus on desirable overall directions in relation to the environment must be reached at the institutional level that coordinates the organization as a whole. Strategic plans and decisions made at the managerial level also refer to the entire organization or to large areas within it. The institutional level encompasses the managerial level, and the latter encompasses the technical level (Ozbekhan, 1971; Susman, 1976). Nevertheless, it has been shown that even at the technical level work can be organized to provide considerably greater scope for self-management than is available in bureaucratic organizations. This need not apply only to basic operating groups. The technical specialists can also function independently without control by higher levels of decision making. This is feasible, for example, when their work is organized around projects that require cooperation among different specialists and between technical and operating groups. In such cases, the basic organizational unit becomes a multidisciplinary team comprised of individuals with distinctive knowledge and skills but who share responsibility for accomplishing project tasks. Once the project objectives, composition, boundaries, and external interdependencies of the team are established, it is possible for its members to organize and manage their own activities in much the same way as groups of operatives, subject only to the same general constraining factor of the team's accountability to the larger organization (Kingdon, 1973).

Similarly, work at the managerial level can be arranged so that executives are able to deal jointly with large areas of organizational decision making that extend beyond their individual divisional or departmental responsibilities by cooperating with one another to achieve common objectives, rather than each executive being subject individually to the directives of the chief executive officer. The pattern of arrangements for technical specialists and managers is shown in Figure 4. As in creating conditions that allow for autonomy and self-management among opera-

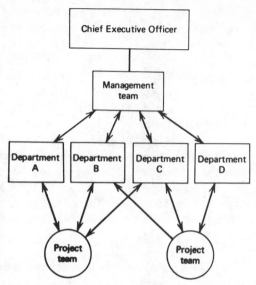

Figure 4.   Organization for cooperative self-management by managers and technical specialist staff.

tors, it is necessary to focus on the set of interdependent tasks and roles requiring coordination. These tasks and roles form the basic unit of organizational design, and it is necessary to locate responsibility for coordination with those persons performing them. Although operators may become competent at performing most or all of the activities that comprise the group's tasks, often it is difficult and undesirable for the members of the technical and managerial teams to attempt to become sufficiently knowledgeable or skilled to perform all the roles involved. Each individual member of a technical or managerial team is more likely to make a special contribution to overall outcomes. The difference as compared to bureaucratic organization is that each individual is judged as much on the basis of effective cooperation and coordination with other members of the team as on the success of the individual's division or department. Effective contribution to overall outcomes may even entail short-term sacrifice of performance in one area in the pursuit of larger shared objectives (Emery & Emery, 1975).

Thus, in organizational democracy, the primary responsibility for decisions and coordination at each functional level is located within that level, a result of recognizing the distinctive contribution that each level makes to the organization and respecting its autonomy. Creating and maintaining conditions in which lower levels can be independent of higher levels depends on the ability of those engaged in interdependent work activities at each level to manage their own coordination, and the higher levels must refrain as far as possible from intervening at lower levels. The institutional level of organizational leadership is concerned primarily with the organization's external relations, leaving those at the managerial level to deal with internal issues of strategy and planning. Likewise, the managerial level concerns itself with broad areas of strategic decision making but not with the details of implementation that are the province of the technical or operative level. When compared with bureaucratic organizations, considerably greater power to decide and act is located at lower organizational levels in democratic organizations (Heller, 1976). Still, many people argue that employees should have even greater involvement in organizational decisions. The institutional and managerial levels set the normative and strategic directions for the organization. Proponents of worker control and worker participation in corporate decision making argue that the great majority of employees still have very limited involvement unless they have control or influence over normative and strategic as well as technical decisions. Although these advocates vary widely in the amount and type of involvement in policy and strategy formulation they seek for employees, they consider that worker control over or participation in the determination of organizational directions at these levels is essential. Initiatives to establish employee representation and participation in policy and strategy formulation have been taken in a number of industrialized countries, for the most part in Europe. In general, such initiatives take the form of councils that parallel existing organizational structures, and they provide for joint consultation and decision making by representatives of management and employees. In West Germany, the government's policy of "codetermination" also requires that workers' representatives comprise half the membership of boards of directors (Jenkins, 1974).

Apart from ideological considerations, there are strong reasons why employees might wish to be involved in decisions concerning organizational policy and strategy. Present and emerging trends in western societies are creating considerable uncertainty about future employment prospects, and employees have an important stake in how organizations respond to these trends. Technological change toward higher levels of mechanization and automation, regional economic decline, withdrawal of firms from industries or geographical areas in the face of economic difficulties, and changing patterns of business investment all raise serious doubts about whether the present employment levels can be maintained—let alone increased. Furthermore, even when business activities are economically viable in the short term, their longer term social and economic consequences may concern people as members of society as well as employees. For example, manufacturing processes and products that are harmful or that consume nonrenewable resources have become increasingly controversial. The employees of these industries are just as likely as other people to be aware of the effects and implications of the products they help to produce. Concern for employment prospects and the social responsibility of business were the motivating forces behind the "Alternative Corporate Plan," which workers at Lucas Aerospace in Britain presented to the company's management through their union shop stewards. This plan proposes a far-reaching conversion from the company's present product base, which has been declining, to some 150 products believed by the authors of the plan to be "technically feasible and socially useful." The products include heat pumps and a diesel-electric unit for city cars that may reduce fuel consumption by 50 percent and almost eliminate noxious emissions, and a road–rail vehicle that runs on both roads and railroad lines and that could have important advantages for Third World countries as well as for densely populated urban areas in the western world. The reasoning of the Lucas workers was quite pragmatic. They wanted Lucas Aerospace to convert from products with doubtful futures, such as those dependent on the conventional automobile industry for market outlets, to developing products in line with the direction of societal trends and needs. They wanted to prevent layoffs and revive the business, and this concern led them to seek involvement in determining the future directions of the company as a whole. (*Self-Reliance,* November-December, 1978)

Although Lucas Aerospace management rejected the proposed plan completely, the plan provides a powerful example of the desire among at least some shopfloor employees to influence the formulation of policy and strategy during times when organizations are confronted with mounting uncertainty in their environments. Nevertheless, the extent of this desire is far from clear, and the most prevalent approaches to employee participation do not achieve their avowed aims.

Evidence that employees wish to be involved in decision making at the institutional and managerial levels of the organization varies greatly and is often conflicting. Some observers such as Derber (1970) report finding little or no evidence that employees wish to participate in decision making at these levels, whereas for others, the assumption that employees do wish to participate seems to be an article of faith. Summarizing their recent British findings, Wall and Lischeron (1977) conclude:

> Workers show a desire for considerable if not complete autonomy *in their jobs.* At higher organizational levels. . . the most prevalent view is that influence should be shared equally between workers as a group and management. Only a minority are of the opinion that decision-making should be the sole prerogative of managers, and even fewer that some form of workers' control (where workers hold the balance of influence) would be desirable. Given the lack of influence respondents perceived *at all but the lowest levels of decision-making* then it is in middle and top-management that the greatest increases are sought. (p. 142, emphasis added)

The studies of Wall and Lischeron suggest a stronger desire for participation in decision making at higher levels than has been indicated by many previous studies, for which they offer two possible explanations. One is that the changes in the social, political, and industrial climate during the 1970s may have influenced workers' attitudes toward greater participation. The other is that they provided in their questionnaires examples of specific decisions associated with the different organizational levels, which may have given their respondents a clearer idea as to what was meant by "participation." This understanding was probably increased through the actual experience of participation provided by organizational experiments. A third factor may be even more significant: The employees who participated in the studies and experiments appear to have placed the emphasis, first and foremost, on control over their own work. When employees considered that they had adequate control over their own immediate work situations, they seem to have been more inclined toward becoming involved in managerial and institutional decision making.

These findings are plausible and consistent with the observations and experiences of others who have found employees to be more interested in autonomy in their workplaces (Emery & Thorsrud, 1969). The growing importance to the future of both employees and societies of policy and strategic decisions and the mounting uncertainty that surrounds these decisions may well give employees more reason to want to become involved at these levels. It appears, however, that for many employees participation begins in their immediate work environment. Equally plausible is the finding that when employees seek participation at higher levels, their desire is to share power with management rather than to usurp it. This finding also suggests a recognition that performance at each organizational level depends on distinctive knowledge, experience, and skills. This need not exclude those whose work involves them primarily at technical or operative levels from participation in making managerial and institutional decisions. It does suggest that meaningful participation by employees must be achieved, first, by ensuring that they are able to control their own work and the factors immediately affecting their work. Next, it raises the question of how employees might become involved effectively in decisions affecting the future directions of the entire organization.

The great majority of designs for employee participation in managerial and institutional decision making are based on systems of elected representation. Workers are represented by their elected union leaders, by fellow employees they elect to represent them in decision-making bodies, or through some combination of both. This approach has been criticized on several grounds. One is that systems of elected representation are often incorporated into organizational structures that are still bureaucratic and amount to little more than attempts to redistribute influence in and control over the higher echelons of bureaucratic organizations. Although some representative systems have been introduced (together with innovations in the redesign of work, as in Norway and Sweden), in many cases the work situations of employees on the factory or office floor have remained largely unchanged (Emery & Thorsrud, 1969). A closely related criticism is that the bodies to which employee representatives are elected tend to become centralist and elitist, providing representatives with avenues of advancement out of the workplace that may

become more important to them than the interests and needs of those they represent. Third, these bodies often do not have any effective decision-making functions, most of them being actually consultative or advisory committees where employee representatives may make inputs to decisions but are unlikely to influence
the final outcomes. For these reasons, the majority of employees in countries
where formal systems of worker representation have been established seem to be
cynical and suspicious of them (Jenkins, 1974).

When employees wish to participate in making managerial and institutional decisions, they are unlikely to have that wish satisfied through arrangements that allow only for indirect and remote involvement. The findings of Wall and Lischeron
(1977) suggest that this may be the case even where employees' representatives
are their own union leaders. They report:

> Participation through personal interaction with management was the choice
> of the large majority of nurses and industrial workers at all levels of
> decision-making and of most Local Authority workers at the middle man-
> agement level. . . . The relative lack of support for participation based on
> trade union representation is notworthy. Among nurses this may be ex-
> pected, but for blue-collar workers (especially those in the industrial sample
> who were all union members and active in this respect) it is less predictable.
> Nevertheless, the explanation is straightforward. To most of these workers,
> pay, security and disciplinary issues defined the normal limits of their shop
> steward's and trade union's activities. Consequently, in relation to partici-
> pation in other areas they looked to other forms of involvement. (p. 145)

There have been important exceptions among trade unions. The shop stewards at
Lucas Aerospace and the local union leaders at Jamestown did not restrict themselves to the traditional concerns of organized labor. They sought ways to involve
their members with management in important strategic decisons. At least
some labor–management committees that participated in a review of labor–management cooperation in the American public sector have developed strong chan-
nels for cooperation on a wide range of issues that complement existing bargaining machinery. In general, however, designs based on elected representation
have not effectively involved employees in the formulation of organizational policy and strategy.

The principal justification for systems of elected representation is that, except
in very small enterprises, the numbers of employees are far too great for every-
body to participate in every decision at the managerial and institutional levels. It
may not be necessary, however, for them even to be represented in every such decision. When the technical and managerial levels have autonomy and the scope to
make their own decisions, under such arrangements as have been described, it is
conceivable that all three levels can exercise mutual or reciprocal control in rela-

tion to one another rather than being locked into a hierarchic al control structure. This system would require, first, that the organization have an explicitly stated philosophy and set of objectives about which there is broad agreement. Emery (1976) suggests that the task of producing a statement of philosophy and objectives should be undertaken initially by the board of directors but should then be negotiated at all levels. Once agreement has been reached as to desirable overall objectives for the organization, each level should be free to discharge its responsibilities, provided that its decisions and actions are in accordance with the agreement. The only time when all these levels need to engage directly with one another is when the agreed-on objectives are not being adhered to and when change makes a significant reappraisal of the objectives necessary. The second requirement is that mechanisms be created for interaction at the interfaces among the different functional levels so that mutual control and cooperation can be exercised.

The two critical interfaces are between the technical and managerial levels and between managerial levels and the institutional level. The relationship between managerial and technical objectives must be worked out and translated into performance requirements at the level of the work groups. Here, the number of employees involved will often preclude direct participation by all concerned, but elected representation is not the only way of dealing with this problem. Core groups of technical and managerial employees can be formed by selecting members at random to serve for a specified period of time. When this period is completed, as a general rule members are replaced by their peers who again are selected at random from among those eligible. To ensure continuity, turnover of members can be staggered. In some instances, key individuals may be needed for a further period of time. Members are drawn from all technical and managerial groups where cooperation is needed to develop and implement the objectives and plans involving both levels. Within these groups, any individual can expect to be called on to serve in the core group at some time, but no one serves for an indefinite uninterrupted period. Such a system can provide the conditions for effective interaction and coordination between the technical and managerial levels while avoiding many of the pitfalls encountered when participation is sought through elected representatives (Emery, 1976).

At the interface between the managerial and institutional levels, the central issue is to establish and maintain a close match between the philosophy and objectives of the organization and management's strategies. The two levels have quite distinct functions and, as with operators or technical level employees, it is unnecessary for the managerial level to be directly involved or represented in all decisions. In determining directions for the organization, the board must take into account the interests of all affected stakeholders. To provide for only managerial level employees to participate or be represented in the board's decisions could, if anything, hamper the board in discharging its full responsibilities. At the same time, interaction between the two levels is essential to ensure that management understands and is willing and able to work out its strategies within the normative framework established by the statement of philosophy and objectives, and that the board understands management's own requirements. Interaction between the two levels for this purpose need not occur as frequently as between the technical and managerial levels. However, an interactive mode in which both levels review objectives, policy, and strategy in the light of major external and internal changes is necessary in addition to the more frequent contact the chief executive officer has with the management team as part of the daily business of guiding the organization's functioning (Emery & Emery, 1975). Even in large organizations it has often been possible for all or most managerial employees to participate directly in these events.

So far, we have discussed in general terms an alternative to bureaucracy for the design and management of single organizations. This alternative involves reversing the bureaucratic principle whereby the work of an organization is subdivided to such an extent that the great majority of employees cannot control and coordinate their own efforts and therefore are made subject to direction and control through hierarchical structures. The alternative is based on conditionally autonomous self-regulating teams whose members are jointly responsible for interdependent tasks comprising whole outputs and for coordinating their activities and external relations, adapting their group organization as conditions or needs change. The basic requirement for democratizing organization is that operators, specialists, and managers have autonomy and scope for self-management with respect to the factors that directly affect their work situation. Beyond this, employees at all levels have a stake in the choices about future directions that are made for the organization as a whole, but they are unlikely to exert effective influence through elected representatives, and direct participation in all such decisions usually is impossible and unnecessary. Given the organizational power self-managing groups have, it is possible for them to exercise mutual control in relation to one another, and mechanisms for periodic interaction between the levels over issues that affect them all can be created. This strategy of organizational design recognizes the role of unions, but whether their role remains limited to traditional bargaining matters or expands to contribute to the active adaptation of the organization depends very much on developing new cooperative relationships between unions and management, such as those established by some of the American labor–management committees. The design strategy recognizes different levels of functions within organizations. It seeks, first, to create conditions for autonomy and control within each level, and second, to provide for strategic participation by all levels in major choices about the future directions of the entire organization.

As organizations move toward organizational democracy, experience and evidence so far suggest that their potential for active adaptation to turbulent environments is likely to increase. The nature and extent of improvement will vary, but it arises from greater commitment and performance capability at the shopfloor level, a reduced burden of internal supervision, greater concentration by management on strategic decisions and adaptation to external change, more effective communication and coordination among departments, and more support for organizational objectives and policies determined in part by employees. For organizations, increased active adaptive potential is evidenced by improved productivity as well as reduced turnover, absenteeism, and intraorganizational conflict. In their working lives employees are likely to experience the psychological and social improvements referred to earlier in this chapter and particularly an increased autonomy in their own work (Jenkins, 1974; Emery & Thorsrud, 1976; Lindestad & Kvist, 1975; Lindholm & Norstedt, 1975; Noren & Norstedt, 1975; Norstedt & Aguren, 1973; O'Toole, 1973; Torner, 1975; Trist, Higgin, Murray, & Pollock, 1963). To the extent that organizations are able to reduce and manage the uncertainty surrounding their choice of future directions through the transformation of bureaucratic structures into adaptive democratic social designs, the capability of societies for dealing effectively with the issues and problems they confront is also likely to increase. However, it is necessary to go further.

The Democratization of Community Governance

Because of the increasing interdependence within and among societies, the major sources of uncertainty cannot be controlled by organizations acting independently in pursuit of their own objectives. The mainsprings of change have moved from organizations to the environment, and not merely to the task or transactional environments organizations are accustomed to dealing with but to the contextual environment that engulfs all sectors, regions, organizations, and communities. Western industrial societies characteristically have responded in two ways to change that cannot be controlled by single organizations pursuing their own purposes. In the early phases of industrialism, the prevalent response of societies was to assume that large-scale change contained a self-stabilizing dynamic and that, after periods of disruption, conditions would return to a state of equilibrium. On this assumption, the best course was to allow a major change in the condition of society to work itself out. Classical economic theory and, for the most part, the economic policies of governments epitomized this assumption and characteristic response modes until the 1930s. Since then, governments have not been prepared or allowed to assume that fluctuations in their workings will contain themselves within limits tolerable to societies. Moreover, governments have undertaken to meet a growing number of social needs and demands that are not met by the private sector. In consequence, the role of government has expanded greatly, and increasing reliance has been placed on government to regulate societies. It is unlikely that western societies will return to the assumption of autoregulation and the philosophy of *laissez faire* unless, in the event of virtually total breakdown and collapse, they are forced to abandon any hope of shaping their future directions coherently and cohesively. The greater worry is that they will persist in reliance on central governments. This persistence has led not only to excessive government but, because government administration in western societies is entrenched in the structure and traditions of bureaucracy, societies are being prevented from developing social designs and strategies through which the issues and problems that beset them might be managed and desirable future directions pursued. Most societies are weighed down by ineffective overgovernment.

The procedures by which elected assemblies and govenment are chosen, the processes of competition and coalition among sectional interests to gain political influence, and the organizational arrangements for the public management of societies' affairs are outmoded. Electorates are represented on the basis of geographically determined constituencies that reflect history and tradition more than the changing patterns of concerns and needs within society. Political parties and organized interest groups reflect sectional conflicts and alignments that are losing their relevance and meaning. The numerous agencies through which governments attempt to work promote strong centralized control through their internal hierarchies but discourage coordination among agencies. Each agency has its own mandate and objectives that all too frequently become self-justifying. Agencies compete for resources and carry out their programs with little regard for one another and for their impact on society beyond being concerned with achieving their particular objectives. As a result, governmental structures are poorly adapted to cope with emerging issues and their complex interrelationships. Lacking alternatives, societies continue to rely upon them.

The issues that have become critical for societies—such as stagflation, urban and regional decline, and environmental deterioration—cut across the previously established boundaries of organizations and other social groupings. Stakeholders in these issues often are dispersed physically or organizationally and do not interact with one another to identify the ways in which their interests are linked and to develop shared aims and strategies for the future. Unable to manage their interdependencies for themselves, they must be regulated from above by governments. New social designs are needed that permit active adaptive response to turbulence to be generated by those persons most directly affected by a given issue or set of issues. The new designs would be based on sets of interdependencies among stakeholders that Trist (1977) has called "domains." The criteria for identifying domains may be geographical, as when the issues in question concern towns or regions. Or they may be functional when stakeholders are linked through common services, such as health and education, or through the activities of particular industries. The domain, comprised of interdependent interests that are all affected by the same sources of uncertainties about the future, becomes the new unit of analysis, planning, and action rather than single organizations. The emergence and activation of domains entails, first, the development of shared awareness about who the affected stakeholders are and the nature of the issues and problems affecting them. As this happens, a domain begins to acquire an identity that is commonly perceived and understood by those persons involved, making it possible for them to agree about the nature of the problems facing them and to seek future directions that it is desirable for them to pursue jointly (Trist, 1977, 1979).

The structures and boundaries of domains are unlikely to coincide with those of existing organizations in the public and private sectors. In the case of Jamestown, referred to earlier, numerous organizations and interests were involved; no single organization provided the means by which they could interact to develop agreed-on strategies for pursuing new directions. I encountered a similar situation when I was engaged as an adviser in planning for the future of an important natural region in Australia. The region was threatened by the uncoordinated activities of more than 30 different commercial, industrial, residential, and recreational groups of users and several local and state government authorities. It was clear that no single, detailed plan for the region could be imposed bureaucratically by any one body because of the fragmented jurisdictions involved. The future of the region depended on the agreement by many different stakeholders to cooperate in determining desirable future directions and regulating their activities in accordance with those directions. No mechanism for collaborative planning existed, however. If active adaptation to a turbulent environment is to occur at the level of domains, structures must be developed to enable the members of these domains to participate in the joint management of their shared futures.

Such structures are based on networks and network nodes through which members of a domain become purposively linked. In his own studies of domains, Trist (1977, 1978c, 1979) emphasizes the importance of "referent organizations," which activate and maintain domains by providing the means for the stakeholder interaction necessary to identify and respond to continuous change. Referent organizations do not have hierarchical authority over their constituent members. Instead, they perform vital functions for members that members could not perform for themselves if acting independently. These functions include (1) providing interactive settings in which shared judgments can be made about emerging trends and issues and in which mutually desired future directions can be determined; (2) enabling members to identify more clearly the domain's boundaries and constituent organizations and groups, to establish the ground rules for their collaboration, and to regulate their relationships and activities; (3) affirming the core values that give collaboration its direction and purpose; and (4) providing infrastructure support by mobilizing resources, facilitating information sharing, and undertaking or providing assistance with projects in the domain (Trist, 1979). Referent organizations can play a central role in linking stakeholders who otherwise would be only weakly connected with one another and, therefore, dependent on government to regulate relationships among them. Such organizations are intermediate between the *micro* level of single organizations and groups that act independently or competitively and the *macro* level of government policy and planning. The Jamestown Area Labor–Management Committee and the Craigmillar Festival Society are examples of initiatives taken to create referent organizations. To the extent that they and other similar initiatives succeed, societies will begin to fill a critical vacuum in their structures. More planned adaptive response to emerging trends and issues will be possible at the more localized level of the domain, with less need for continuous direct intervention by state and national governments (Berry, Metcalfe, & McQuillan, 1974; Emery, 1976; Friedman, 1973; Metcalfe & McQuillan, 1975; Schon, 1971; Trist, 1977, 1978c, 1979).

Because referent organizations cannot control the members of domains by hierarchical means, collaboration among members must be achieved through non-hierarchical negotiation. Several different patterns of relationships between referent organizations and domain members have been identified so far. For example, an organization that already exists in a domain may become the referent organization for that domain. An example is a voluntary organization sufficiently broad in the scope of its aims to be acceptable to the other domain members. Conversely, a new referent organization may be created by members of the domain, as happened in Jamestown. Similarly, referent organizations may differ according to whether they have an official public mandate or are voluntary. The Craigmillar Festival Society is a voluntary referent organization brought into existence by residents of the community, whereas the growing number of ad hoc advisory committees created by governments to express the views of stakeholders in policy issues have official public standing. Referent organizations also may be well established and may function to preserve what already exists; examples are historical and conservation societies. Or they may emerge in response to new situations and needs and function as agents of social innovation. As a final example of variation, in some domains only one referent organization may be present whereas in others there may be several referent organizations. The presence of multiple organizations could mean, however, that conflict and competition among stakeholders is more prevalent than consensus about common aims, as appeared to be the case when a team of students working with me studied patterns of interest group relations in West Philadelphia. Whatever types of relations between domains and referent organizations are developed, the latter are likely to be successful only if they embody the linkages among most if not all members of the domain and do not usurp their members' prerogatives and functions. Domain members must be able to control the referent organization collectively and be free to pursue their own purposes while cooperating in areas of mutual concern, rather than being controlled by the referent organization or dominated by particular members (Trist, 1977, 1979). An effective referent organization is a means of achieving mutual self-regulation. It is an alternative to excessive hierarchial control of governments and to narrowly conceived and fragmented interest-group politics.

To date, only a few innovative referent organizations have been in existence for a significant period, but these display several marked similarities that may be more generally applicable to the process of domain development. In each case, a critical situation such as economic deprivation or chronic economic decline has existed and has not been coped with effectively through established structures. These situations have not been unique to the particular groups of stakeholders involved. They have become widespread throughout societies, but at local levels they take on concrete meanings. Moreover, in local settings the complexes of interacting factors that produce such situations can be traced through, making it possible to address the situations in their entirety. If the situation is economic decline, all the contributing factors and consequences (and the interrelationships among them) can be tackled rather than attempting to treat them separately and piecemeal. In each case, the activation of new initiatives has been caused by a few key individuals involved in varied interest groups who, in other circumstances, may have little in common. They recognize, however, that all interests are affected by the critical situation and attempt to bring them together. The innovating organizations that have grown out of these initiatives have been independent of statutory bodies and also of the major local power groups. Instead, they derive their strength from wide bases of support in the domain. Their claims to recognition, including financial assistance from government authorities and other sources, rest on their distinctive capability and potential for accomplishing what cannot be achieved by traditional means (Trist, 1978c).

As with single organizations, the prevalent approach to regulating societies is bureaucratic. Policies are centrally formed, and resources are allocated to programs through structures that are dominated by party politics and that exclude the great majority of the population from active involvement in the management of their own affairs. The administrative organizations through which policies and programs are implemented are differentiated from one another to such an extent that cooperation in areas where their objectives intersect and coordination of interdependent activities is difficult or impossible. In pursuing their objectives, the administrative organizations rely heavily on narrow technical expertise and on the imposition of controls. They attempt to treat as being discrete problems that in reality are intermeshed, and most agencies tend to have their own particular "clienteles" comprised of the organized interests with which they have the most dealings. Bureaucratic regulative structures leave societies' members powerless to do much about the conditions affecting them. There have been active negative reactions against such structures, among the most recent being the tax revolts in the United States exemplified by Proposition Thirteen in California. The more pronounced trend, however, has been for societies' members to dissociate themselves passively from the policies and programs of their elected governments.

The emerging alternatives display a very different pattern. For the most part, they are developing away from the centers of power on the peripheries of the political arena. They require that power be shared among local stakeholders and government bodies. The political processes of decision making cut across party lines, and issue-centered community politics becomes more important than party politics. The referent organizations through which groups of stakeholders interact are controlled by the stakeholders and provide the means for self-regulation as an alternative to imposed governmental controls. These organizations confront the complex interrelationships between problems and issues whereas established government political and administrative structures largely ignore or are unable to deal with problems and issues. In contrast to agencies that specialize in particular regulative and service functions and in dealing with particular sectional interests, referent organizations are concerned with the interdependencies among varied objectives and with achieving collaboration among interests to address holistically the issues affecting their future. For individuals, referent organizations offer the prospect of active participation in pursuing mutually desired futures in place of the existing bureaucratic social designs that leave them largely powerless and with little option but to withdraw into a private existence (Trist, 1978c).

The predominant bureaucratic organizational pattern in western industrial societies prevents the societies from effectively dealing with the forces that threaten their future. Active adaptation to turbulent social environments is impossible within that pattern. The innovations in the design of work organization and the emergence of new socioecological designs and strategies for dealing with larger systems of interacting problems and issues provide ground for hope that societies can reduce the uncertainty surrounding their choices of futures and can embark on new positive courses. At each level of social organization and in all sectors of society, the basic principles of redesign are essentially the same. Whereas bureaucratic forms of social design render the great majority of societies' members largely powerless and evoke maladaptive responses from them as a result, democratic designs are open to the influence of those who participate in them. They provide the means for people to become involved actively in the management of their future, first by creating the conditions in which they can develop localized responses in order to control the changes directly affecting them, and second by redefining relationships among the varied functional levels within social systems so that each has a degree of autonomy to manage its distinctive concerns and reciprocal control with respect to the other levels. In the case of the single organization, the democratic alternative to bureaucracy is based on conditionally autonomous, self-regulating work teams at the operating and managerial levels, and on forms of interaction at the interfaces within and among all levels to determine mutually the directions of the enterprise. At the socioecological level in a democratic design, the policies and programs of governments are concerned primarily with assisting local active adaptive responses through collaboration among members of domains linked by referent organizations that they control collectively. As with the institutional level of management in single organizations, democratic governments provide the resources necessary for internal self-management and then concentrate their own leadership endeavors on managing external relationships and transactions. Social designs with these characteristics have far greater potential trenched patterns of single-loop learning, which are characteristic of bureaucratic organizations, inhibit or prevent new learning and the discovery of active adaptive responses to changing and uncertain environments. The learning patterns of individuals are bureaucratized.

Therefore, a central issue in transforming bureaucratic organizations and institutions is to democratize learning. To do so entails providing the conditions under which individuals in collaboration can acquire new understanding of their environment, explore potentially adaptive alternatives to existing social designs, and plan to pursue new directions by redesigning the organizations and more extended domains in which they participate. In the case of single organizations, the need is to release their members from the confines of the familiar bureaucratic world and provide them with the freedom, guidance, and support to engage in new inquiry and planning. When stakeholders are dispersed in extended domains such as communities and regions, temporary settings are required to stimulate new inter-active learning and planning. The settings in both cases are "social islands" where participants work together, usually for several days, to accomplish the task of discovering the possibilities for active adaptation. The objectives and structuring of the task embody the logic of active adaptation to turbulent environments. The organization of the social island embodies the values, ideals, and design principles of participative democracy. The settings are designed to provide optimal freedom for participants to engage in new learning and planning while acquiring direct experience of democratic alternatives to bureaucracy.

Since the early 1970s, beginning with the work of Fred Emery and a group of social scientists in Australia, many such learning events have been conducted (Emery & Emery, 1975; Emery, 1976; Crombie, 1980.) Chapters 3 through 5 provide an account of designing for active adaptive learning and innovation in a large major organization on the basis of continuing experience over several years. Chapter 6 extends this experience to designing for learning and active adaptation at the domain level where many stakeholders are involved. However, while the work with organizations and domains was developing, it had to be recognized that the barriers to active adaptation encountered by many individuals were not caused only by the restrictive forces presently operating in their work and the other contexts of adult life. The roots of their inability to engage in new learning and active adaptation lay deeper in their early socialization into bureaucratic organization and, in particular, in the effects of formal education. If, through education, individuals learned only the organizational world of bureaucracy, they would hardly be prepared to participate as adults in the transformation of their societies to manage uncertain transition. Conversely, if education could be redesigned to prepare individuals for active participation in work and community life, many more might enter adult roles able and willing to undertake the challenge. Therefore, the fo⁾ lowing account of experience with designing for learning and active adaptatⁱ begins in Chapter 2 with redesigning education.

for active adaptation to turbulent social environments than bureaucratic organizations.

The Democratization of Society as a Design for Active Adaptive Learning

Western industrial societies are at a crossroads where they must choose between alternative future directions. The choice is between persisting with the bureaucratic social designs of the industrial age and developing new social designs based on participative democracy. This is a fundamental choice because the two social principles are basically incompatible. Choosing the first direction, of attempting to strengthen bureaucratic hierarchical structures, will lead to intensified societal crises and breakdown. Cumulative experience with the second alternative of participative democracy has proved it to be as universally applicable as bureaucracy, and it is both feasible and far more adaptive in the present conditions of turbulent transition. Nevertheless, despite the many diverse innovations in developing participative-democratic social designs, bureaucracy remains the dominant organizational pattern.

Several reasons may be given for this predominance of bureaucratic designs. First, in the face of mounting evidence to the contrary, the belief continues to be held that the problems and crises of industrialism are temporary and that the present industrial order will survive unchanged. Conversely, others are so convinced as to the inevitability of collapse that they believe nothing can be done to prevent it. Both views express an inactive posture of doing nothing to transform the basic social designs of societies. A third response is to recognize that major change is occurring and to exploit immediate opportunities with little understanding of, or regard for, the likely eventual consequences. Opportunistic tactics are employed within bureaucratic frameworks. Fourth, attempts to transform societies' institutions and organizations are resisted because of the practical difficulties and perceived risks involved in fundamental innovation. The problems of active adaptation vary greatly among and within societies as do the kinds of response to change that are feasible and acceptable. Theoretical alternatives tend to be distrusted by those concerned with practical affairs, and demonstration through examples of what others have achieved in different circumstances is often received with skepticism. Reluctance explore alternatives to existing social designs will be even stronger when those involved perceive that their own interests, power, and security are threatened. The inclination is to react to change in the environment by persevering with and attempting to strengthen existing organizational structures (Ackoff, 1974; Emery, 1978; Maccoby, 1976).

A deeper source of resistance may be the fear that any move toward participative democratic designs will generate more rather than less upheaval, conflict, and disorder. Bureaucratic principles of social design are taught formally only to a few of the industrial societies' members, but these principles are learned experientially by the great majority, first through schooling and subsequently by work and other life experiences that reinforce the schooling. Although confronted with mounting uncertainty about the future and the awareness that existing bureaucratic social designs are failing, their most probable reaction is to retreat still further into bureaucratic structures, which are the only structures they know. When unfamiliar alternatives are proposed, they cannot understand them except, perhaps, at a level of abstraction removed from their personal life experiences. They may know that existing, familiar structures and strategies are failing, but they will persevere with failing structures rather than experiment with basic alternatives. Beyond the more obvious and limited reasons for resisting active adaptive innovations, the fear of searching for and discovering new choices of future directions reinforces passive dependence on bureacratic social designs even when the failure of these designs increases the prospect of societal breakdown and collapse (Emery, 1978).

Rational analysis and empirical experimentation have revealed a basic general alternative to bureaucracy but in themselves are insufficient to stimulate and sustain the diffusion of active adaptive innovation. This is often the case even in organizations where experimental redesigns are carried out. Redesign has usually been attempted through demonstration pilot experiments in single organizational units and evaluated according to explicit criteria after a specified time. If the pilot is judged successful, commitment to further innovation throughout the organization may be announced. Despite many successful initial experiments, several critical difficulties have arisen. The usual practice is for pilot experiments to be designed by outside researchers or consultants. Resistance may come from members of the units selected for pilot experimentation who perceive the redesign proposals as being imposed or are suspicious of the reasons for introducing them. When change is initiated in one unit, tension and conflict with other units may arise. Supervisors, managers, and staff personnel could well regard the increased autonomy and scope for self-management as threatening their functions. Even when an experiment is evaluated as successful, other members of the organization have difficulty in understanding the redesign, and there are likely to be doubts as to whether similar innovations would work as well under different operating conditions. Managers of other units and departments may feel under pressure to introduce redesigns in their own areas but without the resources and support given to the initial pilot project. For these and other reasons, implementation of redesign is difficult. When diffusion throughout the organization does not occur, experimental innovations remain isolated and threatened with extinction (Herbst, 1976; Walton, 1977). The obstacles to active adaptation through redesign in large domains involving many different organizations and groups are likely to be even greater.

Whereas the replacement of bureaucratic structures with participative-democratic designs is central to active adaptation, the discovery and development

of effective democratic social designs entail processes of continuous and open-ended learning. When the development of new social designs is left in the hands of outside researchers and consultants, the outsiders may learn a great deal, but those who have to live with the new designs usually learn very little. In consequence, they are poorly equipped and possibly poorly motivated to maintain the new designs and to develop and modify them as conditions and needs change. It is not enough for outside researchers and consultants to think through the problems and to produce the new designs. The prospects for active adaptation to turbulent environments through social redesign will remain unfamiliar, abstract, and perhaps threatening to many people unless they can come to grips with such possibilities through their own inquiry and learning. The challenge for outsiders is not to find the available active adaptive alternatives for people but to design the conditions in which people can learn to discover these alternatives themselves. The task expands from redesigning organizations to designing for active adaptive learning, which in turn might lead people to redesigning their own organizations based on their understanding of what it will take to pursue desirable future directions in turbulent environments. To acquire the understanding necessary for active adaptation, they would have to engage in new learning. Active adaptive learning entails searching into trends in the contextual environment, assessing how wider change is affecting future prospects, identifying inadequacies of existing organizational designs, and developing proposals for redesign. The knowledge and experience of outside researchers or consultants can assist an organization's members, but they must convince themselves of both the need and possibility for active adaptive innovation in their particular situations and take the leading role in implementing their proposals for redesign.

A major difficulty is that bureaucratic organizations induce and reinforce the kinds of learning behavior that sustain those organizations. As individuals learn modes of behavior that produce desired outcomes or avoid undesired outcomes under certain conditions, they tend to persist with those modes. When major change occurs, the individuals continue to pursue familiar courses of action rather than breaking out of established patterns to engage in new learning. Argyris and Schon, following Bateson, have described the learning that is typical in bureaucratic organizations as "single-loop learning" (Arygris & Schon, 1978). Members of the organization react to change in ways that retain the central features of the existing organization. To respond adaptively to change arising from turbulent environments, they would at least have to engage in "double-loop" learning. Such learning would lead them to question the established purposes and objectives of the organization and also its social design. Moreover, they would need to undertake such inquiry more or less continuously, which would depend on their becoming self-conscious about their attempts at new inquiry and about seeking to improve their potential for continuous learning and active adaptation.

CONCLUSIONS

The challenge of learning to manage the future can be thought of as occurring at three levels. First, individuals must acquire the ability and willingness to engage in new learning and active adaptation more or less continuously, and the task of developing this capability should begin with their initial education. Second, continuous new learning and active adaptation are necessary at the level of organizations. Third, active adaptation to turbulent environments depends on new interactive learning and planning among dispersed stakeholders in the future of extended social fields. Varied issues in active adaptation arise at each of these levels and in different contexts. The basic aim of participative design is to enable those individuals involved to learn how to address the issues of change affecting them, to discover and pursue positive new directions, and to learn how to do this continuously for themselves.

The emergence of turbulent environments in western societies gives rise to the need for active adaptation to act on and to influence the basic directions of change. Bureaucratic organizations and technocratic approaches to planning reduce the prospects for active adaptation to manage future directions. Active adaptation depends on new understanding of how change in the environment is affecting future prospects, the emergence of new and widely shared values to guide choices of future directions, and the transformation of societies' organizations and institutions to enable those involved in them to take a much more active part in responding to the trends in their environments. Many active adaptive initiatives have been taken in a number of countries, and the general characteristics of participative democracy, as a basic alternative to bureaucracy, have been established. However, bureaucracy persists as the dominant organizational form of western industrial society. If active adaptive innovation is to occur more quickly and on a larger scale, and if new initiatives are to survive and develop, those who are affected by them must be involved effectively in the process of social redesign. Participative design has evolved as an educational methodology that attempts to create the conditions under which new learning and active adaptation through social redesign can occur. Experiences with attempting to create these conditions in education, organizations, and more extended social fields are reported, discussed, and evaluated in the following chapters.

Democracy in Learning

2

Educational systems and their component organizations have a special responsibility for helping societies' members to develop the learning capabilities they need in order to meet successfully the challenges of their times. Although learning occurs and must occur in all spheres of life it is, or is supposed to be, the *raison d'être* of formally organized education. Certainly, the years spent in schools and other educational institutions significantly affect individuals' potentialities for learning and adaptation in future life situations. Beyond the knowledge and skills individuals acquire, education serves as an agent for the socialization of individuals into wider social structures and processes. Education provides individuals with their first sustained experience of organizational life. Unless is it adapted to the fundamental changes occurring in societies, not only will individuals be poorly equipped with knowledge and skills, but they will be unprepared for participation in transforming the institutional and organizational structures of their societies.

The trends affecting the future of western industrial societies have at least three important implications for education. First, the knowledge and skills that will be relevant and necessary in the future cannot be predetermined with as much confidence as they were until recent times. It is becoming impossible for educators to anticipate the demands and opportunities students will encounter in their later lives. Technical knowledge now becomes outdated very quickly. Equally important, many more people than in the past are likely to find it necessary or desirable to change their occupations and careers in later life. Therefore, education no longer can be based on the assumption that knowledge and skills acquired early in life will, with marginal updating, remain adequate. Second, the growing interconnectedness between the complex problems and issues societies face seriously reduces the extent to which issues can be treated independently from one another and on the basis of specialized fields of knowledge. Specialized training and education make possible the concentrated development of specific capabilities within narrow ranges of activity. This development is achieved at the expense of leaving most individuals who acquire such competence lacking in understanding of and unable to deal with the interrelationships among their own fields and other disciplines. Third, increasing uncertainty about the future direction of change in society not only undermines confidence in existing empirical or factual knowledge; it also gives rise to normative confusion or uncertainty and conflict about what kinds of futures are and ought to be desired.

Given these trends, the specific knowledge and skills individuals acquire through initial education become less important than their willingness and ability to seek new knowledge and understanding. As the knowledge within particular fields becomes inadequate to illuminate issues that increasingly are intermeshed, the ability to inquire into and comprehend larger, changing patterns of interrelationships comes to be at least equal in importance to specialized expertise. We need new strategies to help us try to understand the environment and the complex changes that are occurring, and we are unlikely to find them in established maps of knowledge based on specialized disciplines. Creating and recreating new frameworks of understanding require searching for new meaning in the emerging patterns rather than interpreting them in ways that are convenient for the existing organization of knowledge. When societies' dominant values and ideals are in doubt, educators should not take them as givens and merely concentrate on developing in individuals the knowledge, skills, attitudes, and aspirations that are consistent with those values and ideals. The valued ends to be served by human endeavor should themselves be opened up to critical inquiry by students as well as their teachers.

Education that helps individuals to develop qualities of thought and action conducive to the enhancement of human potential during turbulent societal transition will be concerned, above all, with helping societies' members to "learn how to learn" (Michael, 1973). The qualities educators will seek to develop in students include: (1) openness to unfamiliar experiences and an active interest in discovering new responses to novel situations by experimenting and learning from experience; (2) awareness that complex, changing problems and issues cannot be understood adequately from the perspectives of particular established disciplines; (3) a willingness to help and learn from others through acquiring and sharing different kinds of knowledge; and (4) the ability to participate in determining the objectives of their own education, making decisions about and accepting much greater responsibility for their own learning (Ackoff, 1974; Holly, 1974; Piaget, 1976). Education can contribute to both individual and social development. It should enable individuals to acquire understanding of the contemporary world and how it is changing as well as the knowledge and skills relevant to meet the challenges of that world. It should contribute also to the discovery within societies of possibilities for creating new forms of social organization to enhance the prospects for active human adaptation that will influence the directions of change and to develop a desirable new social order out of the present uncertainty. For education to serve both these ends, it must be redesigned to embody the social principles of active adaptive organization.

For the most part, however, education is organized and conducted according to the same bureaucratic logic that pervades other sectors of western societies. It prevents individuals from understanding their world and from acquiring the necessary capabilities for learning and active adaptation. The majority of societies' members enter adult life knowing only the organizational world of bureaucracy. So long as education remains bureaucratic, it will continue to reduce human potential for survival and development in the era beyond industrialism.

BUREAUCRATIC EDUCATION AND ITS CONSEQUENCES

Contemporary education in western society is as much a product of industrialism as is the factory. Its evolution has been influenced greatly by the requirements of the industrial system and by the desire of societies' members to share in the material wealth that industrialism can create. Industrial societies require masses of individuals who are mobile in the new labor markets rather than being tied to the traditions of local community life. They also require technicians, scientists, professionals, administrators, and managers in ever-growing numbers. On the supply side, there is no shortage of recruits, and education has come to play an important mediating role between the demands of industrialism and the aspirations of individuals. The result has been a great increase in the number and size of schools and tertiary educational institutions. Moreover, in order to meet the increasingly diverse demands of a growing variety of occupations and careers, education has become more and more specialized. Distinctions are made between students expected to enter the general work force and those destined for careers in the higher echelons of the industrial order. Curricula have evolved to match the training of individuals to the requirements of the different vocations they are expected to pursue. As governments have assumed the role of providing education for the majority, these curricula have been standardized as the basis for planning and control through administrative hierarchies.

To a considerable extent, education has succeeded in satisfying the more immediate manpower needs of societies by ensuring that individuals are available for employment in the types and quantities required. The material standards of living enjoyed by many people also has increased significantly, although this is less true for groups that were already the most severely disadvantaged. Now that western societies are passing beyond the industrial era, the education that has evolved to meet their requirements during that period is unable to help individuals to develop the learning capabilities now needed in the new and emerging conditions. In the buildup to full industrialism, educational systems have responded to change by changing the content of curricula, but the underlying logic of their organizational design has not changed. Further updating of the content of education is not enough to meet the fundamentally different conditions of the new age. Bureaucratic education produces in human beings bureaucratized patterns of learning behavior, in contradiction to the new social designs needed for successful management of turbulent societal transition.

The basic unit of bureaucratic educational organization is a teacher instructing a class of students of similar age and presumed levels of ability. The subject matter the students study is divided into segments such as English, mathematics, history, physics, and so on, and each subject is treated separately from the others. In secondary and tertiary education, the staff concentrate on teaching their own particular specialties as far as possible. The daily and weekly routines are programmed into timetables with fixed periods spent on each subject. During these periods, the same information is given to all members of the class at the same time and in identical sequence. The students' task is to reproduce what they have been told or shown, and they are assessed according to the accuracy and completeness of their reproduction. The emphasis is on the content of the subject matter and on the students' capacity to absorb and repeat that content. Students are rewarded or punished for their individual performance in each subject and for the degree of their compliance with the institution's rules and norms relating to general conduct. Decisions about the subject matter to be taught, the methods by which students are required to reproduce the content of their instruction, and the timing and duration of tasks are determined by the staff within the constraints of the curricula, the timetable, and their individual responsibility for particular subjects. The staff are themselves coordinated through hierarchical organizational structures. Thus, there is minimal involvement of students in determining the objectives and methods even of their immediate classroom activities, and larger decisions about curricula, institutional organization, and educational policy are made at still more remote levels (Ackoff, 1974; Herbst, 1974; Holly, 1974).

Most contemporary education is based on the compartmentalization of knowledge into subject areas, standardized instruction in each subject area, and passive imitation of that instruction by students. This process develops in students little more than the ability to perform as directed by their teachers. The students learn to depend on the staff to tell them what to do and how to do it. Some students accept this situation in expectation of later extrinsic rewards. Preoccupied with obtaining favorable grades, and finding themselves in competition with one another for the approval of the staff, they want only to know what the staff require of them. To help a fellow student would bring the risk of competitive disadvantage, and what one might learn from other students is to them irrelevant. Curiosity about matters outside the formal study program would entail spending time in activity that does not increase the students' prospects of obtaining higher grades. Similarly, because the content of their education is segmented and imparted to them by subject specialists who display little or no interest in the interrelationships among subject areas, students working for higher grades in expectation of the career prospects that will follow are unlikely to concern themselves with exploring possible interrelationships. Such inquiry would bring no extrinsic rewards. The safer path is to concentrate on each subject in turn as independent from the others and on satisfying the demands of the teacher who provides the instruction in each subject. Because of the emphasis placed on specialization in higher secondary and tertiary education, the pressure on students to focus their attention on only parts of the field of knowledge increases as they move toward completion of their formal education. At the same time, many of the tasks students are required to perform often lack meaning or relevance for them, and staff preoccupation with competitive individual performance is in conflict with cooperative social instincts and values. Students are made to be passively dependent on the staff at a stage in their lives when many of them desire greater independence from adults and more fellowship with their peers. Although some students accept this dependency as a price to be paid for anticipated rewards, others reject it and rebel against their situation. However, because they have little power to change it, their probable reaction is to become indifferent and to await the time when they can, with relief, leave the educational system (Holly, 1974; Jamieson & Thomas, 1974).

Whether students are happy or unhappy with the passive submissive role imposed on them by most formal education, the longer they remain subject to these psychological pressures the less likely they are to develop the capabilities for active learning and innovation needed in western societies today. If this is the effect bureaucratic education has on students, the effect on many teachers is even greater. Their primary involvement in the educational system is as subject specialists recruited to teach predefined areas of knowledge in accordance with the requirements, rules, and procedures of the institutions that employ them. In general, teachers have little involvement in formulating educational objectives, policies, and strategies.

Teachers have a degree of autonomy in the teaching situation itself, but it is largely a negative autonomy that exists because it is not feasible to supervise teachers closely. Teachers tend erroneously to equate the absence of supervision with academic freedom and professional autonomy, which it is *not*. True professional freedom is a right to *decide* that is conferred upon individuals engaged in certain occupations because, by virtue of their exclusive possession of distinctive skills and esoteric knowledge, only they are considered competent to make the necessary decisions (Nokes, 1967). Even in occupations such as medicine that traditionally have enjoyed professional autonomy, this exclusive status is being questioned and challenged. Teachers, particularly in secondary schools, have never attained such autonomy beyond a few superficial symbols of authority and status. Many of them work hard at protecting their image as experts and authority figures, however. For example, in his study of teachers' attitudes and behavior, Pellegrin (1976) concludes:

In terms of ideology, it is clear that most teachers are virtually obsessed with guarding their prerogatives over individual autonomy. . . while teachers may relinquish control over the affairs of the school and the school system, they are more concerned about their autonomy in the classroom than they are about any other matter. . . the desire of the teacher to control classroom management is so strong that the individual teacher wishes to protect this jurisdiction in classroom decision-making from the authority exercised both by his colleague group and by those in administrative positions. (p. 361)

Beyond their concern with status, there may be several reasons why teachers desire this autonomy. They may be reacting against the pressures of the classroom situation by attempting to maximize their personal authority over and social distance from the students, a reaction also common among prison staff (Thomas, 1972; Thomas & Williams, 1977). More positively, some teachers may be attempting to protect the teaching situation from administrative interference.

Whatever the motives, however, staff preoccupation with individual autonomy appears to have at least two negative consequences. First, many teachers not only desire autonomy from the larger educational organization, but their insistence on having exclusive control over the teaching situation excludes the students from any active role in making decisions about their own learning. This attitude strengthens the image students often have of staff as demagogues who impose their will on students by requiring them to work on tasks the staff have decided should be performed and by the methods the staff dictate. When students have little or no opportunity to influence the design of their own education, it becomes external to and alienated from them. Although some of the tasks the students perform may have some intrinsic appeal for some of them, any appeal is left to chance. It is likely that just as many students are ''turned off'' by what they are doing and are working only for extrinsic rewards or in order to avoid punishment. Moreover, in a society that is changing rapidly and in which there is increasing uncertainty about the future, the presumption that individual teachers alone are the best judges of what students should learn and how they should learn it is highly questionable. As they grow older, students become aware of the changes occurring in society and of the growing uncertainty about future propsects. These problems are seldom addressed in their formal education. Apart from the constraints imposed on the subject matter of education by the curriculum, teachers preoccupied with their specialties and with maintaining their superior status are unlikely to engage willingly in areas of inquiry where their own knowledge and understanding may not be much greater than that of their students. For students who are concerned only with getting through the curriculum as directed by staff, this may not be a problem. Nevertheless, their formal education ignores many of the changes and issues students should be aware of and should attempt to understand. Some students, however are not only aware of the changes occurring around them but find these changes sufficiently important, interesting, or disturbing to want to learn more about them. To such students unresponsive teachers become symbols of an educational system that is outmoded and dogmatic as well as authoritarian.

Second, because the autonomy the staff wish to maintain is highly individualized, it reinforces the segmentation of education and compounds the obstacles to comprehending relationships among different parts of the field of knowledge. Although societies increasingly require understanding of and strategies for responding to complex, changing systems of interrelated issues, most educators display little active interest in the interdependence that exists among their subjects. As a result, students also acquire a fragmented orientation toward knowledge. The division of knowledge into the present categories of disciplines and subjects is the product of a historical process. As a way of classifying knowledge into units for intensive study, it reflects the scientific philosophy that has dominated western society for 200 years or more. Like earlier frameworks for organizing knowledge about the world, it loses its usefulness when fundamental discontinuities in the evolution of societies occur and make new modes of understanding necessary. However, the prevalent reaction of academics and educators is to resist change and adhere to the disciplines and boundaries familiar to them. In Ackoff's (1974) words: 'Disciplines are craft unions preoccupied with preserving their academic prerogatives. Academic departments do not organize knowledge; they organize teachers and disorganize knowledge'' [p. 92]. The disintegration and specialization of knowledge may have served the progress of societies during the industrial age, but the search for relationships and holistic ways of comprehending them are necessary now. Most academics and educators, on the other hand, appear to be more concerned with their established areas of autonomy and expertise within the confines of the existing organization of intellectual and educational activity.

The outcomes of education are becoming less and less acceptable to societies. The levels many students attain in basic skills and knowledge are declining. Violence, destruction, student apathy, and absenteeism are adding to the already high costs of education. Students who persevere with their formal education beyond secondary school often have not developed the learning capabilities needed for further academic work. Even many graduates of higher educational institutions are merely highly trained single-loop learners. The malaise of contemporary education has been described well by the UNESCO Commission chaired by Edgar Faure (1972). In its Report, *Learning to Be,* the Commission states:

> For the first time in history, education is now engaged in preparing men for a type of society which does not yet exist. This presents educational systems with a task which is all the more novel in that the function of education down the ages has usually been to reproduce the contemporary society and contemporary social relationships. The change can be easily explained if the

relative stability of past societies is compared with the accelerated development of the contemporary world. . . . A system designed for a minority when knowledge was slow to change quickly becomes out of date when employed for mass education in times of whirlwind change when the volume of knowledge increases at an ever faster pace. The system finds it difficult to keep up with the demands of an expanding society; the people it educates are not properly trained to adapt themselves to change; and some societies reject the qualifications and skills when these no longer answer direct needs. (p. 14)

Widespread dissatisfaction with education has led to many demands and proposals for reform, but with a few outstanding exceptions they have been addressed to the content and methods of education and not to its organization. The crisis in education identified by the UNESCO Commission is a product not merely of outmoded curricula and teaching methods, but of a bureaucratic organizational design that develops, reinforces, and rewards bureaucratic patterns of behavior in staff and students. These behavior patterns are hardly adaptive in conditions of uncertain historic transition. Because bureaucratic education produces individuals who are largely incapable of active adaptive learning and innovation, it is necessary to change the organizational design of education. If societies' members are to participate effectively in the transforming of their institutions and organizations, they must have opportunities to experience, experiment with, and learn about alternatives to bureaucratic social design. Education has a responsibility for providing them with such opportunities.

REDESIGNING EDUCATION FOR ACTIVE ADAPTIVE LEARNING

Education must be redesigned organizationally to create the conditions under which active adaptive learning can occur. These conditions include (1) student participation in determining the objectives of learning as well as the methods to be employed in learning activity; (2) freedom to experiment with different methods and strategies of learning; (3) a supportive environment in which "mistakes" are more likely to be valued positively as contributing to learning rather than as occasions for punishment; (4) encouragement of collaborative learning, which enhances the knowledge and understanding of all rather than rewarding competitive individual performances; and (5) timely feedback on the outcomes of attempts at learning to enable learners to adjust their behavior to increase their effectiveness (Ackoff, 1974; Crombie, 1976; Emery, 1977; Lewin, 1951). Creating such conditions entails redesigning education around the task of helping students to discover what they need to learn, to become motivated to learn continuously, and to learn how to learn for themselves in the face of uncertainty and in cooperation with others. When these conditions are created, not only are individuals more likely to develop the capabilities for continuous adaptive learning needed to cope with turbulent transition, but they will experience a very different organizational form from that of bureaucracy. In effect, they will be learning from direct experience about active adaptation through participative organizational democracy.

My own explorations of the possibilities for redesigning educational organization to serve these ends commenced in 1974 with three management courses in the University of Western Australia that dealt with the theory of organizations. For several years prior to 1974, increasing attention was given in these courses to the emergence of turbulent environments and their effects on organizations, and to innovations in organizational design (see Chapter 1). However, I went no further in the courses than attempting to teach students *about* the changing nature of organizational environments and the alternative strategies of active adaptation that were being explored. Beyond informing students about environmental trends and innovations in organizational design, I now recognized that it was possible for them to experience directly the democratic alternative to bureaucracy. The existing course design presented a paradox. Students were studying alternatives to bureaucracy within course structures that were still highly bureaucratic. The redesign entailed moving away from the traditional organizational structure of the courses to a design based on groups of students who had as their task the education of themselves, using staff and other resources to accomplish this task. The redesign concept is summarized in Figure 5.

In the traditional design, lectures and tutorials were used as the primary means of imparting information and knowledge to students. In the lecture mode, large numbers of students were entirely dependent on staff to decide what material

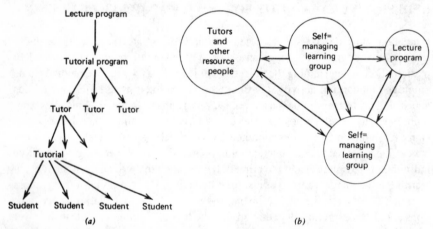

Figure 5a. The traditional bureaucratic course design.

Figure 5b. The democratic course design.

would be presented. The tutorials, consisting of one staff member and approximately 10 students, provided potentially greater scope for student participation. Much depended, however, on the nature of the tutorial tasks and the particular combinations of tutors and students. Many of the tutorial tasks were simply extensions and applications of the lecture material and required students to present papers or to undertake case analyses and exercises. The small number of students was supposed to facilitate more personal interaction between them and the staff, but the tutorials largely functioned to reinforce the downward flow of communication from the lectures. The staff members played dominant roles in directing task performance, and the students were given little opportunity to participate actively in determining the direction of their learning. The majority of students behaved passively and confined their efforts to reproducing the content of the lectures and the assigned reading.

The organizational redesign focused on the tutorial groups because, although traditionally they had been dominated by the staff and by the lecture programs, they offered the most likely area in which students could assume greater responsibility for their own learning. In the tutorial settings, it was intended that students would make decisions about learning objectives, appropriate activities, forms of internal group organization, use of staff and other resources, and criteria and methods for assessing task performance. Lectures were still considered to be important as one means of making information and knowledge available to students, but the relationship between lectures and tutorials needed to change so that the content of lectures could be adapted to the learning objectives and requirements of the tutorial groups. Initial lectures were used to explain the overall objectives of the courses and the philosophy and structure of the new design, as well as to provide introductory coverage of the general subject areas. As the tutorial groups became clearer about their own interests and objectives, the remainder of the lecture programs were to be developed to support them. Thus, the new design was intended to embody the organizational characteristics of participative democracy. The tutorials, as self-managing learning groups, were considered to be analogous to the conditionally autonomous groups in work settings, and the roles of the staff were redefined to emphasize their potential value as resources to the students rather than as authority figures.

In developing the new design, certain contraints had to be accepted. The innovations were being introduced within the context of the larger university organization, as shown in Figure 6. The three courses involved in the redesign were located in the Department of Commerce, a component department of the Faculty of Economics and Commerce. Two of the three courses, Organization and Business Management 200 and 300, were undergraduate courses taken predominantly by students studying for the Bachelor of Commerce degree, which required successful completion of 10 courses over a minimum period of three years. The third course, Organization and Management 509, was offered within the Master of

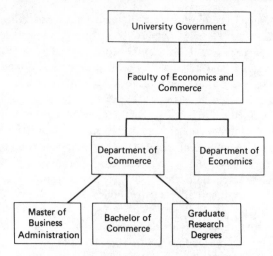

Figure 6.   The university organizational structure.

Business Administration program, which required successful completion of 16 courses over a minimum period of two years. In 1974, 210 students, most of whom were in the second year of their studies, were enrolled in Organization and Business Management 200. Seventy-five students who were in their final year were enrolled in Organization and Business Management 300. Both courses were conducted over a full academic year divided into three terms. Organization and Management 509 was a second semester course taken in the first year of the MBA program; 43 students were enrolled in 1974.

The organization of the department, faculty, and university restricted the scope of the redesigns in two main ways. First, students were required to attend classes at fixed times and to submit to formal examinations. Other university requirements limited students' choices of courses, and both staff and students were subject to institutional rules, regulations, and norms. Second, students were taking several courses other than the three in question, and these courses were not affected by the redesigns. In fact, responsibility for Organization and Business Management 200 and 300 was divided among several different staff members, each one being officially responsible for particular segments of the courses throughout the year. Implementation of the redesign concept in these courses was limited to about one third of the academic year, during which I was officially responsible for them. This situation restricted students' opportunities to experience and experiment with the democratic alternative to bureaucratic organization and also their scope for exploring interrelationships among subject areas. Conversely, as Weick (1976) has pointed out more recently, the traditional university structure and culture did provide sufficient autonomy to allow significant innovation to be attempted within these confines. In other words, the high degree of independence of courses from one another limited the scope of the redesign. Nor did it help students to develop more holistic approaches to learning and understanding. It also, however, reduced the prospect that implementation of the redesigns would be obstructed by opposition from the wider university organization.

Several steps were taken to initiate and implement the organizational redesigns within the two undergraduate courses. First, discussions were held with five staff members who were to be involved as tutors in these courses to explain the redesign concept, explore the implications for their roles, and to ascertain whether they were willing to work with students in the proposed way. Second, in lecture meetings during the first week of each experiment, the redesign concept was explained to the students who were invited to use their tutorial meetings to identify and discuss their learning aims and possible ways of pursuing them. In the lecture meetings, the staff members described areas of knowledge in which they felt competent and able to assist students, but the students were encouraged to determine for themselves the directions their learning should take and to use people other than the course staff to help them. Third, meetings were held in the second week at which all the tutorial groups in each course were asked to present their learning aims and proposed learning activities, to indicate the subject matter that would be relevant to them in lectures, and to state their wishes as to how their task performance should be assessed. From there, the conduct of the courses was based on the development and progress of their tasks by the tutorial groups, with staff assisting the groups and adapting the lecture program to support the groups' learning activities.

In the graduate course, Organization and Management 509, I was the only staff member involved, and tutorials were not formally established as part of the traditional course structure. As with all courses in the Master of Business Administration program, a staff member was assigned sole responsibility for a particular course and, apart from meeting with the whole class for three hours each week, had discretion to organize the course in any manner. Also, the majority of students were studying part-time while working in managerial, administrative, and professional occupations. The smaller class size, the greater autonomy within the existing structure, and the varied characteristics of the students made both necessary and appropriate certain departures from the approach to redesign employed in the undergraduate courses. The redesign concept was introduced in the same way as in the undergraduate courses, but because of the students' previous and (in most cases) current contact with work situations in organizations, it was suggested that they could design their learning objectives and tasks around organizational issues with which they had had direct experience and which were important to them. They were encouraged to attempt to identify concerns and tasks that several students could share as a basis for collaborative learning activity in small groups, with meetings of the whole class being used for lectures and discussions intended to stimulate and support the groups.

The redesign was introduced first in Organization and Business Management 200, then in Organization and Business Management 300, and finally in Organization and Management 509. Students' reactions to the redesign in each course was gauged from three sources of information. First, by the end of the second week, the groups had presented their learning aims and proposals for pursuing them, which provided some indication of their initial reactions to the redesign. Second, staff members made their own observations of developments during the period of the experiments. Finally, toward the end of each experiment, a questionnaire was distributed to the students. Statistical analysis of their responses provided a general estimate of student satisfaction and dissatisfaction and also revealed two basic patterns in their reactions to the redesign. Using these three kinds of feedback, it was possible to assess the redesign in terms of the students' attitudes and learning behavior.

Implementation of the redesign concept in the two undergraduate courses began with the meeting of the staff members to be involved. Their reactions to the redesign concept were mixed. They found it difficult to envisage how the redesign would work in practice, some were doubtful as to whether the students would be able to make major decisions about their own learning, and one staff member thought that the change would be perceived by students as a guarantee that they would all pass. On the other hand, one member was supportive, and they all agreed to try the redesign.

Organization and Business Management 200.

The first lecture was used to explain the redesign concept and for the course staff to describe briefly the subject areas in which they were most knowledgeable. It was emphasized that the staff saw themselves as resources in this respect and that students were free to pursue their own interests and objectives in the course. If the students' interests and objectives could not be supported adequately by the staff, the students were encouraged to look further afield for the people who might be able to assist them. Also, it was emphasized that the function of the lectures was to provide information and knowledge relevant to the tutorial groups' learning aims and chosen tasks, and that the lectures were secondary in importance to the pursuit by the groups of their own learning objectives in feasible and appropriate ways. In tutorial meetings during the first and second weeks, the staff members assigned to each group were available to answer students' questions and provide assistance and guidance as requested, but they generally left the groups to work by themselves.

The meeting to discuss the tutorial groups' learning objectives and proposed strategies for achieving them was held at the end of the second week. It was impossible to involve all 210 students in this meeting. Therefore, each tutorial group was asked to appoint two of its members to present its objectives and proposed activities. Other students were invited to attend as observers. Following a brief introduction to reaffirm the purpose of the meeting, the groups' representatives presented their learning objectives and proposals for accomplishing them, suggested subject matters and speakers for inclusion in the lecture program, and stated their groups' preferences concerning assessment of performance. In attempting to determine their learning objectives and strategies, the majority of the students evidently had been highly constrained by their previous dependence on staff for direction and by their familiarity with the conventional structure in which tutorial activities closely followed the lecture program. They had not identified learning objectives of their own but, rather, had limited their choices to selecting topics from the subject areas in which the staff had claimed to be competent. These areas were mentioned six times more frequently than other possible areas for inquiry. Similarly, in deciding how to plan and organize group learning activities, the students had merely planned a series of discussions to follow lectures on the topics they had chosen from the areas described by staff. This arrangement was suggested five times more frequently than any alternative proposals in which the groups' own learning activity took priority over the lecture program. In effect, the majority of students were asking the staff to continue to exercise almost exclusive control over their learning. On the question of assessment, they were more ambivalent. Not all the groups commented on this issue, but the majority of those that did generally expressed dissatisfaction with traditional criteria and methods of assessment. Although they were prepared to leave decisions concerning assessment to staff, the issue did appear to raise doubts and discomfort about depending on the staff to decide the students' educational fates. Possibly, therefore, the inclination among most students to retain the existing organizational structure of the course reflected their inability to use the increased scope for self-determination that was offered to them rather than satisfaction with the traditional structure.

Although most students reacted to the introduction in the foregoing way, not all of them did so. Some students were critical of the large size of the lecture classes and preferred smaller classes and greater interaction with lecturers. Also, there were several requests for lectures from managers and union leaders in addition to those given by staff, and a number of tutorial groups wanted to involve staff in their discussion on the basis of personal interest in particular topics rather than having the same tutor all the time. These students had made some attempt to explore ways of modifying the traditional course even though they accepted it as the basic organizational framework. Moreover, 30 students did introduce a significant innovation by opting for self-determined projects that they intended to undertake individually or in groups, and they made arrangements with two staff members to obtain guidance in designing and carrying out their chosen learning tasks.

Toward the end of the experiment, staff members were asked to provide feedback on how the groups had functioned. According to these accounts, most groups had persisted with traditional learning patterns. A small number of groups had moved, or attempted to move, into alternative learning tasks and settings, including several new groups that had been formed by students who had discovered mutual interests and learning aims. Some groups had become confused by wanting to remain in the traditional, familiar educational pattern and the temptation to explore alternatives. The groups that reacted negatively to the redesign were described by the staff as "unable to work in uncertainty" and as "lacking knowledge of what they wanted to learn." When groups responded positively, this was attributed in one case to "a strong and experienced leader." Another group was described as "more aware of the problems involved in learning" and "more open and self-analytical." A third group found by the tutor to be unresponsive before the redesign was reported to be "still slow but more friendly." The comment of one staff member provided a reasonable summary of student behavior during the experiment. He observed: "on the whole the students are unhappy and worried about the outcome. A small proportion are pleased and are enjoying freedom for the first time in their scholastic careers."

Most staff members reported that their own roles had become more difficult. They commented that they were busier and had to try to fill gaps in their knowledge, that it was difficult to help the groups, and that many students were not committed to learning about the subject. One remarked, "My status as a tutor has certainly fallen below that of tutors in other courses." In general, staff roles became more difficult when student demands on the knowledge of staff members changed and when groups were unable to provide their own leadership. Staff members became emotionally uncomfortable when the redesign gave rise to confusion and resentment among the students.

Analysis of students' responses to the questionnaire administered at the end of the experiment provided a check on staff observations of how they had reacted to the redesign and revealed two quite distinct patterns of attitudes toward learning. These patterns are shown in Figure 7. In the first pattern (Figure 7a) reliance on the staff to provide direction was central. Students in this mode sought personal advancement through traditional education, depending on the staff to direct and stimulate them in lectures and tutorials. The students were motivated by the desire for rewards the staff controlled, notably grades. They perceived themselves to be in competition with one another and did not regard their peers as individuals whom they could learn from as well as help. For them, the staff alone held the key to their educational progress, and they evaluated the staff members strictly in terms of how well they performed their traditional roles. These students also tended to be young and to have entered full-time university study direct from secondary school. Their whole pattern of attitudes testifies to the efficacy of prolonged subordination to bureaucratic educational organization in producing a young bright élite trained to perform as directed by their superiors.

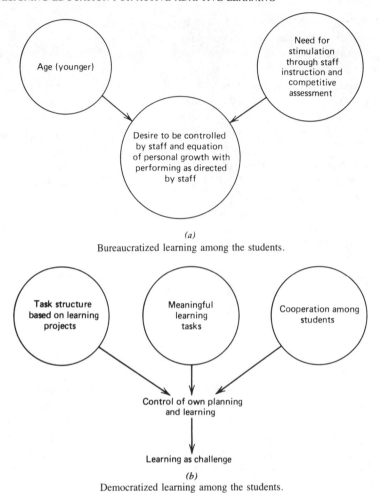

(a)
Bureaucratized learning among the students.

(b)
Democratized learning among the students.

Figure 7. Attitudes to learning among students in Organization and Business Management 200.

In contrast, the second pattern indicated that some students were prepared to plan and control their own learning by participating in setting objectives, designing tasks, experimenting with different approaches, and pursuing desired outcomes in cooperation with other students. For them, the most appropriate paths to new knowledge and understanding were self-determined projects, often undertaken in the wider community, that provided them with the room to explore and manage their own learning. Access to information and opportunities for discussion were the main resources they needed to support them in their tasks. Once they had adapted to the new design, they found little difficulty with the unit. In fact, working on interesting tasks in cooperation with others and being able to control their own learning activities seemed to enable these students to redefine difficulty as a challenge they were willing to meet.

Further analysis of students' responses gave some indication of the proportions of students oriented toward each learning mode. Surprisingly, 48 percent were inclined toward the democratic mode whereas 52 percent remained in the traditional pattern. A stronger bias toward traditional education had been expected. Possibly more students wanted to pursue new learning opportunities than the staff had observed to be doing so. The search for meaningful tasks and experimentation with alternative ways of working takes time and requires organizational and group settings that support the learner. The structure and culture of the university limited the extent to which these conditions could be created. It is at least possible that, given more time and freedom from constraints outside the course, more students would have taken the first steps toward learning to manage their own learning.

Organization and Business Management 300.

The redesign was carried out in a similar manner but with one important difference. With an enrollment of 75 students, it was possible to hold a meeting with them all to discuss their learning objectives and tasks. This meeting quickly took on the atmosphere of a "market day," as groups displayed descriptions of their proposed activities on the walls of the lecture theater and students wandered from one display to the next, questioning one another and discussing their ideas with the staff. When compared with students in Organization and Business Management 200, these students were able to gain direct information about all the proposed learning activities, and it was easier for them to identify other students with whom they wished to work. Most of them wanted to move away from the traditional structure and to engage in learning projects in the wider community. Associated with this tendency, some broadening of the students' perceptions of staff members and other potential resource people was evident. Students who chose to undertake projects in the community expected that key resource people would be found in the organizational and other settings they planned to study, and that consultation with staff members would occur when needed. They were comfortable with a greater degree of independence from the staff and did not restrict their expectations of staff members to traditional relationships based on fixed periods spent in the classroom.

Staff members' accounts of trends during the experiment suggested a similar picture. They reported that half of the students were engaged in projects outside the university and 20 others had planned their own reading and discussion programs. A small number had maintained the traditional arrangements. One staff member reported that a tutorial group he was working with had become confused and passive. Most staff members observed negative as well as positive reactions to the redesign, but, in contrast to Organization and Business Management 200, most students had managed to develop their own learning objectives and strategies for pursuing them.

Analysis of students' responses to the questionnaire again revealed two clearly distinct orientations toward learning that were very similar to the patterns that emerged in Organization and Business Management 200, as summarized in Figure 7. Students in the bureaucratic learning mode relied on staff direction, the pressure of assessment, and competition with one another for their motivation to learn in the traditional way. The emphasis was entirely on the organizational structure of education, which they had grown used to, suggesting a fear among some students of taking more initiative for themselves and of coping with the resultant uncertainty. These students, who were almost at the end of their formal education, seemed to be saying that they could not conceive of education being any different from what they had always experienced. Also, because they were in the final year of their quest for educational qualifications, they may well have been more preoccupied with simply "getting through" than with questioning their previous learning and seeking new learning experiences. Several students said to me that the freedom to direct and control their own learning had come too late. Once more, the persistence with bureaucratized learning behavior was more prevalent among the younger students who had entered university direct from secondary school.

Conversely, students who were oriented toward the democratic learning mode not only desired control over and responsibility for their own learning, as in Organization and Business Management 200, but they expressed awareness of the possibilities for continuously enlarging their learning aims and choices. They were less inclined to regard the redesign as presenting them with a finite increment of autonomy. Rather, they saw it as a vehicle for progressive self-development through working on challenging tasks in cooperation with one another. Their responses also confirmed the impression given at the beginning of the experiment that they had a different perception of the staff, regarding them not as authority figures but as resource people whose exprience and knowledge were important to their own success. Analysis of the distribution of responses indicated that 55 percent of students were in this learning mode whereas 45 percent preferred the traditional structure. However, a significant number of students were away from campus working on field projects when the questionnaire was distributed and did not complete it. Had they done so, it is likely that the orientation toward democratized learning would have emerged more strongly.

Organization and Management 509.

The redesign was introduced and students were advised that they might draw on their personal experience of work organization to identify learning tasks that were interesting and important to them. A framework for organizational analysis and redesign that highlighted the essential differences between bureaucratic and democratic structures was presented, and some relevant literature was recommended. On the basis of information about students' work experiences, tentative groupings of individuals were suggested, but the students were encouraged to modify these to suit their own purposes. The overall structure of the learning program is shown in Figure 8.

During the first few weeks, the groups worked on identifying their learning objectives and developing their task organization. I was available for consultation during this period. Then the groups were paired into mirror groups, with one group presenting its task to the other group and receiving feedback. The next stage was a meeting of the whole course at which the first half of the group projects were presented and discussed. The groups then returned to the mirror situation where the roles were reversed, and finally the second half of the projects were reviewed by the whole course.

The experiment started slowly. The students appeared to be neither anxious nor enthusiastic. They merely worked through the stages passively, occasionally asking questions. Some groups were having difficulty in identifying learning tasks that would interest all their members, but there was little movement into or out of the groups. The pairing of groups seemed to achieve little, and the meeting of the whole course to review the first half of the group tasks was dull. However, when the groups returned to the mirror situation, they became considerably more active and discussion of the second half of the projects by the whole course was much better. This suggested that the students had taken some time to master the unfamiliar learning enviroment but had eventually done so.

Because only I worked with the students in this experiment, I asked them to provide feedback about their reactions in their own terms as well as to complete the questionnaire. Much of the unfavorable comment focused on lack of staff direction at the comencement of the course. Students reported that there was widespread confusion about what was expected of them, that time was wasted by the groups on "idle and irrelevant discussion," and that, wanting to identify quickly problems worth working on, they became impatient with the time spent on searching for learning tasks during the first few weeks. They also had difficulty in understanding the functions of the groups, and for some students inadequate direction created anxiety about assessment and a lack of enthusiasm. Some of the learning

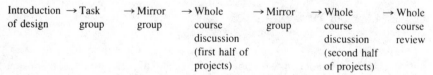

Figure 8. Design of the graduate course program.

tasks were not widely shared among group members, and there were complaints that the tasks lacked depth and that group members did not contribute equally to them. There were several comments that the weekly meetings were not long enough, that staff members should have been more active in the groups, and that groups were presenting their learning tasks before the tasks had been sufficiently developed.

Although the students reported considerable difficulty in working autonomously in groups, many of them felt that the groups had provided the most valuable learning experience in the course. They considered that the groups became more effective over time, that individuals' experiences and viewpoints were broadened through interaction, and that their communications and decision-making skills had improved through working in groups. One frequent comment was that leadership roles were shared widely among group members and that relations generally became progressively more cooperative and supportive. Finally, as the groups became more comfortable about working on learning tasks they had chosen for themselves, this approach to designing for learning became increasingly attractive to many of the students compared with the traditional structure of formal education.

Once again, the strong tendency toward either bureaucratic or democratic learning modes was evident in the patterns of responses to the questionnaire. About 30 percent of the students preferred the traditional learning mode but apparently for two distinct reasons. First, some students saw in bureaucratic educational structures the means of competing against one another. They wanted to be told what was expected of them and then to prove that they could perform designated tasks more successfully than other students. This form of competition provided them with their motivation. The second reason seemed to be a belief, held particularly by the younger students who had not been out of the educational system for very long, that the staff knew better than the students what they should learn and how. It is likely that both motives were linked in all three courses to produce the conservative reactions displayed by some students, but the responses among the MBA students revealed more clearly that the preference for bureaucratic structures had dimensions of both competition and dependence.

Conversely, 70 percent of the students were attracted to the democratic learning mode in the same general way as were the undergraduate students. They were inclined toward having greater freedom to determine learning objectives and to pursue them in cooperation with one another. However, they went even further. In the undergraduate courses, the central educational outcomes of intellectual stimulation and personal growth were seen as highly dependent on the staff. The majority of second-year students defined the staff members as authority figures, whereas most third-year students saw them as more experienced and knowledgeable resources. The greater maturity of many MBA students was reflected in the stronger perception that intellectual stimulation an personal growth could come through their interactions with one another. Although they may have been unsettled at first by the lower degree of staff direction, eventually they learned to seek more solutions to their learning requirements in cooperative working relations with their fellow students.

Summary of the Redesign Outcomes and Ongoing Developments

The organizational redesign of the courses evoked two basic patterns of responses from the students. They consistently tended toward either continued reliance on the traditional bureaucratic structure of education or the active search for new learning and understanding in cooperation with one another and the staff. Various forms of compromise between the two were sought by some students, but for the majority the choice seemed to be quite clear. The proportions of students who adopted each orientation are summarized in Table 2. In the first mode, students regarded their education primarily as a means of personal material advancement and defined it in terms of instruction and repetition as directed by the staff, ignoring or competing with one another in their efforts to obtain favorable assessments. Students in the second mode accepted an active role in making decisions about their learning requirements, redefined their education in terms of planning and controlling their own learning, and perceived one another as potential coproducers of new knowledge and understanding. Variations in these learning patterns among the courses suggested further insights into the characteristics of the two modes, but the basic distinction was between bureaucratic and participative-democratic orientations toward learning.

Since the courses were first redesigned, students taking them have consistently tended to display one or the other orientation toward learning. Each year during the first few weeks considerable uncertainty and stress have been experienced by both students and staff. The difficulties experienced initially have been central to the process by which students try to move from the familiar relationship of depending on the staff to accepting the challenge of directing and controlling their

TABLE 2. Estimated Percentages of Students in Bureaucratized and Democratized Learning Modes

Course Name and Number	Bureaucratized Learning	Democratized Learning
Organization and business management 200	52	48
Organization and business management 300	45	55
Organization and Management 509	30	70

own learning and developing their own ways of working effectively with one another. At the outset, they expect a course structure based on a clearly defined curriculum determined in advance by staff members who will lead them through the curriculum by means of formal instruction, assignment of tasks, and establishment of performance criteria. Each course does have a structure, but the structure is incomplete and develops only as the students become involved in making decisions about learning objectives and tasks. In consequence, conflict has been evident during the early weeks among the students and directed toward the staff. The conflict arises from the absence of a detailed curriculum and from anxiety about assessment, which is experienced all the more acutely when students encounter difficulty in reaching consensus about learning objectives and tasks and in developing their own work organization. At the same time, there have been enough students in each class who accept the design readily, are able to work in uncertain situations, and who manage to establish positive directions with their peers. A stage must be reached at which students are sufficiently clear about desired ends and the means for achieving them, after which they become more comfortable in their new relationships with one another and with the staff. In this process, the uncertainty that staff members themselves experience is necessary and unavoidable. The design of the courses raises issues in group and organizational life that the staff cannot resolve for the students. Were they to try to do so, they would merely establish the traditional dominance-dependence relationship. For students who overcome their initial difficulties, the learning outcomes are of two kinds. Not only do they acquire new knowledge and understanding of subject matter, but many also become more conscious of their own learning individually and in groups. They become aware of and interested in their learning behavior as they realize the extent to which they themselves can direct and control it.

Some students respond positively and immediately to the freedom to learn in new ways, or at least they begin to explore the possibilities in the organizational design of the courses. Others become anxious and are unable or unwilling to take an active part in managing their own learning. Whether students respond positively or negatively to the democratization of the courses seems to reflect both psychological factors and the influence exerted by the wider educational organization. The main psychological variables are students' prior experiences of education and their ability to change these expectations. The difficulties associated with taking control of and responsibility for one's own learning tend to be greater for students who enter a university directly from secondary school with little experience of organizational settings other than those of formal education. Many of them are highly constrained by the prolonged uninterrupted periods they have spent in bureaucratically designed educational systems and by a passive sense of purpose with respect to their future. They expect important decisions about their education to be made for them, and they do not know how to become involved in learning with staff members and one another except through relationships mediated strongly by bureaucratic organizational structures (cf. Paskow, 1974; Sanford, 1976). Moreover, many students who enter a university directly from secondary school do so on the basis of little information and less critical thought. They have difficulty in conceiving of any alternative to bureaucratically designed education, and their decisions to continue with their formal education are taken mechanically and automatically. Confronted with an educational design that offers them greater scope for choosing both the learning objectives they wish to pursue and the appropriate means for pursuing them, they are uncomfortable about exercising that choice.

Not all the students who enter a university directly from secondary school display this paralysis in the face of freedom to learn. However, the pronounced tendency for them to do so raises serious questions about the effects of secondary schooling on individuals' learning capabilities and the desirability of encouraging them to undertake formal education for such long continuous periods early in life. The learning patterns of the Master of Business Administration students generally have been quite different. It is no coincidence that these students not only have reentered the educational system after several years of postgraduate work experience but that the great majority are studying part-time while continuing to pursue their work careers. They have decided to seek further education on the basis of personal judgments about their aspirations for and prospects in the future. Such decisions are seldom taken without some critical thought, and they may be reversed quickly if the actual learning experiences are judged to be irrelevant to the student's interests and aims or not worth the personal sacrifices involved. Similarly, a proportion of students in the undergraduate courses have sought tertiary education, often on a part-time basis, after spending several years working for a living. On the whole, these students display more purposefulness in their education, and, when confronted with possibilities for designing and managing their learning, they are more likely to overcome initial difficulties and to pursue these possibilities successfully.

The inability of many young full-time students to cope with uncertainty and their greater tendency to continue to rely on staff members to direct and control them support my earlier contention that schooling has disabling effects on individuals' learning capabilities. The difficulties students encounter in making choices about their learning objectives and tasks are in contrast not only to the learning behavior displayed by older part-time students, but also to the behavior of the children who participated in the design of the White Gum Valley playground discussed in Chapter 1. These children were able to work efficiently and effectively with one another and with adult resource people, they exercised positive initiative when confronted with complex planning issues and conflicts of interest, and they demonstrated a strong sense of responsibility to others who might be affected by their proposals. Their learning capabilities were evidently still relatively undamaged, and they were highly responsive to the challenge of a meaningful task. When children whose formal education has only just commenced can learn to participate actively and cooperatively in planning processes, whereas many young adults approaching the end of their formal education have great difficulty in doing so, we cannot avoid concluding that students' experience of education during the intervening years in secondary school may in fact reduce rather than develop their ability to manage their own learning.

It seems equally likely that most, if not all, of these students should not enter a university directly from secondary school. The practice of enrolling students in school as early as possible and keeping them there as long as possible ignores the different stages of human development individuals go through. During different periods of their lives, they are subject to different expectations. Different needs and interests take priority, only some of which can be met through their formal education. The longer their initial period of full-time education lasts, the more likely it is that their development in other respects will be delayed, or that their attempts to satisfy other expectations, needs, and interests will be in conflict with the demands of education (Thompson, 1973). Secondary education must be redesigned so that it will develop rather than restrict individuals' abilities to take control over their own learning. However, periods of uninterrupted formal education should be shorter and distributed throughout their lives rather than dominating the years from childhood to early adulthood. So long as education remains bureaucratized and students are subjected to it for such prolonged periods, societies will continue to produce young adults who are unprepared to engage in the new learning and constructive innovation needed for active adaptation to mounting uncertainty about the future.

The difficulties some students encounter in attempting to learn how to manage their own learning are not caused solely by their own psychological condition. The redesign of the courses has been introduced within a larger traditional organizational structure and culture that sets limits to what can be achieved. The values, performance norms, and organization of the redesigned courses contrast markedly with the approaches taken in most other courses. Particularly in the undergraduate courses, which are conducted over the whole academic year and of which the redesigned part is only approximately a third of the whole, these differences have been brought into sharp focus. Some students have recognized them as reflecting more than differences of subject matter or the idiosyncrasies of individual staff members, and they have asked why basically different approaches are adopted in the same course. However, the dominant structures and cultures of traditional educational institutions do not lend themselves to deep exploration of such issues. To work through the question in an open dialogue with staff and students would require the staff to share their individual prerogatives over subject matter and educational methods to an unprecedented extent. Although the institution sanctions experimentation and innovation by individual staff members, it does so only to the extent that the norms, standards, and regulations continue to be observed and that other colleagues are not affected in their own areas. Therefore, the students' question is to a large degree undiscussable (cf. Argyris & Schon, 1978). In the graduate courses, fewer problems of this kind are encountered because graduate courses are conducted as semester units and are relatively more autonomous. Nevertheless, given that most students have difficulty in learning to work with the participative design, the persistence of bureaucratic educational design in the wider institution appears to exert a further restraining influence on the ability and willingness of some students to do so.

Developments in the internal participative design of the courses have made it possible to provide students with more effective initial support in their attempts to define their learning aims and to manage their own learning under conditions of greater freedom and uncertainty than most of them have been used to. In the University of Western Australia courses, two main developments have strengthened the conditions and prospects for active adaptive learning to occur. *First,* the broad objectives of the course have been defined in such a way that students still can identify their own learning aims and plan to pursue them while obtaining guidance from a general framework. The objectives are sufficiently positive to provide a general rationale and direction for the activities of all course participants, but they provide students with a great deal of scope to interpret the objectives in terms appropriate for them. On entering the courses, students are confronted with the basic propositions developed in Chapter 1—namely that societies are in a state of turbulent transition, that the most prevalent modes of response to uncertain change are maladaptive, that potentially active adaptive response strategies are emerging, and that the course is intended to help the students learn more about such alternatives. With respect to their learning projects, they are then invited to think through what they need and wish to understand about their world and the changes occurring in it. Given their initial tentative choices of preferred areas of inquiry, the propositions may be used as guides to the kinds of questions they could ask about those areas. Initially, students attempt to identify their individual areas of interest and concern. For the purpose of bringing them into interaction to explore and negotiate possible shared learning objectives and collaborative tasks, the "market day" has proved to be the most effective mechanism. Even in the Master of Business courses, where prior knowledge of students' occupations and work experiences is available to the staff, the market day provides for a relatively unfettered exercise of choice that is superior to imposing any staff-determined criteria for the formation of self-managing learning groups. This mechanism has also been found to be workable with larger numbers of students than it was originally thought it would be.

Second, along with the more definite articulation of general course objectives, there has been some redefinition and clarification of the respective roles of staff and students. The main responsibilities of staff are (1) to introduce the course objectives and proposed organizational design, (2) to provide lectures and other resource material relevant to the general propositions, (3) to be available to assist with the design and implementation of learning projects, (4) to progressively adapt the lecture program to students' learning aims and requirements, and (5) to provide feedback to students about their progress with learning, including responsibility for final assessment. Students' main responsibilities are (1) to identify personal learning objectives; (2) to find common ground if possible on which to base collaborative learning projects, (3) to design and carry out the projects, (4) to master the general subject matter of the course as this relates to the projects, and (5) to contribute to mutual learning through cooperation with one another around learning projects and other course activities. Apart from staff and students being clearer about what expectations they might have of each other, the main change from the original design is that the staff accept responsibility for providing stronger initial guidance, for example, through lectures on the general subject matter, in parallel with students working on their own learning projects. Recognizing that the identification and sharing of learning objectives and the development of effective project organization not only takes time but is experienced by many students as a period of difficulty, frustration, and anxiety, this arrangement provides for the students a greater sense of making progress from the beginning. It is then critical to judge when the projects have developed sufficiently for students to express their learning requirements and adapt the courses to them.

The organizational design of the courses will continue to evolve and change because the intention is that they should acquire and develop the characteristics of learning organizations capable of continuous active adaptation. So far, the design might be described as "guided democracy." Although suspicions might be aroused by the association of that term with Sukarno's dictatorial regime in Indonesia, in the context of education it means that staff members accept a *temporary* role of providing intellectual leadership while creating the possibility for students to assume progressive control over the substance, direction, and management of their own learning. Since the initial redesign in 1974, there has been a general decline in the anxiety and frustration displayed by students in the courses and a marked increase in the proportions of the student groups who move more readily toward assuming control over and responsibility for their learning. At the same time, students who are unable or unwilling to break out of the bureaucratic learning mode generally are able to work more comfortably while at least being exposed to the concept of active adaptation to turbulent transition. In general, the level and quality of learning activity in the tutorial groups and the groups formed around projects have increased greatly, and these groups have become the centers of course activity. One reason for the change in orientation evident among the students may be that, compared with the early 1970s, many more students are aware of and concerned about emerging issues in societies' future. The pronounced shift toward active adaptive learning, however, appears to be a result also of an educational design that provides students with more effective possibilities for learning to manage their learning.

Two major constraining factors remain, but experience in attempting to deal with them has revealed ways in which they may be reduced or overcome. The first concerns assessment and the student anxiety associated with it. Assessment becomes a barrier to learning when student concern about it begins to distract them from their efforts to identify and pursue their own learning objectives in collaboration with one another. It must be recognized that not only do societies and their component organizations and communities expect educational systems to provide such assessments, but many students also demand that their educational performance be evaluated. The criteria and procedures educators employ in evaluating students appear to be disputed more than the question of whether the students should be assessed at all. It will never be easy to reconcile tension between the roles of teacher and judge in a participative democratic education. In the courses we have designed at the University of Western Australia students generally have taken the view that assessment of their performances ultimately should be the responsibility of the staff. However, given that the students are able to define their learning objectives and to design tasks for pursuing them, they are in a position also to make decisions about the criteria for evaluating task performance and the forms of assessment appropriate for their chosen objectives and tasks. In bureaucratic education, more or less common tasks and evaluation criteria are imposed on students by the staff, and individual students' performances on those tasks are compared. In democratic education, students are assessed on their performance in relation to the objectives and tasks they have chosen to attempt, and they have the right to propose and negotiate the design of their assessment with staff members. Beyond this, assessment causes fewer difficulties once students and staff accept that the primary function of assessment is to help students to make progress toward their learning objectives. Although educators are expected to make "final" assessments of task accomplishment, their more important contribution to students' learning is to help them to achieve the highest levels of skill, knowledge, and understanding possible by providing continuous constructive feedback about the students' efforts at inquiry. Assessment is still an issue in our courses, but it becomes less intimidating to students once they begin to make progress with their chosen tasks and their observations of the staff's behavior confirm that the primary concern of the staff is to assist their attempts at new learning rather than to impose tasks and sit in judgment over task performances.

The second constraint is that the contribution education makes to the development of active adaptive learning capabilities among students will remain severely limited so long as the opportunities for such learning are confined to a few independent courses. The redesign of education must encompass relationships among subject areas, the various educational levels through which students progress, and the structure and management of educational institutions and systems in their entirety. The redesign of education must provide the conditions necessary for the integrated holistic development of knowledge and understanding of a changing uncertain world, together with experience of organizational designs that allow for active student participation and collaboration not only in specific learning tasks in particular subjects but in all dimensions of students' education. Over a period of several years, experiences with a new graduate program in the Wharton School of the University of Pennsylvania has demonstrated some important possibilities for enlarging the scope of educational redesign in these directions.

The Social Systems Sciences Unit was conceived by Russell L. Ackoff of the Wharton School. It offers graduate programs for students with backgrounds in any discipline. Within the unit, courses are offered in three main areas: philosophy of science and the scientific method, systems theory and planning, and social and organizational design. The usual credit requirements based on course work plus dissertation apply. However, although students may be encouraged to take certain courses, they are required to take only four courses within the unit and may choose the remainder from any fields. The four required courses consist of two learning cells and two research cells. The design concept of the cells is similar to that which guided the redesign of the organization and management courses at the University of Western Australia. However, the scope for students to learn holistically and in new ways is made considerably greater by the affiliation of the teaching program with research centers. If they wish, students may take reduced course loads and work as paid staff in the research centers for 30 hours a week. Students from other graduate programs in the university also are eligible for such appointments. The two centers most closely associated with the teaching program are the Busch Center and the Management and Behavioral Science Center. Both centers are staffed by faculty who teach in the program, nonteaching research staff, and students. In itself, this is not an unusual arrangement in American graduate schools, but the basic orientations, research strategies and organizational designs the centers have adopted greatly increase the possibilities for active adaptive learning by all who are involved.

The centers' activities are concentrated on action research projects that have as their overall objective the simultaneous advancement of scientific understanding and improving future prospects within societies. Toward this end, they undertake research sponsored by such clients as business and government organizations, associations, and communities. The preferred mode of sponsorship, particularly in the Busch Center, is contractual with the emphasis on reaching agreement between the center and the client with regard to the formulation of the client's problems, appropriate approaches to examining and resolving them, and criteria for evaluating project outcomes. From the client's perspective, usually the primary concern is to resolve or dissolve the problems and issues with which it is confronted. The centers undertake research projects in the wider society to generate the resources necessary for sustaining and developing the centers. However, there must be sufficient intellectual challenge and social importance in the projects to justify their staff becoming involved. A project is launched when both criteria are successfully integrated in a shared formulation of objectives. The centers carry out research into complex real-world issues in ways expected to produce important achievements for the clients sponsoring the research and for the advancement of social scientific understanding. Typically, the issues and problems the centers accept are characterized by high levels of uncertainty and risk of failure. More straightforward problems generally are regarded as appropriate to traditional academic research or to consultants. The centers provide university-based resources to address and attempt to resolve important and novel issues and problems that cannot be dealt with adequately by traditional means. The orientation is toward research that produces new learning, not only in the discovery of solutions, but in increased understanding of the nature of the issues and problems in question and the forces that give rise to them (Emshoff, 1977).

Opportunities for students to participate in the centers' projects adds a dimension to their education that is not present in their individual courses, no matter how democratically these may be designed and conducted. The learning experience they acquire also is different from that gained through the role of the traditional research assistant. The organizational nucleus of the centers is the project team, which is composed of the staff members most able to contribute to the project. Once agreement on broad objectives and approaches has been reached between the center and the client organization, the project team usually works closely with a team from the client organization on the development and implementation of the project. Because of the complex and uncertain nature of project undertakings, the centers generally draw on a range of disciplines and experiences in developing formulations of and approaches to the problems with which they are concerned. The design and conduct of their research is based on exploratory forms of inquiry and on interactive learning both among disciplines and between researchers and clients. Students comprise the majority of staff members of the project teams, they are involved actively in all phases of the project, and it is not unusual for them to take the role of team leader. Project leadership is determined primarily on the basis of commitment and competence, rather than academic status. Involvement in center projects provides students with experience in field research in a manner that engages them with holistic research designs and strategies, drawing on a variety of disciplines and integrating them into the project contexts. Students often develop their dissertation work on the basis of the research project to which they have contributed, and because of the close affiliation between the centers and the teaching program, the experiences and knowledge gained from the projects provide learning material for the courses as well. Through the teaching program and the centers, conditions are established for students to learn how to manage their own learning in collaboration with others in the process of acquiring knowledge of subject matter. The centers also enable students to integrate different fields of knowledge around uncertain and complex project tasks in the world beyond the university.

In sum, experiences with the redesign of the organization and management courses suggest that, when confronted with the challenge of managing their own learning in unfamiliar and uncertain situations, individuals tend to respond in one of two basic ways. These response modes correspond to the two social design principles of bureaucratic and participative-democratic organization. Negative responses to the participative redesign of the courses seem to be associated with prolonged experience of bureaucratic education, which reduces students' ability and willingness to direct and control their own learning. Over the years, there has been a pronounced increase in the numbers of students moving toward the participative-democratic learning mode. This trend suggests that, although past learning experience constrains individuals in situations that require new learning, such constraints can be overcome. Many years ago, Hartmann (1942) argued:

> . . .present learning is less dependent upon previous experience and the adequacy of earlier skills and information than upon the clarity, field properties, and excellence of organization of the learning material itself. (p. 206)

The participative design of the courses has been clarified and strengthened to provide students with more effective general direction and support in assuming progressively greater control over their learning. Although several factors may account for the trend toward active responsibility by students for their learning, improvements in the organizational design of the courses has provided greater opportunities for it and many more students have responded positively. To this extent, progress in the democratization of education to help students to develop active adaptive learning capabilities has been made, but further progress requires much broader redesign strategies. The Social Systems Sciences Unit, the Busch Center and the Management and Behavioral Science Center in the Wharton School have developed a form of organization at the departmental level of teaching and research that makes possible more holistic learning based on multi- and interdisciplinary inquiry and enlarges the potential scope for active student participation in the design and management of their education.

DIMENSIONS OF EDUCATIONAL REDESIGN

Turbulent historic transition gives rise to requirements for new learning and understanding through which to discover and develop strategies of active adaptation. Such learning entails changes in knowledge and changes in human values, attitudes, and motivations. Bureaucratic organizations prevent new learning and, instead, reinforce the patterns of learning behavior that sustain them. What individuals learn and how they learn are influenced in large part by what is rewarded by the organizations in which they participate. By persisting with bureaucratic educational designs, societies are making rods for their own backs. New social designs are needed to increase societies' potential for active adaptation so that they can reduce and manage uncertainty about the future. Students, on the other hand, are emerging from their initial period of education with skills, knowledge, attitudes, and values that might be considered appropriate for bureaucratic organizations but certainly are not appropriate to the challenges that must be met. Lewin (1942) once stated:

> Autocracy is imposed upon the individual; democracy he has to learn. . . .Learning democracy means, firstly, that the person has to do something himself instead of being passively moved by forces imposed upon him. Secondly, learning democracy means to establish certain valences, values and ideologies. Thirdly, learning democracy means to get acquainted with certain techniques, for instance, those of group decision. (p. 231)

Bureaucratic education rewards student dependence on and submission to the authority of teachers and educational hierarchies and the acquisition of imitative skills, narrow specialization, and competitive individualism. As students discover this, they may reject or accept the bureaucratization of their learning, but either way they do not learn democracy through their formal education. At a stage in the development of societies when the active participation of their members in the shaping of future directions is most needed, societies' educational systems are on the whole producing individuals who know only the organizational world of bureaucracy and its technocratic outgrowths and are not prepared for active participation in making a desirable future.

Failure to create the learning conditions that foster the development of the qualities of thought and action necessary for active adaptation in turbulent environments threatens the future of educational systems themselves. The declining performance of these systems lends credibility to Reimer's pronouncement that "school is dead" and Illich's call for the "deschooling" of society (Illich, 1971; Reimer, 1971). Certainly, the educational systems of western societies no longer receive the support or respect they enjoyed previously, but the failure of bureaucratic education does not leave societies with only the alternatives proposed by Illich, Reimer, and similar critics of education. Their argument derives its persuasive force from the observation that bureaucratic education prevents active adaptive learning and that such learning, insofar as it occurs at all, does so largely outside of formal education, as will increasingly be the case if educational systems do not change. Societies have another choice of educational futures, however. They can transform their educational systems to provide the conditions for active adaptive learning and the development of human potential for creating desirable future states out of present crises and uncertainty.

The experiences with the redesign of the organization and management courses at the University of Western Australia and the social systems sciences program at Wharton provide grounds for optimism without detracting from the magnitude of the task that lies ahead. Over a period spanning the best part of a decade, these programs have demonstrated the possibility of stimulating and guiding the development of active adaptive potential both through the orientation they give to learning and the conditions of social organization they create. Many other educational innovations have displayed similar characteristics of social design. The contrast between these emerging designs and bureaucratic education presents a fundamental choice of educational alternatives. Herbst (1974) has offered a scheme of analysis that highlights many of the important dimensions of educational design on which this choice must be made. These dimensions and their interrelationships are summarized in Figure 9. Table 3 summarizes the characteristics of bureaucratic and democratic education on each dimension.

Democratizing education requires the redesign of both the task organization within subjects or courses and the relationships among them. At the outset, tasks are minimally specified within courses. Students participate in the formulation of objectives and the choice of learning tasks, they are provided with scope and encouragement to experiment with different methods of performing tasks, and assessment provides feedback to support learning. Subjects are treated as interrelated, and exploration of their relationships is encouraged. Staff and students interact on the basis of joint responsibility for and control over learning. Although

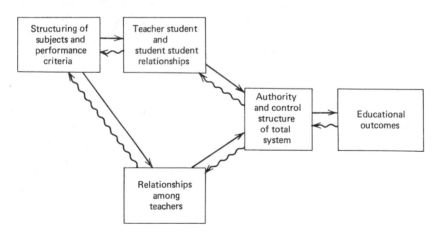

Figure 9. Basic dimensions of educational design. Adapted from Herbst (1974). Wavy arrows indicate reinforcement of the basic organizational characteristics.

TABLE 3.   Differences Between Bureaucratic and Democratic Education on the Basic Dimensions

Dimension	Bureaucratic Education	Democratic Education
Structure of subjects and performance criteria	Prespecified tasks, instruction content, and methods	Minimum initial specification with student participation in determining objectives, content, and methods
	Subjects isolated from one another	Subjects treated as interrelated
	Assessment rewards accuracy of reproduction by individual students	Assessment provides feedback on progress with chosen tasks and supports cooperative, continuous learning
Teacher–student and student–student relationships	Dependence based on teacher's hierarchical authority, control of assessment, and possession of esoteric knowledge	Joint responsibility and control shared by teachers and students
	Competition among students	Cooperation among colearners
Relationships among teachers	Individual autonomy, competition for resources	Interdependent and collaborative
Authority and control structure of total system	Control imposed through bureaucratic hierarchies	Control developed and maintained within learning settings
Educational outcomes	Dependent, competitive, narrow elitists; alienated drop-outs	Individuals who are able and motivated to manage their own continuous learning in cooperation with others

it is accepted that, initially, staff have greater access to knowledge than students do, the objective is to eradicate this inequality. It is assumed that staff and students are equal in their potential ability to learn (without denying differences among individuals, in either group), and the use of esoteric, mysterious language that creates artificial status differences between staff and students is rejected in favor of communication the students can understand. When relations between staff and students change in this way, it is possible for relations among students to change from competing for staff approval to cooperating with one another as well as with staff. Similarly, task-mediated relations among staff members change when the relationships among their various subject areas are recognized as central to the educational process. It then becomes possible and necessary for them to collaborate with one another on common educational objectives, interacting with students on an integrative basis rather than, or as well as, conducting the courses separately.

CONCLUSIONS

Taken together, experiences with the University of Western Australia organization and management courses and the Wharton School's social systems sciences program demonstrate that basic redesign on the dimensions discussed in the foregoing paragraph is feasible. In order to make further progress in redesigning education, the larger organizational structure of authority and control also must be transformed. Redesign on these dimensions makes possible and requires change from organizational structures based on externally imposed control through dominant hierarchies to designs that provide for control to be developed, maintained, and adapted within the primary learning groups, supported by matrix or network forms of organization to achieve overall coordination at higher levels. To the extent that the required changes on all these dimensions are accomplished, the results of the education process are likely to be different. In general, we could expect that more students will emerge who have learned how to manage their learning and who are better prepared to seek new knowledge and understanding over time under varying and uncertain conditions and in response to changing needs. Moreover, education would then be making its contribution to helping students to prepare for their roles in creating their societies beyond bureaucratic industrialism.

Educators such as Holly and Piaget have shown quite clearly that the arguments for the democratization of learning apply to all disciplines and all educational levels (Holly, 1974; Piaget, 1976). As educational systems attempt to respond to the growing demand for recurrent education arising from the increasing changes and requirements for new learning that adults are encountering in their lives, the relevance of these arguments and concepts should be even clearer. Adults are hardly likely to meet the learning challenges of their times through educational designs that regard them as infants. Societies have wider needs for the kinds of learning that make active adaptation to turbulent transition possible. These are the learning needs that manifest themselves in the crises and challenges confronting organizations and larger systems in all spheres of collective human activity. Redesigning education for the young increases societies' potential for active adaptation in the future, but the conditions likely to produce that future are emerging in the present. The conditions must be understood and acted on by today's adults in the settings in which they arise. The initiatives toward designing for active adaptive learning on the part of students have provided invaluable experience with the sustained development and management of possibilities for active adaptive learning. In the next three chapters the account of this experience is extended to encompass attempts to meet the challenge of active adaptation through learning among adults in work organizations.

3

Designing for Organizational Learning

The present and emerging trends in the environments of organizations place a high premium on their capability, through the efforts of those who participate in them, of continuous learning and active adaptation. How an organization's members learn and with what results depends to an important extent on the characteristics of the organization's basic social design. Organizations depend on the learning of their members. Through the ways in which organizations are designed, however, they also exert strong influences on the kind of learning that occurs and the contribution that learning makes to organizational functioning.

Bureaucratically designed organizations influence the learning of their members in at least three main ways. *First,* choices about the values and purposes to be served by organizational activities are separated from the performance of these activities, and the involvement of most organization members in making such choices is very limited or nonexistent. *Second,* the learning required of members of organizations is largely restricted to performing narrowly defined tasks and roles according to specific predetermined procedures. *Third,* feedback about performance is fragmented into evaluation of individual task accomplishments with the result that individuals are unable to relate their contributions to those of others. Bureaucracies reduce the variety of purposeful behaviors of their members and reward and reinforce their reliability in single-loop learning. In consequence, bureaucracies must also depend on elaborate information systems and control structures to maintain overall monitoring and regulation, but these structures become ineffective in turbulent environments. Insofar as their members are unable to learn in ways that increase their understanding of the changes affecting them and their ability to produce active adaptive responses, bureaucratic organizations themselves lose the capability of reducing and managing turbulence.

Democratically designed organizations increase the variety of purposeful behaviors of their members. They continuously seek to improve their own learning and active adaptive potential by encouraging and supporting learning among their members, which leads to constructive organizational innovations. Members are involved in determining the ends to be served by their efforts, they have freedom to develop and modify appropriate strategies and methods of task performance, and feedback about performance is based on their joint contributions to organizational purposes and objectives. In democratically designed organizations, new learning that leads to changes in norms governing performance, as well as improved ways of satisfying established norms, is regarded as central to survival and development. Moreover, members develop shared awareness of how they learn and what facilitates or inhibits adaptive learning, and they seek to improve the conditions and behaviors that produce such learning (Argyris & Schon, 1978).

There is almost a paradox here. Bureaucratic organizations are highly resistant to the kind of learning that would result in their transformation. I argued in Chapter 1 that rational analysis and experimental demonstration alone are not sufficient to overcome the sources of resistance to active adaptive redesign of organizations. Learning that produces new understanding of the environment, the inadequacies of bureaucratic designs in the present and emerging environment, and the feasibility of adaptive alternative designs must occur among organizational members themselves, but this is extremely difficult in organizations that are already bureaucratized.

Early in 1976 an opportunity and challenge to address this issue arose in the unlikely context of a request from the Australian Telecommunications Commission for assistance in designing and conducting a new management training program in Telecom Western Australia. The request appeared, at first sight, to offer few prospects for achieving significant organizational change because conventional management education and training programs have seldom if ever had such effects on organizations. These courses have taught managers *about* theories, concepts, and techniques through lectures, discussions, and simulated exercises—most of which have been contrived with little account taken of the settings in which the managers actually have worked. The trend has been to remove the managers physically and psychologically from their work worlds, place them in the hands of educators responsible for imparting new information to them, and expect (or not expect) them to make use of this information on their return to the organization. This approach has not provided adequate opportunities to *practise* new theories, concepts, and techniques or to test their meaning, relevance, and validity through the personal experience of using them in the circumstances under which managers must make decisions and act. Although knowing about a theory or concept is indispensable to using it, such knowledge is not sufficient to ensure understanding of the theory or concept and skill in its application (cf. Argyris & Schon, 1974, 1978).

As theory had become separated from practice, so the task of educating managers became divorced from that of managing the organization. Training and development sections have proliferated in organizations, but they have remained tangential to their central operations. Despite the growth in official support for management education, in practice managerial attitudes often have been characterized by polite tolerance or by cynicism and indifference. Senior management support and involvement usually have been confined to approving proposed courses and allocating resources to them, leaving to relatively junior staff members the important responsibility of identifying and satisfying learning requirements in the organization. Training staffs have tended to look outside the organizations needing learning skills for ideas and knowledge that would assist them to design courses. Or they have looked for courses already offered externally, and then they have attempted to "sell" these within the organization. Frequently, decisions to release individuals to attend courses have been made grudgingly or on the basis of whether the persons could be spared rather than on the basis of any definite expectation of future benefit to the individual and to the organization. Even when participants have discovered something in the course content that they wished to explore further through application in their work, they have often found themselves returning to organizational situations not conducive to experimentation and innovation. In consequence, the function of training and development as stimuli to new learning has been stifled and their influence on organizational directions severely limited.

If a management education program was to make any significant contribution to managerial learning and organizational innovation in Telecom Western Australia, radical departures from conventional approaches were necessary. The design of the program would have to take account of both the ways in which bureaucratic organizations prevented or inhibited active adaptive learning and the tendency of conventional management courses to reinforce the barriers to new learning. In fact, it would not be a management education or training program in the traditional sense. Rather, it would be an intervention directed toward mobilizing the learning capabilities and initiatives of the organization's members in new ways. The task was both similar to and different from that of redesigning formal education as discussed in Chapter 2. It was similar in that it was necessary to break with the assumptions, beliefs, and designs of conventional education in order to create the conditions for active adaptive learning. The program would have the same basic characteristics of enabling participants to engage in active adaptive inquiry and gain direct experience of participative democracy. The main difference was that participants would be able to focus on the change and uncertainty affecting their organization and on developing adaptive alternatives to its present design and strategies. Whereas many of the students discussed in Chapter 2 had only very general learning objectives, the Telecom managers could ground their searching and learning more in their experience and observations of how wider trends were affecting their particular organization. Also, they could direct their efforts at active adaptation toward concrete issues in the organization's future. Telecom's approach at this stage was not a fortuitous coincidence. Tom Alford, who was then responsible for training and development in Telecom Western Australia, had experienced as a part-time student the redesign of the organization and management courses at the University of Western Australia. He saw clearly the possibility of extending that design strategy for active adaptive learning to an increasing number of managers in a single organization confronted with managing change and uncertainty in its environment. This led to my involvement.

TELECOM AUSTRALIA

Evolution of Telecom in its Environment

The function of the Australian Telecommunications Commission, which trades under the name Telecom Australia, is to provide, maintain, and develop telecommunications services throughout Australia. From federation in 1901 until 1975, this function was performed by the Postmaster General's Department (PMG), which also was responsible for postal services. Telecom was created in 1975 as a result of recommendations to the Australian government by a commission of inquiry into the Postmaster General's department, which concluded that the postal and telecommunications services should be organizationally separated. The commission further recommended that the two new agencies should be set up as statutory authorities rather than as government departments. Statutory authorities were considered to be different from government departments in four main respects: (1) the cabinet minister responsible for each function would not be involved in the day-to-day administration of the agency, which would be accountable to Parliament on an annual basis, (2) management of a statutory authority would have greater freedom to make business decisions because it was less constrained by annual budgets and the Treasury, (3) management would have greater authority over organizational and staffing matters whereas government departments were subject to the regulations of the Public Service Board, and (4) statutory authorities had greater latitude for involving persons outside government employment in contributing their skills and experience to the overall direction of the enterprise. As a government department, the PMG was subject to political control and pressure and tended to be insensitive to other external factors. Strategic planning and management were hampered by the vagaries of the political process such as changes of government and fluctuations in the annual amounts appropriated for its functions. The main reason for establishing Telecom Australia as a statutory authority was to provide it with autonomy to operate more in accordan ce with business principles although it would remain subject to the overall authority of Parliament.

The Telecommunications Act of 1975 defines Telecom's responsibilities as: (1) to provide, maintain, and operate telecommunications services which best meet the social, industrial, and commercial needs of the Australian people and to make its services available throughout Australia so far as is reasonably practical, (2) to cover current expenses and meet at least half of capital requirements through revenue earned each year, and (3) to keep services up to date, operate them efficiently and economically, with charges as low as practicable. In addition to the national telephone network, the services to be provided by Telecom include international subscriber dialing, the public telegram service, data transmission via telecommunication lines, and facilities for broadcasting and receiving radio and television programs nationally and internationally for the Australian Broadcasting Commission. To perform these functions, Telecom has fixed assets of $6009 million and employs 87,500 full-time employees. It is the largest employer in Australia.

The formal organizational structure of Telecom Australia is shown in Figure 10. The Board of Commissioners is responsible for policy making and direct oversight of the organization. It is serviced by a secretariat that reports to the Managing Director, who is a board member. The Planning and Finance Directorates also report to the Managing Director and are responsible for developing corporate and financial policies. The Chief General Manager is responsible for the operation of Headquarters departments and the Deputy Chief General Manager is responsible for the functioning of the State Administrations. The Coordinator Management Reporting Systems keep both informed of the organization's performance against objectives and targets. The basic departments of Telecom are Engineering, Customer Services, Accounting, Supply, Personnel, Industrial Relations, Information Systems, and Research.

The structure of the State Administrations is shown in Figure 11. In general it mirrors the division of functions in Headquarters. The State Managers meet quarterly with senior national management in Headquarters. Individually and as a group they have significant influence in the organization. In 1977 the State Administrations underwent a major change with the creation of an Operations Department responsible for the key functions of technical installation and customer services. The purpose was to achieve better communication and coordination between the two functions that have the greatest direct effect on delivery of service.

Telecom's work force is comprised of several main occupational groups. Engineering and technical personnel account of 58 percent of all employees. They perform the functions of designing, planning, installing, and maintaining the telecommunications network. Professional engineers are the dominant force within this group because of their educational qualifications and positions in the

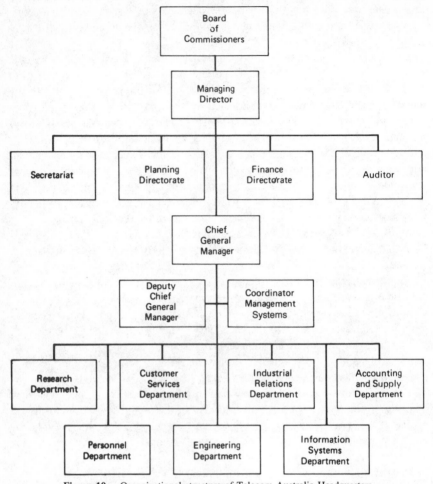

Figure 10. Organizational structure of Telecom Australia Headquarters.

organization. Prior to the creation of the Operations Department, they occupied all management positions on the technical side and have continued to do so in the Engineering Department. Technical staff members are responsible for the planning, installation, and maintenance of telecommunications equipment. They are trained by the organization to high levels of technical expertise. Linemen comprise the largest occupational category in Telecom. They are semi-skilled people who construct and maintain the bearer paths of the system—namely, cables and aerial routes. Their work consists mainly of digging trenches, laying cable, and maintaining the cable.

The majority of employees in departments other than Engineering and Operations occupy administrative and clerical support positions, ranging from senior

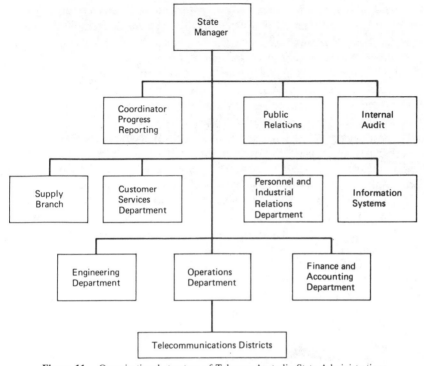

Figure 11. Organizational structure of Telecom Australia State Administrations.

management to clerical assistants and typists. Promotion is based on knowledge and ability acquired mainly through experience in subordinate positions, but educational qualifications are important in areas such as accounting and data processing. Although it is possible for these persons to be highly mobile among departments and functional areas, they tend to specialize in the areas in which they were recruited.

A much smaller group of operators handle the manual operations of the network. Telephone operators provide the assistance necessary to connect calls when this cannot be done automatically. They also connect long distance calls from public telephones and assist in setting up international calls. Phonogram operators accept telegrams for transmission by telephone and also transmit telegrams received from other places to addresses in their areas. Telegraphers transmit and receive telegrams over the telegraph. Their services will be required for a long time, but telegraph traffic is declining, causing staff reductions and feelings of job insecurity and anxiety about moving to quite different work.

Telecom has retained the strong career orientation of the PMG. Most occupational categories have career paths, and the majority of employees seek to pursue careers within the organization. On the one hand, this practice has the effect of increasing employee competence and commitment, particularly as their length of service and associated career investment increase. On the other hand, it tends to reinforce parochialism and adherence to outmoded conventions. In consequence, Telecom has entered what many hope will be a new era with several strong conventions that carry over from its past and that may not be conducive to the pursuit of new directions.

The general conventions of Telecom derive from the former PMG and the Australian Public Service. Whereas officially espoused objectives and formal organizational structures may be changed relatively quickly, conventions tend to persist in the behavior of the people who have been conditioned by them. One major convention in postal organizations is that the mail must get through. The PMG's record in this respect was good, and new employees were indoctrinated in the department's standards, which frequently were reinforced through official communications. As the telecommunications function grew, a similar ethos developed. Telephone and other services were highly maintained, and any breaks in service received the highest priority. However, this pride in performance could have also led to organizational arrogance, or to the attitude that the Australian public was fortunate to enjoy the services of an agency that could provide it with the benefit of continued technological innovation. Such attitudes reflect a general public service outlook that government agencies should decide how best to meet society's needs within the legislative scope of their functions, and that their accountability to Cabinet and Parliament are sufficient to ensure that they would act in the public interest. In the case of Telecom, the tendency toward unilateral organizational action was strengthened by a kind of technological determinism. That is, policies and decisions were determined mainly by those persons having technical expertise and by the direction of scientific and technological development. The concern of technical experts to build the telecommunications network, rather than an active interest in discovering and meeting needs in society, appears to have been the primary orientation.

A second set of conventions arose from the employment conditions offered by the Australian Public Service. Recruitment to the service traditionally has been mainly through public service entrance examinations. Competition for employment usually has been strong, but once employment has been attained, job security has been almost inviolate. On the other hand, educational distinctions have acted as barriers to promotion for many employees and have limited their career horizons. Moreover, for many years seniority was the main criterion for promotion, which tended to frustrate the aspirations of younger staff members and to dampen initiative within the organization. "Efficiency" officially replaced seniority as the main criterion in the 1960s, but remnants of the old policy have lingered on. Moreover, by virtue of the amount of legislation through which they are controlled, government departments are very regulation conscious. The lower employees are in the organizational hierarchy, the more likely they are to be enveloped in regulations with little or no scope to respond to members of the public as individuals with particular needs. At the same time, junior employees have the greatest amount of daily contact with the public. Secure in their employment but lacking authority and incentives to use initiative, many employees have felt powerless to improve their performance or have used the anonymity a vast bureaucracy confers on them to ignore or deny criticism.

In Telecom itself, one other convention has important implications for the future, namely, the dominant influence of engineers in the organization. Engineers usually attain junior management positions within five years of commencing their careers. Their rapid rise and dominating influence are due partly to the importance of their technical expertise. Also, promotion has provided a means for individual engineers to avoid keeping abreast of technological change by assuming administrative and managerial responsibilities, and engineers in charge of other engineers generally have fewer difficulties in communicating with their subordinates. The resources for which engineering managers are responsible far exceed those of nonengineering positions, and the amount of information available to them generally is much greater than that possessed by other departments. Telecom's engineers have made an enormous contribution to developing a telecommunications network comparable to the most advanced in the world, but their strength lies predominantly in their ability to plan and control by technical means, and their dominance within the organization adversely affects those who perform other functions. Linemen are managed directly by engineers and, although technical staff may advance through several supervisory levels, they have little discretionary responsibility and all decisions other than minor ones are made by engineers. Their range for development is limited and narrow, yet the work they perform is critical to the delivery of Telecom's services. Administrative and clerical staff members are responsible for a wide range of nontechnical functions, including customer relations, and in the technical areas, they provide essential support. They too, however, are overshadowed by the engineers. They lack professional status and receive little encouragement to acquire higher qualifications. They have little knowledge of the physical network for which they are often criticized by engineers and the technical staff. Their advancement in the organization is slow, and the extent of individual positions open to them usually is much narrower when compared to that of engineers. It is difficult for them to understand how their performance relates to others and to the organization as a whole, and many feel that they do not have sufficient authority or status to influence other areas. Their work has traditionally emphasized accuracy, standardization, and detail which, together with the narrow scope of individual positions, limits their initiative.

The creation of Telecom as a statutory authority and the further reorganization in 1977 is reducing the inhibiting effects of its traditional structures and culture. Educational restrictions on advancement have in principle been reduced considerably, particularly for technical staff whose opportunities for promotion to managerial positions in the new Operations Department appear to be greater than when they were under the control of Engineering. As a statutory authority, Telecom should be subject to more general legislative control and fewer detailed regulations, allowing management and staff to exercise greater initiative in responding to the needs of customers and the general public. With the organization's functions and objectives more clearly defined and with greater emphasis on efficient and effective performance, Telecom employees may develop an identity apart from the undifferentiated category of public servants and the associated image of them as incompetent, insensitive bureaucrats.

However, Telecom's apparent new autonomy and greater visibility also bring into sharper focus the challenges it faces in its environment. As a young industrial country, Australia's future is fraught with uncertainty. Up to World War II Australia's economic growth depended primarily on agricultural exports, and it imported manufactured goods, mainly from Britain. The war gave considerable impetus to technological development, and the manufacturing base was broadened and deepened. From 1945 onward, successive governments pursued programs of industrial development supported by policies aimed at attracting overseas capital investment, quickly increasing Australia's population through assisted immigration, and protecting local manufacturers from import competition. Major petroleum and other mineral discoveries provided further stimulus to economic growth. Now the assumptions, values, and strategies of the post-war economy and society are being challenged by trends such as increasing unemployment, inflation, and environmental deterioration. Australia remains highly vulnerable to international developments and is affected greatly by the same sources of uncertainty as other industrial societies. It is confronted with major questions about its future directions. Technological change and innovation, including telecomunications, will influence those directions greatly. The integrated advancement of computer technology and communications is widely regarded as the next major stage of basic technological innovation in western societies. The implications of this technological revolution for societies' future are enormous, but they are far from clear. As the central provider of telecommunications and the largest employer in Australia, Telecom is caught up in the technological revolution and its uncertain implications for the society's future.

Progress toward large-scale integration based on microprocessors, the development of domestic satellites, and innovations such as optical fibers are at the core of this revolution. These innovations hold the promise of a great increase in the range of services available not only to business and government but also to households. They offer the prospect of vastly increased speed, capacity, quality, and reliability of communications systems together with a marked reduction in energy consumption and cost. Proponents of the impending technological innovations anticipate significant productivity increases and the opening up of many new market opportunities. They also see a potential for the decentralization of economic activity within and among societies, the relief of growing numbers of people from monotonous work, increased involvement of managerial and nonmanagerial employees in organizational decision making, and much greater scope for people to use technology to serve their own purposes and to regulate their life situations.

Conversely, although the central importance of telecommunications to life in society is recognized, the communication needs of societies are hardly understood at all. Enthusiasm about the prospect of a new wave of basic technological innovation has undoubtedly overshadowed serious consideration of what those needs might be. Because of the unprecedented pace with which new technological possibilities are emerging, together with their uncertain implications, public policies for regulating the application and use of new technology have not been able to keep up with the changes. Similarly, managements within organizations are confronted with making decisions about the introduction of new technologies that they do not understand sufficiently to know what the effects and their required responses will be. The emerging innovations are expected to open up many large new markets and this expectation is giving rise to strong demands for minimum regulation by governments. Uncertainty about the wider consequences of technological innovation and concern over possible abuses of people's rights and interests, however, have led to counterclaims that favor close monitoring and control. The effects of technological innovation on employment are particularly cloudy. The contention that the new technologies will create new and better jobs and careers is contradicted by the view that employment will decline, that many of those who retain their jobs will lose control over their work and suffer deskilling, and that growing numbers of unemployed people will experience severe economic disadvantages in society. Older employees, women, young people seeking to enter the work force, and ethnic minorities are expected to be the hardest hit.

Already Telecom is encountering tension and conflict arising from uncertainty about the effects of technological innovation. The current thrust of its development is toward centralized automation. Commercial engineering and economic arguments clearly favor automation of telecommunications, but the human and social implications are not so easy to resolve. On several occasions Telecom has been criticized for imposing technology on the Australian public. There are other problems, too. The prospect of competition from companies such as IBM has increased, and in 1977 and 1978 Telecom was involved in a long and bitter dispute with its technicians' union, which virtually paralyzed the society. The dispute arose over Telecom's plans to centralize telephone exchange maintenance and automate large numbers of manual exchanges—a course of action that would reduce labor requirements, lower costs, and restrict many of the remaining technical jobs to monitoring and replacing components. The dispute was resolved, at least temporarily, only when Telecom management agreed to negotiate with the union over technological change within frameworks that included considerations of effects on society and quality of work life, as well as economic, engineering, and technical assessment considerations (Hull, 1980).

The directions Telecom takes in the future will have a major impact on the society. It has a great need to seek new understanding of its environment and of its social role. Such understanding must be acquired through the learning of its members. The traditional structure and culture of Telecom are not conducive to meeting the challenge of reconciling the possibilities created by technological innovation with the human values necessary for societal guidance in the future. Telecom's structure is centralized and bureaucratic. The organization's culture is strongly influenced by public service conventions and a tradition of technological determinism. The major task of the new management education program is to provide the conditions that will allow participating managers to acquire new understanding of their organization in its environment, to discover possibilities for introducing adaptive organizational innovations, and to learn from the experience of acting to transform the organization's structure and culture.

DESIGNING FOR THE SELF-EDUCATION OF TELECOM'S MANAGERS

Telecom had been conducting conventional management courses since 1960. These were residential courses built around lectures, case studies, and exercises. In the early 1970s, growing dissatisfaction with the courses was expressed that centered on the difficulties participants had in translating abstract conceptual material into terms relevant to their work situations. Telecom's first response to criticism of the courses was to offer a highly unstructured alternative that dispensed with all formal lectures and predetermined tasks and instead asked participants to draw on their own experience and ideas to address the question, "What is management?" This alternative provided insufficient definition of course objectives and inadequate frameworks within which participants could organize themselves around learning tasks. It was rejected by most state organizations, and in Western Australia the one course conducted in this manner gave rise to considerable frustration and dissatisfaction. Evidently the course designers had defined their choice as being between the conventional course structure and practically no structure at all. It was, and perhaps still is, a common misapprehension among educators to regard bureaucratic and *laissez faire* designs as the only alternatives available to them. Participative democracy is a third alternative. Its structure is based on a clear definition of learning objectives and the broad stages to be used in achieving them, a division of responsibility between staff and participants, and evaluation of task performance. The structure differs from that of conventional education in that participants take a more active role in defining objectives and tasks, they have scope to plan, experiment with and control their learning, and the purpose of feedback is not to reward or punish but to assist learning (see Chapter 2).

Because of negative experience with the unstructured course, Telecom headquarters produced a new proposal, the main features of which are summarized in Figure 12. The basic format provided for the linking of theory and practice through a series of three residential workshops interspersed with two periods during which participants would carry out assignments in the course of performing their normal organizational roles. The purpose of the first workshop was to prepare participants for on-the-job assignments by introducing theories and concepts drawn from several areas of management thought. After this experience, they were expected to review their own roles leading to the identification and planning of assignments aimed at effecting improvements in their managerial performance. In the second workshop, they would examine their experiences with the assignments and receive further theoretical inputs. In the next period back on the job, it was envisaged that the managers would build on their experience with the initial assignments and use the inputs from the second workshop to overcome any difficulties they had encountered before. In the final workshop there would be another review of the assignments and an exploration of the relations between Telecom and its external environment. Then participants were to develop recommendations to senior management concerning desirable future changes based on the content of the course and their own attempts at innovation within the organization.

The general design was sent to the state organizations. As was customary, the states were encouraged to modify it to suit their own conditions and requirements and to seek assistance from local external resource people. In Western Australia this responsibility was primarily Alford's who, reflecting on his experience as a student in the university courses that had been redesigned, suggested to me that we collaborate to produce a design for Telecom in that state. The new structure at least promised to facilitate learning through managers' experience of efforts to resolve issues in the organization that were important to them, but it was possible to go further than the headquarters design in several ways.

First, the headquarters design appeared to have restored partly the old practice of having the staff determine in advance the educational material to be presented, which placed participants in the essentially passive role of reacting to what they heard and read. The experience with the university experiments and with the par-

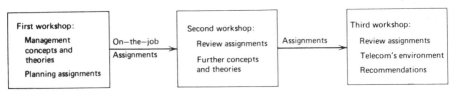

Figure 12.   Format of new management course in Telecom Australia.

ticipation design workshops and search conferences suggested that there was another way in which to build the initial framework within which participants could do their own planning. It was decided that the first workshop should begin with participants as a group searching for trends in the wider society, exploring the implications of these for Telecom's future role in society, making judgments about desirable directions for the agency, and assessing its present strengths and weaknesses with respect to pursuing those directions. The participants should then be able to identify the issues requiring resolution in their own areas of responsibility and plan for change in the light of their wider shared awareness. Consistent with open-system thinking, which stresses the importance of context, they would be approaching the task of organizational redesign from the outside in. Serious consideration of Telecom's environment was more appropriate to the first rather than the final workshop, as had been suggested by headquarters. Moreover, from a very early stage in the program, participants would have the opportunity to take an active role in the management of their own learning rather than enduring a period of exaggerated and inappropriate dependency on the workshop staff.

Second, it was essential that senior management in Western Australia be closely and continuously involved in determining the organizational objectives the program should serve, and thereby accept that ultimate responsibility for Telecom employees' learning and growth rested with them. Participants were to be drawn from relatively junior ranks of middle management, which was acceptable because they were sufficiently close to the organization's base to influence daily operations through direct intervention. However, if primary responsibility for the program was left with the agency's training staff and external resource people, this in itself could create enough uncertainty to defeat the central purpose. Without active involvement of senior management, participants might well wonder how much credibility the program had and in particular whether they could take seriously the invitation to learn by experimenting and innovating within the organization. Equally important, the relevance of the program depended on how it related to the challenges that Telecom was likely to face in the future and to senior management's strategies for meeting them. Although the senior group at the state level was by no means completely independent of headquarters, it was well placed to inform the program staff and participants about emerging wider developments and probable future requirements. For both these reasons it was important that senior management take an early and continuing active role in the program, while allowing participants adequate freedom to determine desirable directions and take initiatives for themselves.

Third, it was important that careful attention be given to the selection of participants. In the conventional courses, selection had been based on the eligibility and availability of individuals. Given the tenuous nature of the relationship between course content and managers' roles within the organization, it did not really matter how any particular participant group was composed. In a program directed toward planned change in the organization, the question of selection did become important. If individual managers were expected to plan and implement strategies aimed at achieving significant organizational improvements, they would need not only the sanctioning of senior management but also the support and cooperation of relevant others in their domains. Therefore, participants needed to be selected, as far as possible, according to the criterion that each individual was interdependent with at least some others because their functions within the agency were linked. Typical of bureaucratic organization, management roles in Telecom were highly differentiated. The scope of individual roles was circumscribed, and managers whose functions impinged on one another often were located in different departments and formally connected only through a lengthy chain of command. Individuals who attended the workshops in isolation might find subsequently that others in the agency with whom they were interdependent and whose cooperation was needed to implement innovations could not share the workshop experience and their commitment to the innovations that had been planned. This might lead to conservative choices of projects or to opposition, frustration, loss of confidence, and declining commitment. Conversely, by identifying networks of established or potential relationships among managers and selecting participants on this basis, it might be possible for them to identify shared change objectives and to pursue strategies of collaborative action.

The final design consideration was the most difficult to resolve. Although the program might stimulate active interest in exploring new ways of managing and producing specific improvements, it was likely that after the final workshop the impetus would decline. The question was how to create conditions that would sustain ongoing learning and adaptation. This goal required an organizational culture in which managerial initiative and responsiveness to changing circumstances were valued and encouraged. Such a culture could not be developed easily or quickly. For example, the growth of understanding and commitment among senior management was expected to take time. Its support for innovation would have to be demonstrated in concrete instances, and such support was likely to vary between projects. Evidence of the strength and scope of sanctioning could accumulate only over some ill-defined period. However, senior management's involvement in the program itself was potentially conducive to the evolution of a supportive climate. It would provide members of the senior group with an opportunity to become more familiar with the kinds of change subordinates desired. The postures the senior group adopted in face-to-face interactions would give participants at least some indication of their seniors' attitudes. It was equally important that participants' immediate superiors have a positive role in the program. If a direct dialogue developed between senior management and participants but did not include the immediate superiors, they could well feel threatened and become alienated from the program and its objectives. As an initial step, it was decided to invite participants' supervisors to the final afternoon of the first workshop to negotiate the proposed projects with their subordinates in a setting free from the ordinary pressures and interruptions of organizational life. A third potential way of building a more adaptive oganizational culture was the development of relationships among the participants themselves. From working together to change the organization in mutually agreed-on directions, a more enduring *esprit* of stimulating and supporting one another might emerge. This prospect would be more likely if, following the first program which the organization was expected to regard as experimental, the decision was made to continue with others. If so, the network of participants could be increased to the point where, it was hoped, a shared tradition of learning and innovation would develop. The problem of sustaining the impact of the program remained unresolved at this stage, but it was possible that the program would become a "shadow" organization through which Telecom managers could learn to criticize the official organization constructively and to discover how to change it.

The design thus sought to bring together managers who were interdependent in their organizational roles, to help them to educate themselves about the possible significance of changes occurring in the wider Australian society, to reflect critically on Telecom's present structure and mode of functioning, and to plan collaboratively for positive change. However, previous experience with the redesign of the university management courses and with other action research interventions in organizations had demonstrated the need to influence the wider organizational forces that affected the possibilities for learning and active adaptation. In particular, the collapse of an organizational development program in a large public hospital immediately prior to Telecom's request for assistance raised the question of whether a different approach to obtaining the client system's sanctioning of change was necessary. Usually, sanctioning had been sought through discussions with the parties whose approval and support was required (Clark, 1976). In the hospital case, several lengthy discussions with senior management had failed to ensure sufficient understanding and commitment. Given this experience, it seemed that genuine sanctioning was more likely if senior management itself searched Telecom's environment, assessed the organization's present state, and from this decided whether the proposed approach to management education and development was appropriate. By involving the senior managers in gaining personal experience of the search mode of learning, we could be sure that they would have a better understanding of the learning processes their subordinates would be working through to produce their ideas and plans for adaptive organizational innovation. The experience and outcomes of senior management's own search would provide a stronger basis than mere explanation and discussion for determining the extent of high-level commitment to the program.

The Search with Senior Management

Subsequent to the discussions that yielded these tentative propositions, a meeting was sought with the senior management group in the state organization. The State Manager gave his approval for the meeting. He did not participate further at this stage but later became closely involved and played an important leadership role.

The senior group consisted of the heads of the Engineering, Customer Services, Accounting and Finance, Personnel, and Supply Departments. The Manager of Development and Staffing was also included because the program came within his area of responsibility. The heads of Accounting and Finance and Engineering could not attend, but the latter was represented by his deputy.

The group met for half a day in April 1976. The headquarters design and the proposed modifications were explained, and initial reactions were favorable. The group then commenced its own involvement through a brief search guided by a simple framework. It focused first on the trends that were becoming apparent in Telecom's environment, then on the broad objectives expected to take priority in the next five to 10 years, on the present strengths and weaknesses of the organization with respect to achieving those objectives, and finally on the kinds of internal changes that might become necessary, including the management capabilities that would be required.

Senior management identified three main trends in the environment: (1) major technological change was expected to continue, (2) the group anticipated that union power would increase with a consequent need for greater consultation and more widespread participation in decision making, and (3) members believed that social change was transforming the lives of individuals, affecting in particular their attitudes toward work. Turning to the future objectives of the agency, the group emphasized that the primary objective would continue to be provision of services to Telecom's customers and that there would be a major emphasis on finding ways to improve service. At the same time, Telecom was already experiencing resource constraints, and these were likely to become more severe. In order to improve service, the group thought that clearer performance targets and priorities, greater ability to anticipate future requirements, more effective internal communication to evoke understanding, commitment, and integration of effort, and flexibility in the use of resources would be essential.

Members of the group then reviewed the proposed management education program and were unanimous that it was highly relevant to the organization's requirements. Having placed considerable emphasis on developing more effective integration within Telecom to meet future demands, the group had little difficulty in accepting the proposition that participants should be selected on the basis of functional interdependencies. For example, the Customer Service and Engineering Departments were involved in the delivery of services, but communications between them at times were inadequate, resulting in confusion and delays. Also, the other departments performed both support and control functions that affected the provision of service. If managers who were linked in these ways could be brought together in the program, it would be possible to orient their thinking and efforts toward issues of mutual concern.

This need was more easily recognized than acted on because of the complexity of the organization, with many functions linked in multiple ways and a large number of specialist positions related only very generally or indirectly to others. A detailed mapping of interdependencies might have helped, but this was not feasible, certainly in the time available. Also, participation in the program could affect a person's promotion prospects, and it would have been unfair to exclude those who could not at the time be located clearly in networks of functional relationships. Moreover, it was always possible that participants would discover linkages for themselves that the program staff had not anticipated. In consequence, the final selection included both managers who were directly related in their organizational roles and others who were not.

Although carried out under severe time constraints, the search with senior management appeared to have achieved its primary purpose. Usually the members of this group interacted in more formal settings where they had to deal with relatively specific issues requiring immediate decisions. Indeed, some had felt that a half-day meeting was too long, given their daily commitments, but there was now general agreement that the experience had been valuable and stimulating. Their interest in the program and its results had increased noticeably during the meeting. For example, one department head stated at the outset that his staff were too busy for any of them to participate, but when discussion turned to the question of selection, he requested at least one place in the program "if it is going to be like this." Having established what they considered to be some of the important general issues that Telecom would face in the future, members of the senior group were developing a shared expectation that the program for middle managers would lead to beneficial change within the organization to help it meet future challenges.

Design of the First Program

Given senior management's firm commitment to the program, the next step was to develop a participative democratic design to stimulate and guide new learning among Telecom Western Australia's middle managers and to enable them to assume progressive control over their learning in the program and the organization. Within the overall format shown in Figure 12, only the first workshop required a more definite design. Decisions about the purposes and design of the second workshop would be made in the light of experience with participants' learning in the first workshop and action phase.

The first workshop was to be of one week's duration in a residential setting. The major purpose was to stimulate new learning and understanding of Telecom in its environment and of how the organization's present state affected the prospects of active adaptation to change, leading to planned innovations aimed at improving both organizational performance and the quality of work life enjoyed by employees. The structure of the workshop is represented in Figure 13. The plan was to engage participants in a search process until they developed shared appreciations of a larger and changing reality within which to develop concrete strategies. Senior management's search had demonstrated that significant change could be expected

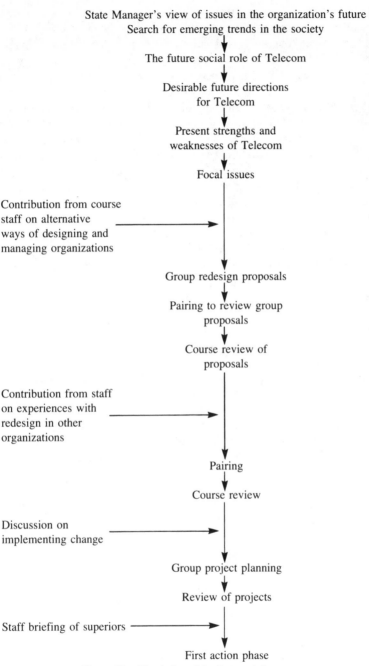

Figure 13. The design of the first workshop.

in the future, but it was important that participants also focus on emergent trends in the wider environment. If they proceeded directly to specific problems, it would be difficult for them to look beyond their immediate situations and past experience as guides for ways of resolving them. The danger was that they would become preoccupied with "fixing" perceived causes of present difficulties and frustrations, seeking solutions within their existing repertoires of responses and accepting established structural and cultural constraints as immutable. When a group plans within a framework of what its members take to be immediate realities, there is a tendency to lose sight of the possibility that those realities are socially constructed and, therefore, can be reconstructed. Although the processes by which social organizations and institutions evolve are complex and may seem historically overwhelming, their design is in large measure a matter of conscious or unconscious choice. Nevertheless, the way in which they are designed usually is accepted as a "world taken for granted" (Schutz, 1964, Vol.1). Searching into the future creates an opportunity to reflect on the possible consequences of persisting with present social designs. It facilitates the development of a commonly held value base from which to consider the possibility of alternative social designs that are more congruent with the pursuit of the desired future.

Participants' basic values were most likely to be expressed if they confronted as large a picture of their future as possible. Therefore, it was important that they begin their search by exploring what was referred to in Chapter 1 as the contextual environment and those change processes emerging in the environment independently of the actions of any single organization, affecting society as a whole but under the control of no particular element. Developing shared awareness of such forces was considered to be essential for effective planning but also for building a learning community. Scanning the environment this widely was intended to provide participants with the opportunity to create perspectives broader than their own immediate preoccupations, which could help to lay the foundations for collaborative planning. Unless their basic values were articulated at this early stage, they could have been lost sight of and, hence, not performed their central function of guiding choices among alternative future strategies.

Searching requires a structure that enables a group of individuals to move to a level of shared responsibility for and control over their own affairs (M. Emery, 1976). In the workshop, it was necessary that the participants rather than the staff members provide the initial contributions of ideas about change and draw conclusions from these. It was not expected that they would possess all the knowledge potentially relevant to the issues that concerned them. The staff would attempt to meet this need later. However, it was essential that the participants accept the task of establishing initial directions as their responsibility and be prepared to assume a large degree of control over their own learning. If they left responsibility for the workshop to the staff, then learning, in the sense used here, would not occur. This did not mean that the staff would be reduced to a passive role. The early sessions of the workshop were to be based on discussion and exchange, which for the staff meant a shift from monologue to dialogue or from delivering prepared lectures to making contributions as issues arose.

This leads to a third point. Although Figure 13 conveys the general logic of the workshop design, periodic reference to the proceedings of previous sessions would be necessary to check for inconsistencies and to review or elaborate on particular themes. The full potential of the early sessions was likely to be realized only if the participants subsequently selected change objectives and strategies consistent with the basic values that emerged in these sessions. As an aid to this process, it was planned to record all contributions to each session on large sheets of paper that, as they were filled, would be hung on the walls of the conference room and remain there for the whole week. By keeping the unfolding record of the workshop in full view of everyone, it would be easier to manage the tendency to lose sight of values and ideals when struggling later with more specific issues and dilemmas.

The remainder of the workshop design provided for a process by which the participants would work—first in small groups and then in plenary review sessions—on the task of identifying desired changes in their organizational areas and developing strategies to achieve these changes. As an intermediate stage in the process, it was proposed that the groups form into pairs and give each other feedback about their respective designs. In this way, each group might receive stimulation from others who were not as closely involved in the particular issue but had potentially relevant experience in the same organization. Managers in the feedback role would have opportunities to learn more about areas and functions of the organization with which they might be relatively unfamiliar. It was also hoped that the pairing of groups would cause managers to become interested in the problems of others in the organization rather than remaining preoccupied with their own concerns, thus helping to foster a broader cooperative learning climate. Progress toward the final project designs and plans for implementing them were expected to take the rest of the week, with the afternoon of the last day set aside for negotiations between the participants and their supervisors. Planned contributions from the staff were kept to a minimum and were intended for stages at which, from past experience, it was expected that they would be relevant and necessary.

CONCLUSION

There is an increasing and urgent need for organizations to pursue strategies of active adaptation in turbulent environments. Such strategies are unfamiliar to them, and therefore it is necessary that their members engage in new learning. Bureaucracy is, however, inimical to new learning and continuous active adaptation. A major problem is how to create conditions for active adaptive learning among members of organizations that presently are bureaucratic.

The learning of managers is centrally important because it is through managers that organizations establish, maintain, and develop relations with their environment. Managers also would appear to be well placed to initiate adaptive innovation within organizations, but conventional management education has had little direct effect on fundamental organizational redesign. Telecom Western Australia offered an appropriate opportunity to address the problem of creating conditions for new managerial learning that might lead to active adaptive innovation in a bureaucratically designed organization that was confronted with emerging critical uncertainty in its environment. The resultant design of the management education and development program provided for (1) active participation by managers in determining the objectives of their learning and in planning and implementing innovative strategies within the organization, (2) positive acceptance by senior management of its primary responsibility for the development of Telecom's human resources and its taking an active leadership role without stifling the initiative of subordinate managers, (3) collaborative learning and planning by managers who were linked through their organizational roles, and (4) developing a shared commitment to new learning and active adaptation within the organization. The overall objective of the program was to stimulate progress toward the participative democratic redesign of the organization through the interactive learning of its members.

The first program began in May 1976. It was attended by 20 managers and staff specialists drawn predominantly from the Engineering and Customer Services Departments, with smaller representation from the other departments. In Chapter 4 we review experience with the first full program. Subsequent to the completion of the first full program senior management decided that the new design should be continued as Telecom Western Australia's approach to management education and development. Chapter 5 traces the evolving experience with the program and evaluates its effects on new learning and development within the organization. A second experience involving an American corporation is then reported, leading to an assessment of the wider implications for transforming organizations.

4

Organizational Learning in Action

Active adaptation by organizations in turbulent environments depends on their being redesigned to embody the organizing principle of participative democracy in place of bureaucracy. Effective organizational transformation entails new learning among the members of the organization, which leads to shared understanding of the necessity and desirability of seeking alternatives to existing social designs, as well as knowledge of the alternatives and how to develop them. The organization's members must have positive reasons for wanting to transform their organization, and these reasons are most likely to be identified and acted on through their own learning. Because bureaucratic organizations do not enable such learning to occur, special efforts must be made to create the conditions under which active adaptive learning among an organization's members is possible.

The management education and development program for Telecom Western Australia was designed to achieve this objective. It was concerned with complex processes of learning among members of an organization. Therefore, assessment of the program must consider not only the results in terms of desired innovations within the organization but also the learning processes that produced or failed to produce them. The program involved managers in these learning processes over a period of seven months. The purpose of this chapter is to report in some depth the experience with the first program in terms of both learning processes and organizational outcomes.

THE FIRST WORKSHOP

The 20 participants came together on a Sunday evening to commence the first workshop. The State Manager of Telecom Western Australia had been asked to attend on the first evening, and after dinner and brief introductions, he made a simple statement about the main issues he thought would confront the organization in the next five to 10 years. He anticipated that increasing economic stringency would make it necessary to use resources more efficiently and effectively, the importance of improving communications among departments would increase, trends in union–management relations would require greater union involvement in organizational decisions, and pressures to improve customer services would become greater. He then discussed informally with the group issues in the organization's future.

The State Manager's contribution at this stage served two main purposes. First, it demonstrated that senior management regarded the program as important and potentially relevant to the organization's future needs. The meeting with members of senior management had established understanding and sanctioning of the program at that level, but the participants so far had been given little reason to regard the program as anything other than another conventional management training course. Although it would have been quite usual for the State Manager to deliver an opening address to mark the commencement of any management course, in this case he made it clear that the program was expected to stimulate improvements within the organization. Second, for reasons given in Chapter 3 it was important that the participants develop as soon as possible shared awareness of change in the wider society and its implications for Telecom as a basis on which to identify desirable future directions for the organization and the internal innovations needed. This could have created difficulties for the participants because traditionally to express value judgments about desirable organizational directions had not been recognized as a prerogative or responsibility of lower middle managers. Given their status in the organization, these participants might have questioned whether it was their place to express value judgments about Telecom and whether, if they did, any notice would be taken. In stating his conviction that the organization would have to pursue new directions and strategies, the State Manager confirmed that this was a legitimate concern of the participants as well as their superiors.

After the first session, the participants and the program staff interacted informally over coffee and in the bar. The next day was spent searching into Telecom's future in much the same way as senior management had done but taking more time and going into greater depth. After a brief explanation of the overall course structure and the objectives of the first workshop, the rationale of searching as an initial step toward formulating more concrete strategies was put forward. The participants then moved to the first stage of the search, where they explored trends in the wider society. Two staff members manned chartboards and recorded individuals' contributions. The unfolding record of work done in each session was kept in full view of participants, affirming that there was room for them all to contribute, providing a sense of making progress with the task and also making it possible to refer back to preceding sessions when necessary.

The group's search into the wider environment and members' responses to the issues that arose provided an initial indication of their basic value orientations. After they had developed long lists of observations about ways in which the society was changing, they were asked to distinguish between trends they thought were desirable and undesirable. There was obviously scope for disagreement, which did occur, but we expected that there would also be a large measure of agreement on basic values when confronting so large a picture of the future (M. Emery, 1976). For the group, the basic issues revolved around reconciling the materialistic and psychological aspects of human well-being and development. Technological progress was seen as a means of satisfying humanity's needs and wants but also as a threat to the physical and social environment through its destructive impact on nature and its destabilizing influence on personal relationships. Central themes of this session were the following:

1 Rational and cooperative use of resources.
2 Subordination of technological innovation to social objectives.
3 The quality of life as embracing nonmaterial as well as material values.
4 Exploring increased opportunities for social and geographic mobility while retaining sufficient permanence and stability in human relations.
5 Providing increased social security but also rewarding productive effort.
6 Developing systems of government based on integration of various interests rather than forced choices among alternatives.

In the next session participants attempted to identify trends affecting Telecom's future. The agency's primary function requires a high level of technological capacity and sophistication, and it was understandable that one theme concerned the acquisition of new technology to increase the quality and reliability of telecommunications services. However, the session was also dominated by a concern with customers and the public, and the issues raised about technological innovation in Chapter 3 became apparent to the group. Although some of the participants emphasized making new services available and finding ways to improve service delivery in an expanding market, others stressed the importance of developing greater knowledge about what customers and the public wanted and adapting to these needs. In other words, the basic issue was whether the organization should be discovering and adjusting to external demands, or itself deciding what services should be made available and influencing public behavior to suit organizational requirements. At this stage it was sufficient that the issue had been recognized. If it became a major point of contention at the level of concrete objectives and strategies, that would be the appropriate time to confront it in greater depth.

Two other themes concerned the structure of the organization and trends in the expectations of Telecom employees. As a consequence of the change in the agency's status, the participants looked forward to greater independence from political control and increased scope to operate as a commercial enterprise. Within the organization, they thought that a more flexible structure would be needed, one characterized by greater decentralization of decision making, improved communication between departments, and reduced emphasis on specialization as an end in itself. An apparent contradiction again arose within the group. Specialization was regarded by some participants as desirable because it promoted functional competence, but others saw it more as a source of parochialism and frustration. Consistent with the philosophy of searching, the staff members were satisfied if potential dilemmas could be identified during these early sessions while avoiding win–lose confrontations. On the question of employee expectations, the main trends were expected to be toward more women in the organization, greater employee participation in decision making, and a greater need among all employees for opportunities to develop continuously.

Against the broad picture of trends in the environment and in the organization, the participants proceeded to identify objectives they considered desirable for Telecom to pursue in the future. They emphasized improving service delivery and the agency's external image, making better use of available resources to improve productivity and profitability, developing a distinctive competence in telecommunications research, improving cooperation among departments, and providing more satisfying work lives for employees. In general, they thought that Telecom was well placed to pursue these goals with respect to its human, financial, and technological resources, but a significant number of the participants regarded the existing structure as a serious potential obstacle.

After the group had progressed this far, it was appropriate to introduce the results of senior management's search as a check on the similarities and differences between the perspectives of the two groups. There was considerable convergence of opinion about broad values and goals. Both groups wanted to increase customer satisfaction, improve industrial relations, develop better staff relationships, achieve more effective communication, operate with greater flexibility, raise productivity and profitability, and gain greater autonomy from political and headquarters control. The senior managers had been more concerned with questions of overall policy, targets, and priorities, and they had perceived communication barriers between upper and lower levels of the organization that the participants did not think existed to the same extent. The participants had directed their criticisms more toward lateral relations, were more concerned with operational issues, and had placed greater emphasis on staff welfare and development. They had also gone further in their criticism of structural rigidity and limited scope for decision making at lower levels in the organization, although they were aware that a reorganization based on multifunctional districts was imminent and might lead to increased scope at these levels. In general, the effect of introducing senior management's statement seemed to be positive. The similarity between the objectives that participants said were desirable and the theme of the State Manager's statement, the previous evening suggests that the group may have been influenced by him. The staff members were not concerned about this because the issues the State Manager raised were critical to the organization and there would have been reason to doubt the adequacy of the search outcomes if the group had ignored them. Moreover, the participants had raised other issues about the social purposes served by the organization, challenging the emphasis on specialization when it was at the expense of effective integration among departments, and pointing to the negative effects of the existing structure on both performance and employee development. Allowing for potential disagreement within the group, the climate at this stage appeared to support the involvement of the participants in constructive criticism as a prelude to organizational innovation.

The way in which the existing organizational structure had been described by the group confirmed that Telecom was structured and functioned predominantly on the basis of the principles of bureaucratic social design. At this point, staff members felt able to introduce the proposition that bureaucratic organizations in general were unable to respond adaptively to change and new challenges and that a basic alternative existed in the form of participative democracy. The essential characteristics of bureaucratic organization were described with the aid of the diagram used in Figure 1. A brief evaluation of bureaucracy's effects on organizational performance and the quality of working life was offered along the lines of Chapter 1. Then the alternative design principle of democratizing work organization was explained, using the diagram in Figure 2 (see Chapter 1). Staff members suggested to the participants that they consider this basic choice of design principles when, in the next stage of the workshop, they began to explore ways of improving their organization.

The participants had spent most of the first day actively developing their own ideas about desired future directions and present organizational deficiencies. At this stage, it was possible for staff members to make a conceptual intervention with little risk that they would be seen as imposing their own preferred theories and dictating to participants the kinds of organizational innovation they should undertake. The participants were in a much stronger position to judge critically the suggestions of the staff, by reference to their own previous work, than they would have been in a conventional course. Already relations between participants and staff were becoming collegial rather than emphasizing the status differences between teachers and those being taught. Therefore, staff members could put forward their suggestions as clearly and strongly as they wished because the process by which the participants assumed control over and responsibility for their own learning was already well under way. Following a brief discussion of the alternative design principle, the participants were invited to form four subgroups to select from the organizational issues that had emerged during the day as being those most relevant to each subgroup's members. They would then have the task of developing designs and strategies to increase their capability for pursuing desired directions in a changing and uncertain environment. Participants who were clearly interdependent in their organizational roles were grouped together in the expectation that the subgroup work would lead directly to shared innovative projects in the organization. For participants who were not directly interdependent on others in the workshop, it was thought that the subgroups would provide learning experiences on which to base individual projects. In any case, the initial grouping was tentative, and staff members explained that the participants were free to change subgroups if they saw other alliances that potentially were more fruitful.

The subgroups worked through the evening, and the next morning formed into two pairs of "mirror groups" as described in Chapter 3. Staff members remained available for consultation with the groups but maintained sufficient distance to allow the participants to assume a high degree of responsibility for the learning tasks. When a subgroup from each mirror group was ready to have its proposals presented to the whole workshop, all the participants returned to the main conference room.

One subgroup had concentrated on the need to improve superior–subordinate and peer working relations. It stressed the importance of increasing opportunities for learning and development in work roles, improving communication to promote better understanding of individuals' contributions to the organization, rewarding successful performance rather than penalizing failure, and establishing new mechanisms to allow more widespread participation in decisions. These directions certainly were consistent with the themes of the first day, but the subgroup had not addressed any particular area of organizational operations in which the directions could be pursued through planned innovation. The second subgroup had investigated the possibility of achieving major cost reductions in providing a telecommunications service for which demand was declining but still considerable. It identified sources of inefficiency and attempted to develop alternative arrangements, but these were largely technical and procedural. The subgroup had defined the scope of its chosen task rather narrowly and virtually ignored the social organization of work. There was little doubt about the importance of the issue, but the proposals reflected the traditional approach to problem solving in the organization. The morale of the employees involved in providing this particular service was very low because of uncertainty about their occupational prospects. The neglect of their needs was a serious deficiency.

The failure of the first subgroup to progress further than discussing highly general issues and, in the second subgroup's proposals, the lack of attention to human or social considerations were interpreted by the staff as evidence either that the subgroups had difficulty in grasping the concepts put forward by staff or that they rejected them. The task of confronting complex issues in their own domain also may have daunted them. As they moved from the broad level of social trends and their values about the organization's future to more concrete strategies, the first subgroup had drawn back from immediate realities, whereas the second had lost sight of some critical values in its engagement with these realities. The difficulties in making the transition from broad value judgments about desirable directions to concrete designs and strategies were to recur in subsequent programs in which Ken Strahan, then a graduate student in management at the University of Western Australia, studied the learning processes. Because his observations and analysis refer to later programs, they can be used here only to speculate about what may have been happening in the subgroups and mirror groups, but it seems likely that participants in the first program were experiencing at this stage difficulties similar to those Strahan later observed.

First, the new program design may have posed more serious problems for the participants than simply the fact that it was at variance with traditional expectations of management training. Nomination for the course would be regarded by many participants as having some effect on their career prospects. To this extent, it would have been important for them to present themselves well, strengthen their reputations, and demonstrate their potential for promotion to senior ranks. Because it had been made clear that they were expected to engage in cooperative decision making and planning, and this apparently had been sanctioned by senior management, they may have felt themselves under some pressure to be consistent with the cooperative ethic. Similarly, they had been told that organizational innovation was, in principle, supported and encouraged but there was also a risk of failure. Such a risk may have appeared to the participants to be all the more serious if they attempted innovation in their own areas of responsibility. They had been given no evidence that risk-taking performances would be rewarded. It is quite possible, then, that some participants experienced a tension between engaging in collaborative projects with others and the wish to protect their organizational situations. Similarly, although the program offered opportunities for participants to enhance their managerial reputations, these opportunities could be exploited only by committing themselves to planned innovative action in the organization with the attendant possibility that this would create difficulties or generate unfavorable repercussions. If these psychological forces were operating in the workshop, they would compound the problems participants faced in developing projects for organizational change and particularly projects that could be shared with others.

Second, the task of developing subgroups' proposals for organizational change depended on qualities of group interaction that could evolve only over time and that were likely to become pathological as much as they might lead to supportive relations around shared tasks. Strahan's later observations indicated that although some subgroups remained mindful of the search outcomes as they moved to the stage of identifying and planning for desirable change, others quickly forgot the search or could not see its relevance to any action they might take within the organization. Building consensus about group tasks was also a problem for some subgroups. Dysfunctional tendencies included concern about producing a well-defined project before the encounter with the mirror group and the report to the whole workshop, allowing one individual to dominate the choice of a project, allowing a coalition to form around planned activities that remaining members could not share, seeking quick compromises in the face of discontent within the group, and downgrading the level of challenge in order to allay members' anxieties. In contrast, other subgroups displayed patience, openness to the contributions of all members, willingness to work through differences and discontent, and an active interest in setting the boundaries of the group task at a level that would present meaningful challenges. The direction in which a group's interactive processes evolved made an important difference to whether its members felt trapped in an unwanted task, did not recognize one another as valuable contributors, were anxious or pessimistic about eventual outcomes or were enthusiastic about their chosen task, comfortable with one another, and confident that they belonged to a group that could accomplish worthwhile ends.

The mirror group mode may have posed further problems for some subgroups. Particularly when a subgroup did not have a clearly defined task widely shared by its members, it was vulnerable to external criticism and forced to expose its internal processes and difficulties. Such a situation could also create problems for the mirror group if, at this early stage, members expected to be confronted with a well-defined project on which to comment. They were then likely to criticize the other subgroup rather than helping it to make progress by offering positive suggestions. By no means all mirror groups behaved in this manner even when their client subgroups were struggling to reach agreement on proposed projects, but in retrospect we believe that the timing of the initial mirroring phase may have been premature in some cases. Perhaps more important, the role behaviors required for mutually supportive and beneficial interactions in this mode may have been more sensitive and complex than some participants were prepared for.

At this stage in the first workshop, staff members did not interpret in this depth the difficulties the subgroups may have encountered although they had expected that the groups would experience some difficulties and that the process of developing their objectives and strategies would take considerably longer. However, the pressures on the groups to develop objectives and strategies could have become counterproductive if sustained for too long. Before proceeding to the remaining group tasks, therefore, a further staff contribution had been planned. The initial presentation on alternatives to bureaucratic organizational design was augmented through examples of attempts to develop participative-democratic designs in other organizations. By shifting the focus away from their own organization for a period, the staff hoped to ease the pressure on the participants while maintaining and stimulating their interest in searching for ways to improve their organization. The examples concerned an experiment in autonomous work groups in a processing plant, the involvement of the White Gum Valley children in the design of a new playground for their school (see Chapter 1), and the organizational design of a new maximum security prison. These examples were selected because I had been closely involved in each of them (Williams, 1979; Thomas & Williams, 1977). By exploring alternatives to bureaucratic strategies in such diverse situations, participants might also acquire a better appreciation of the imagination usually required for organizational members to break with well-established assumptions and beliefs. We hoped as well to emphasize the essential simplicity of most successful redesigns. On the whole, the effects of this intervention seemed to go in the intended direction. Discussion of each example was vigorous, and although many participants adopted questioning attitudes, the attitudes were positive rather than negative. In other words, skepticism and conservatism began to be replaced by active scrutiny. A stronger interest in exploring alternatives was becoming evident.

The participants returned to the mirror groups to work on the tasks being considered by the remaining two subgroups. One of these closely resembled the concerns of the first subgroup that had reported (i.e., the improvement of working relations within and between work units), but three of the members were able to use the interdependencies among their organizational functions to identify particular target areas for work redesign. The further opportunity to explore and digest the concepts put forward by staff had also helped them to produce a coherent redesign strategy. This strategy entailed moving from a structure based on the performance by individuals of fixed specified tasks to a multiskilled group responsible for the whole function of the section. There was also a corresponding redefinition of supervisory roles to incorporate greater involvement in unusually complex problems previously dealt with by management and in the training of their subordinates to assume higher responsibilities. Two other members of this subgroup could not participate directly in the project but wished to remain associated with it while they were developing their ideas for individual projects. In turn, the three managers directly concerned with the project were willing to spend time helping with the individual projects.

Unfortunately, the fourth subgroup had become enmeshed in detail without developing an innovative overall design concept. It was attempting to find ways of improving cooperation between two sections of the organization with the aim of providing a better service to customers. Inadequate communication and coordination were generating frequent confusion, frustration, and dissatisfaction for both customers and employees, but the group's ideas for improvement were restricted to changing formal communication procedures. Because the flow of work between the sections was subject to considerable variance, a strategy that sought solutions in standardized procedures seemed inadequate to achieve the required degree of mutual adjustment (cf. Thompson, 1967).

Although three of the subgroup tasks appeared to be deficient in important respects, our staff members lacked detailed knowledge of the situations to which they referred and could respond to them only in general terms. Moreover, it was clear that they were not genuine group projects but directly concerned only one individual in each case. The other members of these subgroups so far had been given little opportunity to develop plans for change that they could pursue in their own areas of responsibility. Therefore, the staff elected to move on to the question of implementing change strategies. We gave a short presentation on the issues involved in initiating organizational innovation (as discussed in Chapter 1), after which the groups considered these issues using the proposals they had so far developed as examples. Their ideas about implementation were reviewed in a plenary session, and the participants moved on to define the change projects they actually planned to carry out during the first action phase of the program. They used the initial subgroups as sources of criticism and suggestions, but new supportive relations emerged as well.

On the final morning of the workshop, the action proposals were presented. Three of these had been designed by small groups and 15 others involved participants acting individually to initiate programs of planned change. In fact, two of the group projects were not based on directly interdependent organizational roles. Members had developed individual projects but wanted to have some indirect involvement in the proposed tasks of their fellow group members. This kind of indirect support was developing between members of different subgroups as well. The workshop had succeeded only to a limited extent in generating cooperative networks among managers whose roles had direct implications for one another, but in a more general way it was successful in developing collective commitment to shared values and purposes. The one project that was clearly group-based involved the three managers from the third subgroup who planned to initiate experiments in autonomous groups, working within their respective units. They planned then to explore possibilities for more effective cooperation among them.

Commitment to organizational innovation was unevenly distributed among individuals and groups, as could be expected. To some extent, this was reflected in the choice and design of projects, which varied markedly in their potential value as learning vehicles and in their likely impact on organizational functioning. On these dimensions, the most powerful design was proposed by the three managers from the third subgroup. Eight other projects were directed toward achieving similar improvements in work within sections, although they did not go as far. In some cases the existing functions of the sections within the organization imposed constraints on what was possible. They were too limited in scope for much improvement to be achieved without considerable redefinition of organizational functions. These matters were beyond the participant's control, but the designs held the prospect that some progress could be made within existing constraints and that implementation of them would be sufficiently challenging for the participants to learn from the experience. The remaining nine projects were directed primarily toward improved information, control, and flexibility in the use of resources. The designs focused largely on technical and procedural dimensions, although several did include provision for some degree of consultation among the parties concerned.

In general, participants appeared to be willing to experiment and to seek constructive change in directions that had been identified as desirable. Such was the climate of the workshop that no participant was prepared to withdraw public commitment to the program. On the other hand, some participants were experiencing private anxiety about their ability to effect desired change and the support their efforts would receive. Although the majority had been able to discern potential relevance in the alternatives to bureaucracy that had been explored (as these related to their broad values), it had been difficult for them to reformulate the general concepts in terms of their own managerial situations. Moreover, they were now confronted with the difficult step of going from talking about action to taking action. Little more could be learned until they engaged with the organization itself, and it was evident that their attitudes varied from confidence and a clear sense of purpose among some participants to uncertainty and caution among others.

Our staff could do one more thing to assist them. In the participant's efforts during the coming weeks, an important factor would be the sanctioning and support they would receive from their immediate superiors. Any doubts the participants entertained on this score would certainly have an inhibiting effect. In particular, it was possible that they would encounter difficulties when they returned from the first workshop if their superiors had been informed about but not actively involved in the program. Together with the daily demands of their work, this could prevent them from making the contributions necessary for the success of the projects. Therefore, our staff had taken the prior step of inviting the participants' superiors to attend the final afternoon of the workshop. This would enable them to acquire some appreciation of the work that had been done and provide an opportunity to discuss the projects in a setting free from the normal pressures and interruptions of organizational life. After lunch on the final day, our staff briefed the superiors on the philosophy and design of the course, emphasizing the importance to both managerial learning and organizational improvement of the attempts at planned innovations and invited them to use the remainder of the afternoon to discuss the proposed tasks with their respective subordinates. The workshop concluded with a dinner attended by senior management as well.

In summary, the program as a whole and the first workshop had been designed on the basis of several propositions about the conditions most likely to stimulate managerial learning and active adaptive innovation within the organization. The propositions were as follows:

1 Managers participating in the program must have freedom to direct and control their own learning and planning.

2 Managers' willingness to engage in active adaptive innovation in the organization would be influenced strongly by their perceptions of the extent to which such efforts were sanctioned and encouraged by higher management.

3 Identification and pursuit of innovations that were potentially adaptive for the organization and its members depended on participants' developing shared awareness of how wider change in the environment was affecting the organization's future prospects.

4 Active adaptive innovations would be those that increased the organization's ability to achieve its objectives while simultaneously enabling employees to satisfy their own needs more fully.

5 Significant organizational innovation would be more feasible if undertaken by managers who were directly interdependent in their organizational roles.

The experience of the first workshop appeared to provide some support for these propositions, although not completely. Some participants had responded very positively to the scope for self-managed learning and planning provided in the workshop, they seemed to be confident of higher level support and encouragement, the innovations they planned to undertake had considerable active adaptive potential, and many participants had developed mutually supportive relations although most of these could operate only indirectly within the organization. Other participants had responded to a very limited extent, which suggested that they had not overcome the difficulties and anxieties that arose early in the workshop and that they felt unable or unwilling to commit themselves to serious innovative attempts within the organization. Conversely, for participants who did not experience difficulties and anxieties to any great extent, or who overcame them, the innovative tasks they had chosen offered significant prospects for their own further learning and for organizational improvement.

THE FIRST ACTION PHASE

The participants returned to their positions in the organization for 10 weeks. Our program staff maintained contact with them through several group meetings at which the participants gave interim accounts of their experiences in attempting to initiate change. They also discussed problems. By getting the participants together within the agency, the meetings were intended to facilitate exchanges of support among them during a potentially difficult period and to reinforce the influence of the first workshop. The feedback at this stage was also to be used in designing the second workshop. Our staff had elected not to make any decisions about the structure and content of this workshop until trends became apparent and provided clues about the participants' further learning requirements. The continuing educational strategy was to develop the program on the basis of the actual patterns of individuals' experience in attempting to act on and change their organizational situations.

From the meetings several impressions were formed about the progress being made and the kinds of problems that had been encountered. As had been expected, progress was uneven. Some participants had proceeded rapidly to implement their planned innovations and, within a matter of weeks, were able to report significant developments. Progress had been made by others but not to the extent that had been anticipated. Some participants had achieved little or nothing. When less had been achieved than had been hoped, it was because of constraints beyond the participants' control, inadequacies in the original designs, or individuals' unwillingness to commit themselves to action that may have contained some risk. Four change projects warrant some discussion. Two of them illustrate the obstacles that confront attempts to change organizational structures and cultures through management learning, and two demonstrate the achievements that are possible.

One participant had appeared to accept the values and concepts developed in the first workshop and had proposed a design for restructuring certain related work roles in his section. He reported, however, that the people concerned had rejected his proposal as unworkable. From discussion, several things became clear. First, he had chosen to intervene in an area marginal to his sphere of responsibility so that the impact would be minimal. Evidently he tacitly denied that organizational innovation was a central component of his managerial role. Like other managers in the organization, he felt quite comfortable with technological change but valued a high degree of stability and predictability in the organizational structuring of work roles. This attitude was further reflected in his attempt to implement the design. He had developed this in detail and then presented it to the affected subordinates. When they pointed out that it did not meet the requirements of their work, the matter was dropped. He did not invite them to explore for themselves ways of reorganizing their work to improve performance and increase the satisfaction they might derive from it. Discussion of several other projects revealed a similar pattern in which individuals' anxiety to control their situations had led them to impose new arrangements rather than allowing participation by those affected in planning the change.

The second case presents a similar picture, but the manager's hesitancy and inability to implement planned change arose from different sources. He understood well enough the concepts of work redesign put forward in the workshop and had grasped their potential relevance to resolving serious difficulties in one section under his control. For some time, the section had been unable to meet its work schedules. It was subject to many and rapidly changing demands for its services, and its inability to cope drew strong criticism from user departments. In turn, the pressure of work and conflict with users had created tension and dissatisfaction among his staff. The manager decided that, by changing from existing work arrangements based on individual tasks to multiskilled work groups with more broadly defined responsibilities, the section would gain the flexibility needed to handle the workload while also providing his staff with more satisfying work and greater mutual support in the face of pressure. He discussed his plan with the section supervisor, who agreed that the proposed design would be better than the existing structure but who argued that it could not be implemented until the pressure on the section was reduced by increased personnel. The manager accepted this argument and did nothing further while waiting and hoping for additional personnel to be approved in the next fiscal year. This manager, too, had been rather anxious about initiating significant change, but the case raises another important issue. Democratization of work is a fundamental alternative to bureaucracy, and its relevance is greatest in conditions of rapid complex changes that cause bureaucratically designed organizations to function inadequately. Ironically, the uncertainty that arises from the mismatch between the existing capability of an organization and the changing demands of its environment can operate to prevent the necessary active adaptation from occurring. Instead of providing the spur to change, it can evoke the maladaptive response of seeking solutions within the existing structure. In effect, the section supervisor wanted to reduce the pressure on his staff through conventional bureaucratic means and then redesign the work organization under easier conditions. The fallacy was in hoping that the march of events would slow down sufficiently for the present structure to be dismantled and rebuilt, rather than recognizing the variety and adaptability present in a work force that can be mobilized to meet the crisis. In other words, the task of transforming an organizational culture includes changing the assumptions its members use to interpret their reality and to guide their selection of responses.

The redesign concept in the third case was almost identical to that of the second, but it was implemented with greater success. This manager's responsibility included a depot that carried out repairs and modifications to equipment. The nature and subdivision of the work had created many seemingly monotonous jobs that compared unfavorably with those available to persons in the same trades elsewhere in the organization. Staff absenteeism and turnover were high, and it was difficult to attract or retain people when special projects were scheduled. Problems of imbalanced workload also often arose. The proposed redesign entailed combining tasks into larger operations that became the responsibility of groups of workers. In addition, the depot had a system of rostered days off, but the days each employee could take were fixed. With the increased flexibility that was expected to be achieved through the group-based work structure, the manager thought that it would be possible for his employees to vary their days off according to their personal requirements. The new design was put to the depot supervisor and foreman, who agreed. The employees generally reacted favorably. Although a few said that they would welcome the increased variety of work, after a period of some six weeks there had been little move toward increasing the variety of tasks the employees performed, which suggested that boredom was not a problem for most of them. Moreover, the employees of the depot had pointed out that they did not feel unduly tied to their work stations and could regulate the duration of their work periods. On the other hand, they made considerable use of the more flexible work arrangements to vary their days off within the constraints of workloads and priorities. One interesting effect was that unauthorized absences declined noticeably. Now that they could vary their scheduled days off they were less inclined to stay away from work on other days. The manager's general conclusion was, "Whereas the depot had been considered to be an undesirable place to work, since the implementation of the [redesign] there has been no difficulty in attracting additional staff." The change and the benefits that accrued to employees and the organization were unspectacular but significant. Five other participants reported similar experiences with their projects. Thus far, the program had stimulated them to search for ways of improving the quality of work life in their areas of responsibility. Their aims and the scope of innovation had been modest, yet the gains were tangible and at least some elements of workplace democracy had been established.

The experience with these projects might suggest that the greatest prospects for achieving organizational change lie in taking small unobtrusive steps, or adopting an "incremental approach" that does not disturb the existing state more than is necessary to achieve very limited objectives (Lindblom, 1959). However, managing the fundamental trends in western societies will require more than merely reducing marginally the extent to which organizations are bureaucratized. The fourth case illustrates it is possible to go further and create the conditions under which an organization's members can become active agents of continuous learning and adaptation. Moreover, it lends support to the proposition that, given initial understanding of and commitment to the concept of organizational democracy, such a transformation can be brought about through managerial leadership and the active participation of those who most stand to gain or lose as a consequence of any change. The success of the innovations reported in the following paragraphs did not depend on outside assistance from researchers or consultants beyond the stimulation of the first workshop. Indeed, it could be argued that the prospects for successful adaptation were enhanced to the extent that the managers concerned and their subordinates learned to design and implement their own alternatives to bureaucratic organization.

The three managers who had proposed working as a team to effect redesign of the work in their respective sections reported highly significant results within two months. Initially they focused on the internal redesign of work in two of the sections. One section received and processed requests for new telephone installations. This work was performed by clerical personnel whose duties were defined in written job descriptions. Different duties were assigned to different positions, which not only established the basis of the division of work within the section but also served as the primary determinant of salary and status differentiation among the clerical personnel, who were distributed through four position levels with corresponding duties and salaries. Prior to the redesign project, the work was organized so that orders passed from initial receipt through a series of processing stages performed by different individuals according to their official job description. Certain ancillary tasks, such as compiling statistics and attending to correspondence, were also the responsibility of different individuals. The second section was an installation depot. Its primary functions were to install and maintain telecommunications equipment, including that used by subscribers and Telecom's own plant and facilities, such as their cable and telephone exchanges. The depot was organized into two sections comprised of several technical grades of personnel, the grades being based on their level of training, experience, and seniority. One section installed subscribers' telephone services and carried out extension and repair work on the external plant facilities (aerial wires and underground cable). The main function of the other section was to install, extend, and maintain Telecom's internal plant, notably the telephone exchanges, and attend to requests for repairs to corporate subscribers' own telecommunications equipment, such as telex facilities. Each section within the depot had a supervisor who scheduled work and assigned tasks. The depot superintendent reported to a district engineer, who in turn was accountable to one of the three managers participating in the project.

Initially, meetings were held with all personnel of the two sections—the sales office and the installation depot—to explain the concept of designing around semiautonomus work groups and how this concept differed from conventional structures in Telecom. In both cases reactions of the employees were uncertain and skeptical. In the sales office, their concern focused on three issues: (1) who would do the unpopular jobs and whether they would always be performed by the same person, (2) whether efficiency would decline if everyone performed every task instead of different tasks being performed by those with the most knowledge, and (3) whether it was fair that people should carry out tasks not specified in their job descriptions, particularly if the tasks were classified at a higher level than they were being paid. The manager encouraged discussion of these issues but emphasized that he was simply offering them an opportunity to redesign their work so as to get greater satisfaction. Over time, the present standards of work quantity and quality had to be maintained, he said, although he accepted that there might be some initial decline while people learned new tasks. He then suggested that the emloyees discuss the possibilites among themselves and let him know their decision by the end of the following week. Interestingly, the section supervisor and personnel in the more senior clerical positions became enthusiastic about the proposal, and the junior employees were the most reluctant to change. One was afraid that she would make more errors in her work and did not want to "mess up anything more." Conversely, another person was generally regarded as efficient and was worried that she would be given too much work to do. The group met with the manager at the end of the following week, but had been unable to reach agreement. There were new fears that, with employees helping one another, in time there would not be enough work for them all, which would result in boredom and eventually personnel transfers they might not want. The manager did not think this would happen, but he insisted that only they themselves could decide whether to change the organization of their work and, if so, how. They met again the next day and decided to redesign their work on a trial basis. At the manager's suggestion, they moved immediately to a location away from the office to discuss concrete proposals, while he and the supervisor remained behind to keep the office open. It took just one hour for the employees to reach a decision.

They developed a design that provided that each individual would select new telephone orders according to priorities and take them through all the processing stages. Having been concerned that unpopular tasks might be neglected, they set themselves daily quotas and usually did them first each morning. One menial task—compiling statistics—could not be integrated with other work, yet the employees knew from experience that too many errors occurred if parts of the task were shared among members of the group. For any given month, it was important that one person do all the compiling even though it was boring work. Eventually, the employees decided to roster themselves for this task to ensure that it was performed correctly, thus sharing the burden of a mundane duty.

Two weeks after the employees commenced working in the new way, the section supervisor reported that they were more effective, had more constructive attitudes, were regularly exceeding their work quotas, and were taking a more responsible approach to complicated assignments. A meeting between the employees and the manager involved in the project confirmed his impressions. They were pleased that no tasks were being neglected, each person felt more responsible for the section's work as a whole rather than only for particular tasks, they had been able to make the system of allocating priorities to orders operate more effectively, and they had been successful in exchanging information and helping one another to learn unfamiliar tasks. One tangible measure of improved performance was a reduction in the average time taken from the receipt of a new service application to issuing a completed order for the installation work to be carried out. Prior to the redesign, this process had taken between 12 and 16 days whereas it now took from 7 to 11 days, representing a reduction in processing time of almost a third. There appeared to be no external factors, such as an unusually low volume of demand for new services, that could have accounted for this result.

Five weeks later, the employees reported that they were still more interested in their work and preferred the broader responsibilities they now had. However, they were worried that there had been some loss of earlier gains, with instances of the priorities allocation system breaking down and occasions on which some tasks had been neglected. The manager pointed out that these problems had occurred before the redesign and that although the workload had been lower than usual for the past week, they had been working with one person less because of an absence through illness. In fact, they had been working under somewhat greater pressure and the meeting brought to light one problem—namely, that the employees were communicating with one another less than before. Even though errors and delays had increased, the employees were much more concerned to rectify them quickly. The meeting had provided them with an opportunity to work through their anxieties, they were still committed to their new design, and it appeared that they could continue to perform at the higher levels that had been achieved initially if good communications could be maintained.

The introductory meeting with the employees of the installation depot also generated some uncertainty and hesitancy. Again, the groups were asked to discuss possibilities of making desirable changes among themselves. The manager who was directly involved in this part of the project stated that he would be available to answer any questions and provide additional information. A week later, the employees requested a second meeting at which they expressed the shared feeling that, because there were no industrial or personal problems in the depot, they could not see what benefits were likely to be gained by introducing a different form of work organization. If there were advantages, they thought the advantages would accrue to Telecom rather than to themselves. The manager replied that he believed there was scope to develop more satisfying work, that depot supervisors might enjoy their work more if they were less involved in detailed scheduling and could concentrate on more challenging activities, and that he would benefit personally from finding out whether there were better ways of organizing work than the conventional way. He openly stated his hope that any change would result in improved quantity and quality of work, but he emphasized that he would be satisfied if, in the longer term, there was no deterioration in the speed or standard of service to the customer. The group still had difficulty in envisaging alternatives to the existing organization and, according to the manager, may have been apprehensive about having greater freedom in their work. As with the sales office employees, there was a concern that unpopular tasks would not get done. The two supervisors were worried that they would lose some of their control while their final responsibility would be unchanged. The manager assured them that they would have the same authority but probably would not have to use it. Although understanding and commitment were by no means shared equally by all the employees, they decided to attempt a trial redesign.

The redesign consisted simply of personnel in both sections of the depot selecting the jobs they wanted to do instead of having jobs assigned to them by the supervisors. Procedures for allocating priorities to jobs were already well established, and it was accepted that they would be observed. Under this general constraint, the main difference between the previous and the new arrangements was that individuals now decided for themselves which jobs to take and in what order. Much of the work, particularly that concerned with Telecom's own plant, consisted of independent jobs each of which required one person, so the principal form of self-regulation available to the depot employees was to match external demands with individual abilities and preferences for particular kinds of work. If a job required more than one person, the employees could determine which people would work together. In either case, they could plan their schedules to reduce traveling time between jobs. This kind of planning would have been a responsibility of the supervisors under the previous design, but it was more easily accomplished by the employees themselves.

Four weeks after the trial redesign was implemented, an open discussion was held with all of the depot personnel. Several trends became apparent. One of the supervisors commented that less skilled staff were selecting more difficult jobs than had been assigned to them previously. As a result, he now spent more time providing them with additional training and was pleased to do so. He had been concerned that he would not have adequate control over speed and standard of service unless he assigned jobs to individuals he thought were competent to perform them. Instead, he found the training role enjoyable, and because junior personnel were requesting assistance on jobs they had chosen themselves, it was easier for him to instill high standards of workmanship. Previously, he had complained that the employees took insufficient care and pride in their work. Now he had greater influence over work performance in his new role of instructing individuals who wanted to learn than when he was attempting to supervise a geographically dispersed work force through the traditional system of rewards and punishments. Moreover, as employees acquired new skills at a pace appropriate to their interests and the demands of various jobs (which was faster than the rate at which those skills were usually acquired in formal training courses), the total work force was becoming more flexible.

Again, there was a difficulty with unpopular tasks, such as packing used telephones and other equipment to be sent to the maintenance workshops for reconditioning. It was decided that these tasks should still be performed by the apprentices but that they had the right to call on other employees for assistance to get the work done more quickly.

The generally heightened work interest was reflected also in greater concern with the standard of service to customers. For example, it was stated in this second meeting that inadequate information on the work order forms and restrictive depot practices were causing installation delays that inconvenienced subscribers. The manager saw this as evidence of a significant attitudinal change because, traditionally, the servicemen had not regarded customer satisfaction or dissatisfaction as any concern of theirs. However, having redesigned their own work, they had a personal stake in the outcomes. Customer reactions provided an important measure of the results being achieved. In general, this had led to greater employee interest in some of the statistical performance indicators, such as the "delay in connection" result for any period. Previously, if an order for the installation or removal of a service had, for whatever reason, been delayed and put aside, the servicemen tended to neglect it. In part, their attitude was understandable because the main causes of delay, such as incorrect or insufficient information supplied on the installation order, often were beyond their control. Nevertheless, they now regarded these delays as reflecting unfavorably on their performance and responded, first, by assigning the delays a high priority and looking for factors over which they did have some control. Second, they became interested in how communications between customers, sales staff, and the installation depot could be improved. Later, in the second action phase, the redesign was extended to encompass this dimension.

The attempts at change by other program participants displayed the same general pattern as the four cases reported in the foregoing paragraphs. Some participants had attempted and achieved little, others had been frustrated in their efforts to achieve more significant change, in some cases progress had been made toward the original objectives but had not yet been fully achieved, and a small number of innovations already had produced important results. The mixed achievements reflected both the various attitudes and motivations of participants at the end of the first workshop and the influence of factors in the organizational situations to which they returned.

THE SECOND WORKSHOP

Using the feedback from the meetings with participants, our staff developed a design for the next workshop. For the participants who had encountered difficulties that seriously impeded or prevented progress with the innovations, there was a need to reassess the original objectives and the strategies that had been employed. Although in some cases factors that constrained the projects were beyond participants' control, questions had arisen about their analyses of existing situations, choices of change objectives, and their willingness and ability to pursue genuine alternatives. In part, then, the workshop would have the purpose of facilitating critical reflection. For participants who had made significant progress, it was seen as a setting in which to consolidate their learning experiences and to plan for further development. The workshop design envisaged that participants would review and share their experiences during the first action phase, question one another about their objectives and efforts at implementation, and help one another to revise their original projects or to develop new aims and plans for achieving them.

There were, of course, dangers in this approach. The participants who were questioned and challenged by their peers were likely to feel threatened, especially when it appeared that some had been more "successful" than others. Our staff decided that this possibility should be raised and discussed with the participants when the proposed objectives and task structure were introduced on the first evening.

In putting forward our proposed design at the beginning of the second workshop, we acknowledged that some participants might experience discomfort, but we argued that without constructive criticism little further learning or progress with innovation was possible. This argument was accepted by the workshop participants, some of whom said that they had been concerned about the workshop being an anticlimax and welcomed the prospect of further challenge and stimulation. At the same time, defensive behavior quickly became apparent. One participant complained that the importance of the projects had not been explained adequately in the first workshop and that this had led him to select a trivial task. He expressed disappointment at having "wasted the opportunity." Another stated that he had been asked to speak for several participants who doubted that senior management support for innovation was as strong as had been claimed. It is interesting to speculate about their reasons for selecting him for this role because he had achieved as much as, or more than, any participant during the first action phase. His comments provoked vigorous discussion that revealed a basic difference between participants who were anxious about senior management attitudes and others who criticized the anxious ones for being too cautious. To our surprise, they were engaging in precisely the kind of exchange that seemed necessary but without the reluctance that had been expected. Earlier than anticipated, the participants were openly communicating critical assumptions, values, and beliefs. When the discussion was exhausted for the time being, our staff suggested that the participants form smaller groups to share informally their personal experiences with the first action phase. The basic differences had not been resolved, but the first evening set the pattern for the whole workshop by sanctioning the open expression of views and the confrontation of conflict.

Discontent, disagreement, and dialogue at this stage were to become persistent features of the program. In many subsequent programs the introduction of the proposed workshop aims and task provoked reactions from the participants that were directed first at us and then toward one another, giving rise to exchanges that at times became quite heated. Behind the reactions lay several fundamental issues that will be discussed briefly. Much of the disagreement seemed to arise from differences between the experiences the participants had with the projects during the first action phase. For some, the projects had provided important new learning that they valued. They could, therefore, readily accept that the projects should continue to be the primary focus of workshop activity. They had gained new information, and had acquired deeper and broader appreciations of Telecom's structure and workings by reaching across departmental boundaries into areas about which they understood relatively little. They had gained new skills through implementing change and, where significant progress had been made, enjoyed an increasing confidence in their managerial capabilities. They returned to the workshop setting excited and eager to go further with the change projects as the central learning vehicles. Others had quite different experiences. The projects were not meaningful to them either because the innovative challenges they had set themselves were downgraded during the initial planning process or had deteriorated during the first action phase. For many, the prospect of continuing to concentrate on the projects not only held the threat of criticism of past performance but also the danger that, unless they did commit themselves to innovative action, their future behavior would also be attacked. In subsequent programs, the frequently expressed demand to be "taught management" instead of being "sucked into coming up with problems and solving them" became a rallying point for the participants who felt themselves caught in this situation. With equal frequency, other participants would reply with statements such as "we have got to have time to get off our bums to do something—we don't get it in our ordinary jobs." Thus, a dialogue developed that reflected varied attitudes toward both managerial roles in the organization and toward learning. These attitudes were consistent with the bureaucratic and democratic patterns of attitudes toward learning described in Chapter 2.

In the first program, our staff interrupted this process with a formal input on the morning of the first full day. Because several change projects were inadequately conceptualized, it was decided that we would introduce further tools for analyzing sociotechnical systems and the problems that arise from the ways in which they are designed. Specifically, the simplified method of sociotechnical analysis developed by members of the Tavistock Institute was presented as being possibly appropriate to many projects (Hill, 1972). Also, in view of the doubts that had been expressed the previous evening about senior management's commitment to innovation, a framework was put forward within which participants might assess more systematically the managerial climate that prevailed in the organization. The instrument developed by Likert seemed relevant for this purpose and was readily available (Likert, 1967). However, the method of sociotechnical analysis received little response and, although the results of the Likert survey suggested that the overall managerial climate was judged by the group to approximate the relatively positive "system three" or "consultative" model, the results were not perceived as having much relevance to the anxieties expressed the previous evening. At this stage, the participants were very concerned about themselves and one another as individuals, and survey results for the group as a whole did little or nothing to resolve these concerns. In retrospect, we saw that the intervention merely distracted attention from what many participants saw as critical issues arising from their efforts, or lack of efforts, to initiate change and improvement in the organization. At this stage, if there existed any means at all for resolving their concerns and conflicts, the means resided with the participants. Therefore, it was agreed that they should move back into the smaller groups that had formed the previous evening to share and discuss their experiences in greater depth.

From this point the small groups and mirror groups became the center of workshop activity. At appropriate stages, plenary sessions were held to reinforce workshop aims and to check on overall progress. Given the variances among projects in terms of learning and progress with implementation, individuals and groups displayed various patterns of behavior. Some remained concerned to present themselves well to the workshop with little regard for the significance of their projects or the progress being made. Others not only were able to use the "free space" of the workshop to reassess their efforts to date and plan the next steps, but they spent some time reflecting on how the projects related to their wider sense of values about Telecom's future directions. The mirror groups generally seemed to be more effective than in the first workshop. The fundamental differences that had emerged during the first evening were not easily or quickly resolved, and they provided an important interactive dynamic in the mirror groups. When listening to other participants' accounts of their experiences with the projects, mirror group members were more sympathetic and willing to offer constructive suggestions than before. As experiences were exchanged, it became apparent that certain issues and problems were common to many projects. Also, what participants had learned through talking to others in different parts of the organization turned out to be of considerable interest. This strengthening of the cooperative ethic did not mute the basic conflicts but made them seem less threatening. Participants were willing to dissect one anothers' attempts at initiating change in the organization but also became more effective at managing destructive antagonisms while working through the problems associated with the change projects. This represented an important stage in the transfer of control over learning from our staff to the participants themselves.

Although some participants remained hesitant, by the final session most of them had made progress with revising their projects and planning for the next action phase. In one case a rather superficial project had been abandoned in favor of a more worthwhile effort. Whereas the original project had been directed toward improving the image of a particular section, the new project promised to give the section a more valuable role within the organization. Conversely, another participant initially had planned a very ambitious program that became unmanageable because of the large number of variables he could not influence. He had redefined the scope of his strategy in such a way that it was now feasible and still highly significant. In many cases the original projects were to be continued, but the participants had identified issues and variables to which they had given insufficient attention previously. Several other projects were changed to allow more broadly based involvement by those who were affected or potentially able to assist. Some participants who had encountered resistance or lack of cooperation from relevant others now planned to take more initiatives on their own while continuing their efforts to convince those whose collaboration was needed for eventual success. Finally, several participants who had already achieved their original objectives planned to extend their efforts to new work areas under their control and to issues in interdepartmental relations.

These outcomes reflected a general tendency throughout for managers who chose significant and difficult projects to set the pace and direction of the second workshop rather than being constrained or distracted by more hesitant colleagues. Indeed, this process seemed to have a positive effect on some participants who previously had attempted little. Although some individuals continued to display mounting anxiety and concern to protect themselves in both the workshop and the organization, others responded to criticism from their peers by actively seeking to achieve previously established objectives or formulating new ones.

THE SECOND ACTION PHASE

During the second action phase, we left the participants to pursue their change strategies, except in one case where we were asked by two interdependent sections for advice and assistance in conducting a workshop to explore ways of improving communications between them. The other main event during this phase was a meeting with senior management to evaluate progress. This meeting reaffirmed support for the course with several members of the group volunteering accounts of ways it had stimulated managerial initiative to a greater extent than was expected. On the other hand, some managers were disappointed that so little formal material on management concepts and techniques was provided, certain projects had encountered obstacles because immediate superiors lacked understanding of the course objectives, and concern was expressed that union officials who might oppose certain changes were not involved. After discussion, it was agreed that training in management techniques was more appropriately provided by other courses and seminars and that the primary value of this program lay in the stimulation of learning and innovation. The senior group also concluded that it could do more to encourage support for the projects among the participants' immediate superiors. The question of union involvement was not pursued at this stage because the program's implications for industrial relations were not yet clear. In any case, some participants in the first program held official posts in their professional and administrative unions, and this was expected to be true of subsequent programs. Therefore, the group decided that union issues should be dealt with as they arose in particular instances. In general, the meeting generated further interest in the prospects for managerial learning and strengthened support for the program as an agent of organizational change and development.

THE FINAL WORKSHOP

It remained, in the final workshop, to review what had been achieved for the organization and the participants and to assess the prospects for ongoing development. Evaluation of concrete outcomes from several projects was still premature. In some cases the results could not be measured quantitatively. In others new initiatives had taken considerable time to implement, and their effects could not yet be determined. Little progress had been made with six projects. When further action had been taken, the participants reported no adverse trends in organizational performance or employee attitudes. More positively, four projects that focused on developing democratic work arrangements had accumulated sufficient evidence for the organization to be confident about the outcomes. The managers who initiated change in the customer sales office and the installation depot reported that the early gains in job interest, cooperation, and performance had been maintained. During the second action phase, they had extended the change to a second customer sales office directly interdependent with the installation depot, and achieved similar results. When staff in this office had redesigned their own work structures, the managers arranged a residential workshop in which sales and installation personnel examined their task interrelationships and developed proposals to improve communication and cooperation. In the first sales office, a new supervisor had been appointed. Being unfamiliar with the new work design, he had attempted to reestablish conventional arrangements, but his efforts were being resisted vigorously by the staff. In three other sections where democratic work structures had been developed, the managers involved reported gains of a similar kind, although not to the same extent.

Beyond specific innovations, the course was intended to stimulate the capability for *continuing* learning and active adaptation in Telecom. In part, this would be achieved through subsequent programs and the innovative efforts of new participants, but the final workshop should provide a bridge between the learning experiences acquired during the program and the ways in which participants approached their organizational roles in the future. The question remained as to whether they regarded the final workshop as marking the end of their own engagement with active adaptive learning and innovation or whether they would seek to learn and adapt continuously.

The issue was addressed by asking the participants to reflect on their experiences with the workshops and change projects to see whether their perspectives on the organization and their roles as managers within it had been affected. They were asked if they could imagine themselves managing differently in the future. Responses were mixed. For reasons similar to those that had led them to question the task of the second workshop, some participants were reluctant to reflect further on project experiences because they had not been meaningful or had been painful. Others thought that they would continue to learn from their attempts at innovation because the innovations had fundamentally changed the situations in which they were now managing and therefore required further learning on their part, or because the original objectives had not yet been achieved. A third group of participants envisaged themselves managing within wider perspectives and with greater knowledge of organizational interrelationships, but they could not give any clear indication of significant change toward actively adaptive values, assumptions, and beliefs. Finally, it was clear that the managers who had already made a lot of progress in transforming their immediate organizational worlds also held the strongest expectations of managing in the future by engaging continually with new learning and the discovery of active adaptive strategies.

CONCLUSIONS

The new management education and development program for Telecom Western Australia was designed to engage the participants in active adaptive learning, through identifying the need for organizational innovation in the context of wider change and attempting to implement planned innovations within the organization. The process of active adaptive learning by the participants entailed the following:

1 Identifying the valued ends to be served by their attempts at organizational innovation in the context of awareness about wider change.
2 Designing specific innovations and planning to implement them.
3 Returning to the organization to initiate the proposed change projects.
4 Learning from the experience and revising or enlarging their aims and strategies.
5 Developing new conceptions of their roles as managers in the organization based on what their own experience had taught them about the directions that were feasible and desirable to pursue.

The workshops were designed to stimulate and support active adaptive learning, planning, and action among the participants. Through involving senior management and the participants' immediate superiors in the program, efforts were also made to establish supportive conditions within the organization itself.

In the first program, progress was made toward the objective of achieving active adaptive innovation within the organization through the learning of its mana gers. A third of the attempts at innovation demonstrably promoted both an improved quality of working life for the employees and a more effective organizational performance. The participants associated with these innovations also appeared to gain the most personal value from the program in terms of learning and potential for future development as managers. Participants who attempted less or who had been unable to achieve their objectives completely comprised another third. They had not achieved as much but seemed to be more aware of both the need for and possibility of constructive innovation in the organization. For the rest, the program appeared to have accomplished little. On balance, however, the first program had made considerable progress toward achieving its aims. Through their own learning experience in both the social island conditions of the workshop and in the organization, a significant number of the participants had demonstrated the feasibility and desirability of participative democratic alternatives to bureaucracy. A greater number were beginning to alter their assumptions and beliefs about their roles within the organization. Although recognizing that the Telecom organization possessed many inhibiting characteristics, in the final workshop they agreed that there was a choice of future directions within constraints and that it was possible for them to achieve more than they had thought prior to their involvement in the program. This was particularly evident when, in the final workshop, they spontaneously reflected on the broad values that had been expressed in the first workshop. Their experience since then suggested to them that it was difficult but not impossible for lower middle managers to influence the social objectives of Telecom Western Australia and that they were not powerless to pursue strategies directed toward desired ends.

Following the final workshop, senior management met and decided that a second program should commence immediately. By late 1980, eight programs involving 160 managers and staff specialists had been conducted. Chapter 5 provides an overview of these programs, evaluates their effects on the organization, and assesses more generally the requirements and prospects for transforming organizations into vehicles of active adaptation through the learning of their members.

5

Democratizing
Organizations Through
Active Adaptive Learning

The management education and development program in Telecom Western Australia is continuing and is intended to stimulate progress toward the debureaucratization and democratization of the organization through the learning of its members. Because bureaucratic organizations reinforce bureaucratized learning, it has been necessary to create new interactive conditions in which active adaptive learning can occur. The residential workshops are designed to provide these conditions. The participants' own efforts at innovation during the action phases are seen as means whereby positive change within the organization can be achieved. The program design is based on the theory that the development of new shared understanding of the organization in its changing environment and a critical awareness of existing organizational deficiencies will motivate managers to attempt to change the organization. Innovations that increase the organization's active adaptive capability will be those that provide its members with greater scope for directing and controlling their own work in cooperation with one another. As the number of such innovations increases, the structure of the organization is expected to be transformed away from bureaucracy and toward participative democracy. Over time, understanding of and support for active adaptive learning and innovation are expected to become more widespread in the organization. The transformation of Telecom Western Australia into a democratized learning organization, capable of continuous active adaptation in a changing and uncertain environment, is regarded as a progressively evolutionary process.

The first task in this chapter is to evaluate the management education and development program in terms of progress toward the foregoing general objectives. Because of the ongoing and open-ended nature of the change processes, evaluation must be based on knowledge and assessment of the *directions* of change rather than on specific before-and-after measurements such as those used to evaluate controlled experiments. The results of particular interventions made by program participants into their organizational situations are important, but the main concern here is with the question of whether more general trends within the programs and the organization are toward participative democratic design and increased active adaptive potential or toward a strengthening of bureaucratic hierarchical control and a consequent reduction of active adaptive potential in a turbulent environment. The direction of these broader trends is the primary measure of increases or decreases in the organization's active adaptive potential.

The development of the program in relation to the organization is depicted in Figure 14. The main features of this development have been the following:

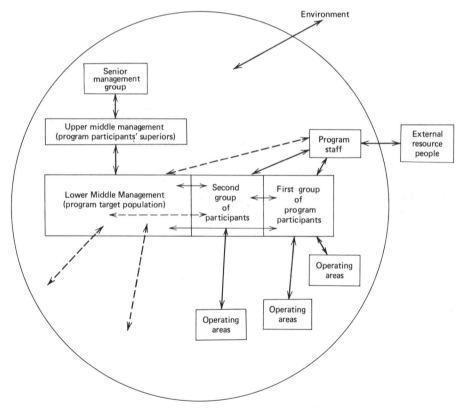

Figure 14. Evolution of a learning organization. Solid arrows show links already established. Dotted arrows indicate potential links.

1   The continuation of the basic program design with the residential workshops being used to stimulate initial new learning among middle managers leading to attempts at innovation within the organization.

2   The increasing number of managers and staff people involved in the learning process and the increasing number of change projects initiated.

3   The continued active involvement of senior management.

4   The involvement of a growing number of nonparticipant organizational members through the change projects arising out of the program.

Continued development of the program has been affected by positive and negative trends in the wider organization. Within the program, trends have emerged over time with respect to the kinds of innovations attempted in the organization and the patterns of learning among participants. These are examined in turn.

ORGANIZATIONAL TRENDS AFFECTING THE PROGRAM

During the five years since the management education and development program commenced, Telecome Western Australia has encountered increasing pressure and challenge in its environment. As a public agency, it has been subject to the Australian government's general policy of more stringent economic management to contain the rate of inflation. This pressure is being felt at all levels of the organization with the result that managers are more constrained in terms of the resources at their disposal. Moreover, Telecom's policies and planning have been affected by union challenges and by political pressures such as the controversies surrounding the introduction of domestic satellites and Telecom's intention to expand into the business market for telecommunications equipment. The organization is faced with demands that it operate with greater economic efficiency in meeting customer and public requirements. It is also being pressed to take employee interests more fully into account but not to expand its operations by entering new markets in competition with private enterprise. Some of these wider forces have been supportive of the program and its objectives. In particular, the dispute with the technicians' union over the automation of telephone exchanges, referred to in Chapter 3, has called into question the organization's traditional technological bias and may have established a precedent for paying more serious attention to human considerations in future planning. Similarly, the challenges to the organization's policies concerning domestic satellites and entry into business markets have emphasized the need to develop a clearer and more widely accepted definition of Telecom's role in the society. These issues were emerging and being recognized when the program commenced in 1976, but more recent developments have brought them into sharper focus. At the same time, increasing external pressure and uncertainty about future directions could work against the program objectives if the organization becomes more conservative and preoccupied with reacting to immediate threats. In consequence, it has never been possible to take for granted the continued survival and development of the program.

Despite economic and political challenges and constraints, senior management personnel have continued to support the program. Initially, the number of managers and staff personnel considered eligible to participate, on the basis of their levels and positions in the organization, was set at 150. Subsequently, it was decided that many more should participate. Prior to the start of a first workshop by each new group of participants, members of the senior management group meet for half a day to search again the organization's environment, develop new shared appreciations of change, and affirm or revise their judgments about future organizational requirements. These search meetings demonstrate senior management's support for the program and acceptance of an active leadership role in relation to it, but they also provide participants in the group with opportunities for interactive reflection on the question of where the organization is and should be going. Such opportunities are not present to nearly the same extent in the more conventional settings in which members of the group interact. The meetings have come to be valued by most members of senior management for this reason, and they now intend to increase the possibilities for searching and planning by holding off-site workshops of their own, each lasting for several days, on an annual or other regular basis. Moreover, they have identified further needs within the organization for learning and development. When Telecom Western Australia, along with the other state organizations, reorganized to establish the Operations Department (see Chapter 3), the new functional management teams worked through the issues raised by the organization in learning settings similar to those provided by the program workshop. At a recent search meeting of the senior management group, it was agreed that the experience with the reorganization should be reviewed, again in settings designed for active adaptive learning and planning. More generally, there has been a trend toward an increasing awareness of the continuing need for learning and active adapation. New events are being planned to enable former participants in the management education and development program to build on experience acquired from earlier attempts at innovation and to engage in further planning to consolidate achievements and meet emerging challenges. Five of the six main departments have introduced the practice of conducting regular workshops for their members to assess organizational changes affecting them and to develop adaptive strategies.

The organization as a whole is far from being debureaucratized, let alone democratized, but the trends discussed in the foregoing paragraph are in this direction. Mounting uncertainty in the environment and increasing pressure on Telecom Western Australia, together with the persistence of bureaucratic and technocratic traditions, are always likely to work against the ongoing attempt to transform the organization. To date, however, not only has support for the program continued, but the program is having a wider influence within the organization. It provides a mechanism for continuing dialogue and learning within and among various organizational levels and departments. The underlying theory of active adaptation through searching and learning has been understood and accepted more widely, and it is being used to address organizational issues beyond the initiatives taken within the framework of the program itself. In this respect, it is important that the stimulus toward extending the possibilities for learning and active adaptation has come from the organization and its members. Our program staff often have been asked to assist, but attempts to meet emerging challenges through participative designs for new inquiry and planning are being initiated within the organization rather than from outside. On balance, therefore, trends in the wider organizational setting so far have been conducive to the survival and development of the program as a design for active adaptive learning and innovation.

TRENDS AND DEVELOPMENTS WITHIN THE PROGRAM

Turning to the program itself, the basic structure of three residential workshops interspersed with two action phases in the organization has been retained. Recognizing the importance of involvement by participants' immediate superiors, a new practice has been adopted of bringing the supervisors together for their own meeting before each new program. In these meetings, the supervisors explore emerging organizational issues from their own perspectives and develop shared definitions of their roles in relation to the participants' attempts at organizational innovation. Supervisors continue to attend the final afternoon of the first workshop to negotiate proposed change projects. The workshops have continued to be staffed jointly by members of the University of Western Australia and Telecom's training and development people. Following the first program, it was evident that certain participants could make valuable contributions in subsequent programs, on the basis of their experience of the learning process as well as their organizational knowledge. As a result, some former participants have been recruited to the staff team. These developments generally have strengthened the program's relationship with the organization.

Development of Collaborative Change Projects

The workshops in each program have been designed and conducted along the general lines described in Chapter 4. In the first workshop, participants explore trends in the wider environment, establish desirable future directions, make critical judgments about present organizational structure and functioning, identify possibilities for adaptive innovation, and plan action strategies. The selection of participants on the basis of their functional interdependence within the organization has been a persistent problem. In each program only a few participants have been able to organize themselves around innovative tasks to which they all can contribute directly within the organization. Nevertheless, there has been a pronounced trend toward collaborative rather than individual attempts at innovation. In part, this trend may have arisen from a perception among participants that innovative projects undertaken by groups were likely to be more effective, in terms both of achieving objectives and of learning. Even when it has been impossible for all members of a task group to "own" a given organizational problem or issue, they have perceived opportunities to contribute to innovative tasks they found important and interesting, and to learn through interactions quite different from their usual work relationship in the organization.

The formation of task groups around these more general shared concerns was facilitated when Glenn Watkins from the University of Western Australia joined the staff team. Instead of attempting to predetermine the groupings of participants in the first workshop, he has employed the "market day" mechanism described in Chapter 2 as a means of enabling the participants to form innovative task groups voluntarily around shared priority concerns identified through the search process. As these groups proceed to define their change objectives and develop strategies for achieving them, they often find it necessary to focus on the concrete organizational situations of particular members. In some cases, this limits the extent to which the other members can contribute to implementation during the action phases. Nevertheless, many participants not directly involved in the situations to which their groups' efforts are addressed have made valuable supportive contributions. Equally important, they have developed a broader knowledge and understanding of the organization than they possessed previously. Given the traditional tendency toward departmental parochialism noted in Chapter 3, this kind of learning is important because it stimulates the development of greater understanding and potential for more effective communication and cooperation among departments. Moreover, in each successive program, at least one task group has formed around an issue in which most or all members are directly involved because of their functional interdependence within the organization. Usually such groups are composed of individuals from various departments. They, too, gain broader knowledge and understanding through the experience of working collaboratively on attempts at constructive innovation. Beyond this, the direct functional interdependence among their members enables them to attempt change projects of greater scope and more far-reaching implications for the organization.

Objectives of Change Projects and Implementation Strategies

The eight programs conducted between 1976 and 1980 have given rise to 81 change projects within the organization. Of the 160 participants who have engaged in these projects, approximately 75 percent have worked in collaboration with other participants. Group-based collaborative change projects, like group-based forms of work organization, generally have greater potential for both effective task accomplishment and learning. The trend away from a preponderance of individual change projects toward group projects is therefore regarded as positive, but much depends also on the *kinds* of change sought within the organization. It has been argued that innovations that increase the active adaptive capability of the organization are those that increase the ability of its members to manage their work activities, the interdependence among them, and the change affecting them. Such innovations require that efforts be directed simultaneously to improving both the technical and human dimensions of work organization. It has been argued also that the redesign of organizations is more likely to be successful if those whose work situations are affected take a leading part in planning and implementing organizational innovation. In terms of the objectives participants have attempted to achieve and the approaches they have taken during the action phases, the change projects have continued to vary considerably.

Approximately half of the change projects attempted so far have placed strong emphasis on achieving administrative and technical improvements, with little serious attention being given to the organization as an open sociotechnical system. The focus has been on formal procedures and technology, seeking improvements in such areas as budgeting, reporting, and equipment. In part, this focus reflects the strength and persistence of the organization's traditional conventions as a technocratic bureaucracy. Like the students who reacted negatively to the democratization of their education, as reported in Chapter 2, the participants who engage in these projects apparently have been influenced so strongly by their experience of closed bureaucracy that they have great difficulty conceiving of the organization in any other way. They may also be reacting against the growing pressures on the organization and themselves. Confronted with mounting change, constraints, and uncertainty, their primary concern is to pursue reactive tactics and strategies by attempting to bring about improvements within the existing organizational structure and the norms governing performance (cf. Ackoff, 1974; Argyris & Schon, 1978; Schon, 1971). As change projects of this kind emerge in the first workshop of each program, they are challenged by staff and by other participants who have already become aware of greater possibilities for active adaptive innovation within the organization. Some projects have been redefined significantly as a result, but the persistence of strong conservative attitudes among a proportion of participants is a restraining factor that inhibits both learning and active adaptive innovation.

Conversely, each program has given rise to change projects that, in different ways and varying degrees, lead to significant innovation within the organization and to new learning among those who participate in them. Many have been similar to the third case reported in Chapter 4, pages (126-127). Established policies and patterns of work organization have been questioned, and at least some aspects of organizational life have been altered in the direction of debureaucratization and democratization. The participants have sought to improve communication, cooperation, and understanding among various departments, they have introduced some positive innovations in the design of work organization within sections, and they have placed greater emphasis on employee development and satisfaction.

In each program at least one project has usually gone further in transforming the organization of work from bureaucracy to participative democracy. The fourth case reported in Chapter 4 (pages 127-132) is one example of innovation leading to the fundamental redesign of work organization on the shop or office floor. In a subsequent program, four managers initiated a change project aimed at transforming the basic relationship between technical training and technical work in the field. The technical training section was confronted with decreasing demand for its courses because of centralized automation of the organization's telecommunications facilities and consequent reductions in the skills required to repair and maintain them. At the same time, the technical staff in the field were experiencing increasing difficulties in servicing corporate customers' equipment. Much of this equipment was supplied by other companies, but Telecom was expected to provide the repair service. A growing problem was that, because of rapid technological change, the technical staff were unfamiliar with the new equipment. The project group developed an arrangement whereby the technical training staff would become mobile in the field. Increasingly, their function would be to stay abreast of changes in customers' equipment and provide instruction to the technical staff by working with them on the equipment itself. A bureaucratic response to this situation would have been to refuse to service equipment supplied by other companies, with consequent losses in revenue and deterioration in customer relations, and to accept the downgrading of the technical training function. The strategy developed by the group was in the opposite direction of increasing Telecom's ability to satisfy its customers' requirements and to provide the technical training section with an important and challenging new role. This innovation was implemented, and recently Telecom Western Australia went still further by enabling the field units to determine their learning and training requirements and obtain the resources necessary to meet them. As each successive program is conducted, usually at least one group of participants conceives and implements a genuinely active adaptive strategy of this kind.

The programs conducted so far have given rise to three broad kinds of change projects within the organization as follows:

1 Projects that focus on narrow administrative and technical improvements, accepting the traditional bureaucratic organization as given.

2 Projects that have involved some questioning and changing of established work organization.

3 Projects that have gone much further toward transforming bureaucratized work arrangements into participative democratic designs to make active adaptive self-management a real possibility.

Many of the change projects aimed at administrative and technical improvements within the established organizational framework have achieved their intended goals. Perhaps as a result of the questioning of bureaucratic organizations that typically develops within the programs, these projects have made progress toward their goals without leading to the strengthening and elaborating of bureaucratic hierarchical controls. They have been concerned with improving information and communications with respect to established and imminent organizational systems and procedures rather than with increasing the degree of external control imposed upon employees. Although such projects do not contribute significantly to the development of more adaptive organizational designs and strategies, they have not hindered progress toward that objective and some appear to have achieved limited improvements. More positively, the growing number of change projects concerned with modifying existing strategies and structures, and especially those concerned with fundamental organizational redesign, are contributing to the progressive transformation of the organization in active adaptive directions.

The second important question about the change projects concerns the manner in which participants attempt to implement them. The great majority of projects undertaken to date have required the cooperation of others within the organization. Even where quite limited administrative and technical improvements have been sought, successful implementation has depended on the involvement of various individuals and groups who are often located in various departments within the organization. In most such cases, the participants have recognized that the pursuit of their change objectives is subject to factors they do not control. They have at least attempted to consult with the other organizational members who are affected by or who are able to affect implementation of their proposals for change. Beyond communicating and discussing their change proposals, most participants also have attempted to involve relevant others actively in developing agreed-on objectives and in taking the necessary steps to achieve them. Moreover, in most programs, some participants have extended the opportunities for learning and planning that they have experienced by conducting workshops with their subordinates and with members of other sections or departments. It has been noted already that this is happening more widely in the organization as managers become aware of the potential of such workshops for communicating with employees and involving them in decisions that directly affect them. The trend toward increasingly widespread direct participation, then, has been a feature of the change projects arising from the programs, and these have stimulated still further attempts to involve employees in planning and decision making throughout the organization.

Learning Experiences and Attitudes

Finally, the programs should be assessed from the standpoint of the learning experiences and attitudes of the program participants themselves. The trends discussed in the previous paragraph constitute evidence that the kind of learning necessary for active adaptation is occurring among a significant proportion of the participants. In the light of new or heightened shared awareness of how external trends are affecting the organization's future prospects, a growing number of the participants are taking initiatives to increase its active adaptive potential through internal redesign in the organizational areas they are able to influence. New understanding of the organization in its changing environment and willingness to attempt active adaptive innovation arise from the participants' learning in the residential workshops and in the action phases. These learning experiences, and the development among participants of positive attitudes toward continuous new learning and active adaptation, are as important as the innovations the participants introduce into the organization during their involvement in the programs. Therefore, evaluation of the programs should be concerned not only with the organizational impact of the change projects they stimulate but also with the participants' learning and their attitudes toward engaging in continuous new inquiry and active adaptation in the future.

The account of experience with the first program in the previous chapter demonstrates that participants display quite different responses to their learning situations in the workshops and in the organization. Similar differences have been evident in subsequent programs. Generally, the different attitudes toward engaging in new learning and organizational innovation correspond to the bureaucratized and democratized patterns described in Chapter 1, and they are apparent in the learning behavior of students as reported in Chapter 2. Some participants are unable or unwilling to question the established bureaucratic organization. Others cautiously begin to explore the possibilities for modifying existing organizational arrangements. Still others are prepared to challenge the present structure and functioning of the organization and are able to conceive and create genuine alternatives. Participants who question the existing organization because of their awareness of wider changes affecting future prospects, and who attempt significant transformation, are likely to gain the most from the programs in terms of their learning as managers and staff personnel. Those who attempt less innovative tasks also appear to learn less, and the participants who remain firmly in the bureaucratic mode seem to learn little.

Insofar as participants do learn from their experience in the programs, what is it that they learn that could be of value to themselves and the organization in the future? The programs are based on the following propositions:

1 Participants gain new and increased understanding by exploring wider changes affecting the organization.

2   Participants discover that they can act on the organization, in their awareness of these changes, to increase its active adaptive potential.

3   Once having engaged in new inquiry and innovative action, it will be possible for the participants to do so in the future as changing circumstances require.

The observed trends within the programs support these propositions in a significant number of cases. The independent study of two programs conducted by Strahan in 1977 and 1978 provides a further check. Apart from observing the workshop processes (see Chapter 4), he surveyed participants' attitudes toward the programs and examined the survey results using the same method of linkage analysis as was applied to the student response patterns reported in Chapter 2. Participants were surveyed twice during the 1977 program and three times during the 1978 program. As was to be expected, the clusterings of attitudes and patterns of relationships among them varied, but several consistent themes emerged. Rather then presenting a detailed analysis of all the survey findings, it is sufficient here to examine briefly the final surveys of each program. These findings represent the participants' own evaluations of their learning against the background of their experiences with all three residential workshops and the two action phases.

The patterns of the participants' attitudes toward the two programs, as obtained from analysis of the final survey results, are shown in Figure 15. At the end of the 1977 program, the majority of participants reached the following general conclusions:

1   They had been able to pursue valued purposes that were important to them and in doing so had learned more about (and had worked cooperatively with) others both in the program and the organization.

2   Existing organizational realities were perceived by half the participants as constraining their attempts at change, but many others did not feel so constrained, most had engaged in projects meaningful to themselves and others, and they perceived the organization as one in which members cooperated in one another's development.

3   In the workshop and in the organization participants had developed task-oriented relationships of mutual support and respect based on the contribution by individuals of their knowledge and experience to the achievement of shared objectives.

4   Through the program and their efforts in the organization, they had acquired greater understanding of relations both between the organization and the society and within the organization.

5   In developing and implementing their change projects, the participants and others had been concerned that the organization move in directions that would enhance the future of the society.

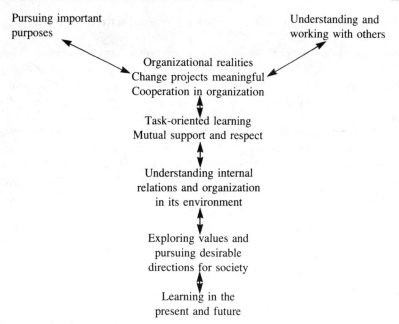

Figure 15. Participants' attitudes toward their learning through the program.

6 The participants felt that their learning in the program would be important to them in the future, that the program was contributing to the development of better future managers, and that their experience of acting on the organization would help them to manage more effectively in the future.

The response patterns for the 1978 program present a similar picture.

The proportions of participants who expressed these judgments about their learning varied, but they were consistently in the majority. Over the seven months' duration of each program, the level of positive attitudes toward active adaptive learning and innovation declined in some respects as was to be expected. As participants engaged in the task of attempting to change the organization, some were bound to experience frustration and disappointment. Also, as was noted in Chapter 4, the participants who undertook projects within the established bureaucratic framework were likely to lose enthusiasm for their chosen tasks fairly quickly, because these projects had a very limited potential for the organization and their own learning. Other participants remained committed to what they were trying to achieve and positive about their learning, but they found it necessary to revise their initial high expectations in view of the organizational realities they encountered. Given that many participants had to contend with organizational constraints, self-imposed limitations, or both, it was all the more significant that positive attitudes toward learning and active adaptive innovation still prevailed at the completion of the programs.

Summary of Program Developments in Telecom Western Australia

In sum, trends and developments in the wider organizational setting and within the programs so far have been largely in the intended direction of transforming Telecom Western Australia into a democratized learning organization capable of continuous active adaptation. The organization has remained supportive of the programs despite increasing pressures. In some important respects, support has grown. Moreover, the programs have influenced the wider organizational context through the continuing involvement of senior management, greater involvment by participants' immediate superiors, the increasing number of change projects, and the stimulation of even more widespread active participation by Telecom employees in managing the conditions affecting their work. Within the programs, the trend toward collaborative change projects has increased the prospects for their successful implementation and their value as vehicles for new learning among participants. The main inhibiting factor has been the tendency for projects to be conceived in terms of established bureaucratic frameworks. However, each program has given rise to significant and successful attempts at active adaptive innovation and there has been a trend toward involving nonprogram participants through consultation and, often, active collaboration. Participants who have questioned existing bureaucratic organizational designs and created genuine alternatives also have gained the most in terms of their potential for continuous new learning and active adaptation, but Strahan's survey findings indicate that there have been positive learning outcomes for other participants as well. From the outset, the programs were designed to stimulate and guide the progressive redesign of the organization through the learning of its members. Although achievements during the first five years have been mixed and there is still a long way to go, considerable progress has been made toward this objective. Equally, if not more important, the new initiatives being planned signify a willingness to continue with and develop strategies for increasing the organization's ability to learn, adapt, and pursue desirable future directions. Management in Telecom Western Australia is recognizing emergent situations that call for new inquiry and novel responses. There has been a growing trend toward involving the organization's members in the search mode which, rather than being regarded as a form of inquiry and learning appropriate only to the programs, is becoming widely accepted as a way of developing participative and collaborative approaches to meeting new challenges.

The question remains as to how far it is posible to generalize from the experience of this one organization in one particular society to other organizations confronted with different problems of active adaptation in other societies. The need to transform societies' organizations has been recognized increasingly over the past two decades. There have been many successful and unsuccessful attempts at redesigning organizations. Has the approach taken in Telecom succeeded to date because it is particularly well suited to this organization and has been favored by special circumstances, or does it have more general relevance and application? What is distinctive about the design strategy for active adaptive organizational learning in Telecom, and why should it be expected to offer better prospects for continuing active adaptation in turbulent environments when compared with other approaches? Ultimately, these questions must be answered through readers' own experiences in attempting to transform organizations into democratized vehicles for learning and active adaptation. However, a partial answer can be offered: first, by drawing on experience with the same design strategy in another organization in a different society, and second, by examining the wider implications of the basic design strategy for transforming organizations.

EXTENDING THE EXPERIENCE

Designing for Active Adaptive Learning and Innovation in an American Corporation

One way of assessing the wider relevance and applicability of the design strategy for organizational learning is to examine its effectiveness for meeting emergent challenges in other organizations confronted with quite different external and internal operating conditions and in different societal contexts. In 1978 an opportunity to make such an assessment arose when an American company requested assistance in dealing with increasing difficulties in its field marketing operations. The circumstances differed from those encountered in Telecom in several important respects. First, the corporation was a private rather than a public enterprise. Second, it was confronted with a situation that could become critical very quickly and required an immediate response. Although major change, uncertainty, and challenge have emerged in Telecom's environment, the management education and development programs have not been forced to address such immediate crises. Third, the American corporation operated in a highly competitive and marketing-oriented industry, whereas Telecom enjoyed a virtual monopolistic situation in many aspects of its business. Fourth, there were important differences in the nature of tasks and task relationships. The focus of the American intervention was on field marketing, characterized by a large number of employees working individually to achieve their sales objectives in the markets for which they were responsible. They were geographically and functionally dispersed with the emphasis being on individual achievement. Telecom was primarily concerned with providing, maintaining, and improving telecommunications services with the dominant emphasis on technology and the conventions of government administration. Some Telecom employees in the field were geographically and functionally dispersed, such as technicians working alone on installation or maintenance work, but the majority of functions were more clearly related when compared with those of field marketing people in the American corporation. Fifth, it appeared that there were cultural differences between the United States and Australia. The differences were difficult to define, but in particular the competitive pursuit of individual self-interest seemed to be more pronounced in American work life than in Australia. Attempting to work with the same basic design strategy for organizational learning and active adaptation under these different conditions would provide one reasonable test of the strategy's potentially wider relevance and applicability to organizations faced with uncertainty about their future.

The corporation manufactures and markets perishable consumer products in North America. For many years it held an unchallenged leadership position in many areas of the national market. Recently, however, it has had to contend with increasing competition and associated proliferation of products and product brands, as well as with wider changes arising from consumer legislation, the energy crisis, environmental issues, and inflation. The company responded to these changes through diversification of its own products and brands and by attempting to improve its information, planning, and control systems. All areas of the company were affected by the changes, but the effects on the field marketing people were particularly adverse.

Effects of Change on Marketing People

Marketing functions in the field were organized in a typical manner. At the base of the marketing organizational structure, field representatives worked mainly through wholesalers to sell the company's products. Each field representative was individually responsible for a geographical area. The areas covered by the field representatives were organized into divisions, which in turn were combined into regions. Field representatives reported to divisional managers, who reported to regional managers, who reported to the vice-president in charge of marketing. Although the field marketing representatives worked in teams for certain purposes, such as special promotions, each representative was individually responsible for a geographical area, and the contribution of his area to the company's total marketing performance was independent from any other areas. Thus, the field marketing people were dispersed and isolated from one another in terms of their functions and geographical locations.

The changes in the company's environment and its responses to those changes affected the field marketing representatives in two main ways. First, the nature of their functions changed, with more time being spent on providing information to corporate headquarters and less on making contacts in their markets. Second, the volume and pressure of work increased because, for example, the diversification of brands and management's increased need for information led to more out of the ordinary requests and unexpected assignments. The importance of the roles of the field marketing people increased as a result of these changes, but the impact of the changes on them and their reactions to these changes were largely negative. They became frustrated with the increased demand for information, which they perceived as conflicting with their function of promoting the sale of the company's products in their markets. The greater workload and the increased frequency of unexpected requests and assignments placed them in a situation where they could not control the allocation of time and effort to their work. They felt that their work had become more demanding and less satisfying, while the support they received from the company was declining, and that their own prospects for future advancement in the company were becoming more uncertain. In consequence, the belief became widespread among field marketing people that company management did not understand their problems and that they were becoming expendable in the competitive struggle.

Marketing management became aware of declining morale in the field and commissioned a university-based study that identified the foregoing problems. These problems were shared by the majority of the field marketing people, and the loss of ability to regulate their working lives was having adverse effects on their domestic lives as well. Morale was low among a significant number of them, and the rate of turnover was increasing. However, although marketing management wished to take action to improve the work situations of the field marketing people, there were no straightforward solutions for several reasons. First, the sources of the problems lay in the company's rapidly changing and unpredictable environment as much as in management's policies and decisions, and the pressures on field marketing people were likely to continue to grow. Second, the problems of the field marketing people were interrelated, and attempting to solve them separately would not improve the situation as a whole. Third, if management attempted to solve problems *for* the field people this might, in fact, lead to further difficulties. Management's judgments might not match the realities of the field situation as the field people perceived them, and their decisions and actions were likely to have unanticipated consequences for the field people. If this happened, the perception that marketing management did not understand the problems in the field might be reinforced. In any case, a one-shot approach to solving problems was not appropriate in a continuously changing environment. Therefore, it was agreed that the field people should be involved in examining their own problems and in developing strategies for resolving them and making the field situation more manageable on a continuing basis.

Developing the Design for Learning and Active Adaptation

Although there was a clear need for a participative design strategy, the organizational and geographical dispersion of field marketing people precluded the identification of functional interdependence as the initial basis for participation. The field people performed similar functions and were affected by the increasing change and uncertainty in similar ways, but they were not directly interdependent with one another. Group-based alternatives to highly individualized work roles were not practicable. This had been a problem with the selection of participants in the Telecom programs, but for different reasons. The Telecom participants were middle managers and staff specialists whose roles had been linked formally only through a traditional bureaucratic chain of command. Selecting participants was a matter of combining, in each program, individuals who could affect each other's performance and who could use their knowledge of such interdependence as a basis for planned collaborative innovation within the organization. In each program this was achieved to the extent that at least one change project had a genuine collaborative basis. The other participants lacked direct interdependence with one another, but back in the organization they were often able to develop innovative designs based on the functional interdependences of their subordinates and on the linkages among functions performed by various work sections or departments. In the American company's field marketing operations no such interdependences existed, and therefore a different approach was required. Although the field marketing people were weakly linked through their organizational roles, they had common interests and were being affected by change in similar ways. The *core management group* concept, as discussed in Chapter 1, could be adapted to this situation as an alternative to participative design based on work groups. This concept was developed to involve employees in managerial decision making rather than decisions about their own work, with members of the group being selected randomly to serve for a specified time, after which they were replaced by other employees. The concept was applied in the field marketing situation by selecting two field representatives from each of the five marketing regions to meet with the university research team in a workshop setting, and subsequently with marketing management in the company's headquarters. The first workshop marked the beginning of a strategy of participative, interactive learning and planning through which field representatives and management could work collaboratively on the challenge of responding positively to the wider changes affecting them.

The Process of Learning and Active Adaptation

The workshop was conducted over three days in late 1978. The proposed task was to examine the effects of external change on the company and on field marketing roles, establish desirable future directions, identify major issues in pursuing those directions, and develop proposals for meeting requirements of the organization and the field marketing people more effectively in the future. Initially, this suggested aproach met with negative reactions from the field representatives. They were very preoccupied with their immediate problems and worried that time spent on exploring wider change would detract from finding solutions to these problems. They were uncomfortable about starting with the search for future trends in the company's environment. For the first hour, discussion was dominated by the voicing of numerous complaints about the situation that had arisen in the field. Compared with the Telecom workshops, the early sessions were characterized by a persistent tension between developing shared awareness of wider change and the tendency to focus prematurely and haphazardly on specific sources of frustration and dissatisfaction. Throughout most of the first day, the workshop was constantly in danger of degenerating into a reactive mode, with the emphasis on redressing past and present grievances and giving little thought to meeting future change. The pressures the field representatives were attempting to cope with in their work situations and their resultant anxieties appeared to be the main factors preventing them from developing a shared understanding of wider change as a basis for active adaptive planning. At several stages during the first day, they would grasp the logic and relevance of the proposed strategy for inquiring into the future of the organization and themselves, but then they would revert to expressing negative attitudes and ''letting off steam.'' For much of this period, the efforts of the workshop staff were concerned primarily with managing this tension. So great were the frustration, anxiety, and anger of some field representatives that its expression had to be allowed, while periodically attempting to redirect the workshop's energies toward more constructive ends. Gradually, and by a rather tortuous route, the participants developed a shared understanding of how wider trends were affecting the organization and themselves. Several main themes emerged around which the participants could begin to explore alternatives to existing organizational arrangements and develop positive proposals for change.

The following broad themes emerged:

1 The need to create organizational conditions under which field marketing representatives could plan and control their work activities and respond more effectively to the changing demands made of them.
2 The need to improve communication and coordination between field marketing and the rest of the company.
3 The need to reassess the career futures of field marketing people in the light of changes affecting their roles, including career planning, performance evaluation, and training.

These themes were clearly relevant to the major problems identified in the initial study. Late on the first day, the participants divided into three groups. Each group examined a particular theme in greater depth and produced draft proposals for constructive innovation. The groups worked through to the middle of the second day, when they came together to share and review the results of their efforts. They then did further work on their proposals to incorporate suggestions made during the review session. On the third day, the groups presented their revised proposals to one another and wrote them in final form for marketing management.

The groups' reports were conveyed to marketing management in an account of workshop proceedings prepared by the university team in consultation with the participants. The reports consisted of 40 proposals. Many were very specific and were aimed at alleviating the pressures that had already built up in the field. For example, pocket dictating machines were requested to reduce the time spent on correspondence. Other reports pointed to the need for fundamental organizational changes that had been created by the company's responses to trends in its environment. The company had responded to increasing competition by diversifying its products. Management had attempted to deal with increasing complexity and uncertainty in ways that required much greater and more frequent information. The introduction of brand marketing teams to develop and promote new products and the proliferation of information functions had led to much more complex and rapidly changing relationships within the organization. Several of the workshop proposals were directed toward improving communications and coordination among the growing numbers of diverse groups—for example, by developing more integrated approaches to planning product introduction and promotion. The general intention was to enable groups to regulate their relationships with one another and to work together more effectively.

Six weeks later, a meeting was held with marketing management to discuss the workshop proposals and their implementation. The meeting was attended by the vice-president of marketing and two senior managers who were responsible for field marketing. The workshop participants were all present to receive direct feedback and to assist with clarification or explanation of particular proposals. The research team leader presented the proposals in each of the three broad areas described earlier. Marketing management agreed with almost all the proposals and responded in the following ways:

1 Informing the field people that initiatives had already been taken to implement some of their proposals.
2 Agreeing to act immediately on certain other proposals.
3 Agreeing with certain proposals and undertaking to try to have them implemented, but explaining that there would be difficulties that would take time to overcome if, in fact, they could be.
4 Explaining why particular proposals were not feasible at that time.

Management also asked the research team to investigate and make recommendations in two areas that required further study—namely, existing reporting procedures and information–decision flows between field marketing and several other departments. Finally, it was agreed that the involvement of field marketing people in this way should continue, initially, by having the same group meet within six months to review progress on implementation of the proposals and to identify further needed improvements and means of achieving them.

Continuing Developments

Six months later the same group of field marketing representatives met with the research team and then with marketing management to review progress with implementation of the original proposals and to develop a strategy for the continuing involvement of field marketing personnel in making decisions and responding to the changes affecting them. As was to be expected, progress with implementation of the agreed-on proposals had been uneven. Several of the initial proposals were directed toward interrelated issues, and implementation of some could not proceed without the others. For example, a consulting firm had been hired to develop a new incentive program, but another proposal that the definition of field representatives' roles be revised to take account of change had not yet been fully implemented. Hence, performance criteria could not be developed as a basis for the incentive scheme. Progress had been made with other proposals, but problems were being encountered. For example, management had advised the field representatives that computerization was expected to eliminate a certain amount of their paperwork, but although progress was being made in this direction, unexpected problems had arisen that would take some time to resolve. In other cases, it was necessary to revise the original proposals. For example, at the field people's request, certain historical information about their markets was being generated in corporate headquarters to reduce pressure on the field people. Now that they were not providing this information for management, however, they discovered that they needed it for their own work. Implementation of the proposal had saved them time but at the cost of losing information necessary for performance of their roles. The revised proposal was that corporate headquarters provide the field people as well as management with this information. Finaly, several proposals had been implemented successfully. For example, the introduction of pocket dictating machines was, in many cases, saving the field people up to 20 percent of their time each week at little cost to the company. In general, there was a shared sense of making progress. The field representatives had not expected more than this, and they were pleased with the results to date. Perceiving that marketing management was attempting to respond positively to their work situations as they were defining them, they approached the task of critical review in a highly constructive way.

As agreed, the research team had undertaken two studies to identify possibilities for improving communication–decision flows between field marketing and other departments and to rationalize reporting procedures. The rationalization study recommended that 42 percent of all reports could be eliminated and suggested improvements to the format of 26 percent of all reports. The findings of this study had been checked with the field representatives prior to the meeting, and management had already taken initiatives to implement several of the recommendations. The first study had not been completed because it involved complex analysis in which the needs and views of several departments were involved, although the information gained so far had been important in rationalizing reporting procedures.

The final task of the meeting was to establish a future basis and direction for cooperative communication and planning between the field marketing people and management. This issue was addressed, first, by identifying further problems that required attention, either because they had not been raised during the work that had been done so far or because they had emerged since the process of participation had commenced. Some specific new problems were identified, and the participants had become even more conscious of a need for continuous direct communication with groups in the company that affected field marketing people and were affected by them. Second, the meeting explored ways of broadening the basis of involvement by field marketing people and developing the participative process. The representatives considered that their superiors should have the same opportunities for interactive involvement in the company as they themselves now had. They also thought that the rest of the field marketing representatives should be better informed and more effectively involved.

The present group had been working for almost a year, and the participants were unanimous that it was essential to the successful continuation and development of the participative management process that other field representatives be involved. They decided that half of the existing membership in the group should be replaced to provide for a balance between continuity and turnover and that representatives from certain specialized markets should be included. Each member of the group would serve for two years, and there would be a 50 percent change of membership each year. The group recommended that field representatives' immediate superiors should have the same opportunities for active participation in decision making and that, until such opportunities were created, the superiors should have the right to nominate the field representatives to serve in the present group. Beyond attempting to broaden the basis of field involvement through rotating membership, the present members had found that many field people did not realize that the innnovations introduced so far to improve their work situations and effectiveness were direct results of the group's efforts. They were remote from and uninvolved in the participative management process. In the coming years most, if not all, of them would become directly involved as members of the group, but immediate steps were necessary to ensure that field people were better informed about and able to contribute to the work of the group. In the first instance, they decided that a bulletin should be circulated regularly to field marketing people to inform them about the group's role and activities and to evoke from the field people further ideas about the issues affecting them and possibilities for adaptive response. Furthermore, they decided that the group itself needed to take a more continuously active and responsible role by organizing group members into task forces to work on the new and emerging issues and problems during the periods between the six monthly meetings with management. Not only would the task forces enable the group to take a more continuous active role, but they would make it possible for other field people to be involved more directly in the work of the core group.

The process of involving the field marketing people in managing the changes affecting them has been developing since 1978. Beginning with the first workshop, the initial task was one of "catching up," or attempting to remedy a large number of problems that had arisen but that had been neglected as the company entered conditions of rapid and continuing change and increasing complexity and uncertainty in its environment. Many of the specific achievements during the first year were mundane but important to the field marketing people. Moreover, it was only as the field representatives and management began to resolve these immediate problems that they became aware of the larger possibilites and issues the participative process was raising. The process is still in its infancy, but it has developed from involving field people in addressing immediate problems in their work toward continuous participative design as a basis of the company's strategies for responding to change in its environment. The core group of field representatives has become a central mechanism for communication and collaborative planning between field people and management. The field representatives' immediate superiors now also meet regularly in the same mode. As understanding of the complex interrelationships between field marketing and other departments increases, possibilities for expanding the scope of participative and interactive management to encompass the critical interfaces in these relationships are being explored.

As in the case of Telecom Western Australia, the question of long-term prospects for the eventual transformation of the company remains open. Developments so far have been consistently toward the debureaucratization and democratization of the oganization achieved under quite different conditions from those encountered in Telecom. The basic concept of designing for the involvement of organizational members in active adaptive learning and innovation was the same. The practical form and process had to be developed and managed to take account of the different conditions. The geographical and organizational dispersion of field marketing representatives made it difficult, if not impossible, to redesign their highly individualized work roles to create self-managing teams. The individualistic and competitive traditions of field marketing, perhaps particularly pronounced in the United States, also seemed to operate against the possibility of developing group-based alternatives in their work organization. The core management group provided another mechanism through which the field marketing people could work with one another and with management in finding adaptive responses to the organization's changing environment.

STRATEGIES OF ORGANIZATIONAL TRANSFORMATION

The experiences with designing for organizatonal learning and active adaptation in Telecom Western Australia and the American corporation suggest that the same basic strategy is feasible under different conditions. The essentials of this strategy follow:

1 Societies are in a period of fundamental transition.

2 The environments of organizations are becoming increasingly turbulent.

3 Bureaucratically designed organizations become less and less viable as environmental turbulence increases.

4 There is a basic alternative to bureaucracy in the form of participative-democratic organization.

5 This alternative offers positive prospects for active adaptation to reduce and manage turbulence and to pursue desirable future directions.

6 Rational analysis and practical demonstration of alternatives to bureaucratic organization are not sufficient to ensure the debureaucratization and democratization of organizations.

7 Democratization is more likely to be achieved if through their own learning, organizations' members acquire greater understanding of how trends in the environment are affecting future prospects and discover active adaptive response strategies.

Beyond accumulating experience with the design strategy under diverse organizational circumstances, experience with the wider implications for transforming organizations should be explored.

Designing for active adaptive organizational learning

Confronted with increasing novelty, complexity, and uncertainty in organizational environments, attempts to debureaucratize and democratize organizations should be based, first, on the recognition that active adaptive social designs and strategies must be discovered through collaborative inquiry and learning. Those most affected by change must be involved fully in all phases of the processes leading to organizational redesign. It is not enough for researchers and consultants to learn *for* them. Indeed, in highly unfamiliar situations where prior research, experience, and knowledge are not well developed, as in the American corporation, it is questionable as to whether researchers and consultants alone could discover and implement workable alternatives to existing organizational designs. Second, it is necessary to conceive of organizational redesign not simply in terms of replacing one set of structural arrangements with another set, but as a process of continuous active adaptive learning by which alternative designs are discovered, maintained, elaborated, and modified as conditions and needs change. Strategies of redesign that are most likely to be successfully implemented, maintained, and adapted are those that organizations' members discover themselves through their own learning.

Designing for active adaptive learning in organizations has three important dimensions, as shown in Figure 16. The first is the general logic of active adaptation in turbulent environments. For an organization's members to learn in ways that enable them to identify the requirements for active adaptation, they must inquire into trends in the contextual and task environment, assess how emergent trends are likely to affect future prospects, determine desirable future directions, critically examine existing organizational design and present strategies, and develop shared understanding of how the organization should change to increase its potential for pursuing desirable directions. In each organization, the problems confronting it are likely to be perceived in more limited and specific terms than these. In Telecom Western Australia, the problem initially was seen as one of improving management education, and it had to be redefined as one of how to increase managers' ability to learn and innovate in a changing and uncertain environment. In the American corporation, the concern was to alleviate growing pressures on the field people, and it was necessary to reinterpret the task as one of finding ways to increase their ability to manage their work situations and relationships in continuously changing and uncertain conditions. The definition of objectives and stages needed to achieve them will vary from one particular context to another, but it must be consistent with the general logic of active adaptation. Unless members of the organization inquire in this way, they will lack an adequate rationale for planned innovation. The rationale is provided by understanding of how wider trends are affecting the organization, knowledge of the probable consequences of doing nothing in response to them, and a shared determination to pursue desirable alternative directions.

The second dimension is the creation of opportunities for the organization's members to engage in such inquiry. They are unlikely to do so within the constraints of the existing organization and their previous learning experiences in bureaucracies. These conditions reinforce bureaucratized learning. Active adaptive

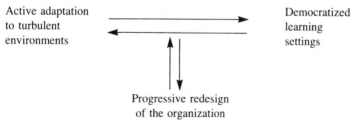

Figure 16. Dimensions of designing for active learning in organizations.

inquiry and planning are more feasible in democratized learning settings. The workshops conducted for Telecom Western Australia and the American corporation are examples of settings in which organizations' members can begin to learn and plan in new ways. The logic of active adaptation, as applied to each orginization's perceived problems, provides the overall task structure. Workshop staff members accept initial responsibility for framing objectives, proposing the main steps to be taken in achieving them, opening up and facilitating discussion at each stage, and suggesting appropriate working modes. They also make judgements about when to make relevant information and knowledge available that workshop participants might otherwise not have access to. These functions are progressively taken over by the participants as they become familiar with the active adaptive logic of the task and confident about their ability to manage their own learning. the workship design, like the educational design discussed in Chapter 2, is intended to provide the conditions under which an organization's members can undertake the cognitive enterprise of planning for its future in a turbulent environment and, through participation in the group life of the workshop, gain direct experience of democratic organization.

The third dimension concerns the effect the strategy of learning and active adaptation has on the organization as a whole. Organizations will not be transformed merely as a result of what happens in residential learning settings. The understanding of the need for active adaptive innovation and commitment to planned change must be transferred to the organization. Unless this happens, not only will the organization remain largely unaffected by what some of its members learn, but continued development of the strategy will be threatened. Insofar as learning in residential settings such as Telecom workshops leads to successful implementation of active adaptive innovations, prospects for continued progress should increase. The experiences with Telecom and the American corporation also demonstrate the importance of establishing and strengthening wider links between the learning settings and the organization. In Telecom, the regular search meetings of senior management and the participants' immediate superiors before each new program, the provision for change projects to be negotiated with superiors, and the involvement of nonparticipants in change projects have been important to the survival and development of the programs themselves. Such has been the effect of the learning design used in the programs that it is now widely employed by the organization for many different purposes. In the American corporation, the regular meetings of field representatives and marketing management as a core group and the more recent innovation of the task forces provide similarly vital links. Through these mechanisms, it is possible to reach out and influence the wider organization in the continuing attempt to transform it. As progress is made in this direction, prospects for continued development of active adaptive potential through organizational learning are increased still further.

Effective participative redesign of organizations entails new learning in accordance with the general logic of active adaptive inquiry, the creation of settings in which it is possible to engage in such inquiry, and the diffusion of active adaptive innovations from these learning settings to the organization. Designing for active adaptive learning requires an approach that is both structured and open-ended. The initial structure is provided by the definition of learning objectives, the steps necessary for their completion, and the social organization of the learning settings. The development of active adaptive learning is a continuous process that depends on establishing mechanisms and networks within the organization through which participation and collaboration in managing change over time can be effected. The conceptualization and articulation of basic alternatives to bureaucratic organization can help to guide the initial learning and the continuing process of organizational transformation. However, the more concrete meaning and relevance of participative democratic alternatives to burreaucracy must be determined and acted on by organizational members themselves. Thus, the strategy seeks to integrate theoretical knowledge of the essential requirements for active adaptation through organizational redesign with the realization of the necessity for people in organizations to identify and act on these requirements through their own learning.

Comparison with other approaches

This strategy seems to go further than other approaches to redesigning organizations. Conventional management education and oganizational research or consulting generally achieve little more than informing organizations' members about alternatives to existing designs and strategies. This knowledge is necessary for organizational redesign, but the presumed expertise of educators, researchers, and consultants is not sufficient to ensure understanding and commitment on the part of those who must implement the proposed changes and live with the consequences. The forces of resistance to innovation discussed in Chapter 1 are more likely to prevail over attempts to implement the recommendations of experts. Techniques for attempting to change behavior in organizations (such as those referred to as "organization development") do not appear to be any more effective. Although organization development interventionists recognize the central importance of learning in organizational change, their focus is usually limited to attitudes and interpersonal relations within the confines of the existing bureaucratic organization. The basic design principle of bureaucracy is not questioned. Seeking to change attitudes and interpersonal relations within a dominant bureaucratic hierarchy will not bring about the democratization of the organization.

The primary objective of the sociotechnical approach to redesigning organization *is* to democratize them. The intention is to transform bureaucratic organizations through designs that enable their members to become self-managing in conditionally autonomous units such as work groups and matrix teams. The redesign strategy has been extended to managerial and institutional functions, providing for both the democratization of managers' work and of the relations among various functional levels of the organization (see Chapter 1). However, although considerable progress has been made toward democratizing organizations through sociotechnical redesign, constraints and obstacles have beset many redesign initiatives. Several writers have reviewed the experience with the implementation and diffusion of sociotechnical redesigns and have drawn similar conclusions concerning the problems encountered. It is difficult to generalize about the many redesigns that have been undertaken, but a central difference between successful and unsuccessful redesigns appears to be whether they are approached as participative and collaborative learning tasks or as social engineering projects in which new designs are imposed on the organization's members.

Walton, for example, has identified several characteristics and problems common among many attempts at sociotechnical innovation (Walton, 1977). It is instructive to compare his findings with the strategy of designing for active adaptive learning in organizations I advocate here. A summary comparison is offered in Table 4. In the strategy described by Walton, innovation is introduced through an experimental pilot project in a single operating unit of the organization. Proposals for redesign of work in the unit are based on sociotechnical analysis of existing operations and work organization, which is usually conducted by researchers or consultants, and are negotiated with management and union officials. The pilot project lasts a specified time period followed by an explicit postexperiment evaluation. If the evaluation is favorable, management and union commitment to further innovation along similar lines throughout the organization may be announced. Knowledge and diffusion of participative-democratic alternatives to bureaucratic organization have undoubtedly been enhanced by the pilot experiment approach, but experience with this approach also highlights several major difficulties.

First, when proposals for redesign are developed by researchers or consultants and approved by management before members of the selected units are asked to try the redesign, the proposals may not be accepted in the workplace. No matter how carefully the proposed changes are explained to members of the units, they often have difficulty in understanding them, they may be suspicious of the reasons for introducing change, and they may not share the commitment and enthusiasm of the originators of the redesign proposals. The redesign is likely to be perceived as foreign and imposed. Second, when change is initiated within one organizational unit, it can lead to tension and conflict with the wider organization. For example, supervisors, middle managers, and other units may regard the increased autonomy and scope for self-management given to the experimental unit as threatening their own functions and prerogatives. Third, even when pilot experiments

TABLE 4.

Comparison of Strategies Based on Sociotechnical
Experiments and Active Adaptive Learning.

Walton	Active Adaptive Learning
	Characteristics
Pilot experiment in a single unit	
Sociotechnical analysis of existing operations by outside researchers leading to proposals for redesign	General commitment to learning and adaptive innovation
Specified time period and explicit postexperimental evaluation	Innovations planned and implemented by the organization's members with some assistance from outside researchers
	Evaluation is continuous and open-ended
	Problems
Resistance or lack of understanding and commitment in the experimental unit	Resistance is not a problem when people invent their own redesigns, but some redesigns may be inadequate
Tension and conflict with wider organization	Tension and conflict are less when others affected by the redesign are involved and when they have opportunities to redesign their own work organization
Constraints on diffusion due to initial failure, lack of credibility, or anxiety	Continuing adaptive innovation is not dependent on the success and credibility of single experiments
Loss of momentum due to perceived decline in top management support	Top management plays a continuing active role

are judged to be successful, diffusion is often constrained by several factors. During the early stages special measures are usually taken to protect experiments from pressures and disruptions that the units involved in the experiments ordinarily would have to deal with. This protection may assist members of the units to become familiar with the new ways of working and to develop the necessary knowledge and skills, but it also tends to create an impression of artificiality and a belief in the wider organization that the new designs would not be practicable without special protection. Attempts to communicate information about the initial experiments in order to encourage further innovation may be met with doubts as to whether the same kinds of changes would be feasible in other areas under different operating conditions. Moreover, the strategy of diffusing innovations on the basis of successful pilot experiments can place those who are expected to follow suit in a difficult position. Successful redesign in one unit does not necessarily reduce the risk of failure in others, but failure of subsequent innovations may be viewed more critically by management than failure in the first experiment might have been. The penalties for failure may even increase whereas the rewards for success, such as improved career prospects, remain the same or even decline. Finally, strategies of organizational redesign based on diffusion from single experiments tend to lose momentum, with the result that the organization reverts to bureaucracy. The course of major innovation in organizations is seldom if ever smooth. As problems, obstacles, and conflicts arise, they sap the energy and commitment of the parties involved. If initial commitment is not sustained long enough for problems and conflicts to be worked through, diffusion from the pilot experiments to the wider organization is unlikely to occur, in which case the early innovations remain isolated and threatened with extinction (Herbst, 1976; Walton, 1977).

The underlying rationale of the strategy is that successful initiation and implementation of pilot experiments in selected work-places will demonstrate to the organization the feasibility and desirability of participative democratic alternatives to bureaucracy. This should produce a ground swell of commitment to democratizing work throughout the organization, but because of the difficulties discussed in the foregoing paragraph, the expected diffusion often does not occur. The strategy of designing for active adaptive learning is different in several important respects. First, the initial commitment is not to a specific experiment proposed by outside researchers but to a structure and process of inquiry that actively involves members of the organization in developing redesign proposals concerning their own work. In Telecom Western Australia, the organization sanctioned the invovement of an increasing number of middle managers in looking for ways to improve organizational performance and employee satisfaction. In the American corporation, management wanted to involve the field marketing representatives in developing more effective strategies for managing the changes affecting them. The broader scope of commitment also means that innovation can occur in many areas of the organization rather than being limited initially to one or a few selected work sites. Second, although outside researchers contribute their knowledge and experience to the development of the learning process and proposals for redesign, they work in a collaborative relationship. Major responsibility for determining desired changes and implementing them rests with the organizational members concerned. Third, evaluation is ongoing and open-ended. Specific measures may be used to assess the outcomes of particular innovations, but evaluation is primarily a matter of judgment by those involved as to whether it is worthwhile continuing. Fourth, the organization's commitment to the diffusion of innovation is based not on the outcome of a single experiment but on its continuing experience with the overall strategy of active adaptive learning and innovation.

These differences affect the nature of the problems encountered in transforming organizations and the prospect of success. First, when employees are involved in developing their own proposals for redesigning their work, they are more likely to commit themselves to implementing the redesign. The greater understanding they have acquired should also enable them to deal with unexpected problems and to maintain and adapt the new work organization with less reliance on outside researchers. The main difficulties that arise concern the employees' ability to invent genuine adaptive alternatives to the existing design. These difficulties must be overcome through learning. In the early stages, outside researchers can contribute to overcoming problems with the development of alternative designs, so long as they do not usurp the employees' key role in the redesign process. Ultimately, new work designs are more likely to survive and succeed over time if the organizational members affected by them have the knowledge and motivation necessary to make them operate effectively.

Second, tension and conflict between pilot experiments and the wider organization arise because the experimental changes in the selected units disturb established relationships and may be perceived as threatening the interests of others outside the units. Resistance should not be fatal when the freedom to experiment with alternative designs is extended throughout the organization rather than being confined, as in pilot experiments, to selected units. New initiatives, such as the change projects in Telecom, may still create problems for other individuals and units affected by the projects, but problems are more likely to be overcome if the basis of involvement in redesign is enlarged to include these others as active participants. The change projects based on functional interdependence within Telecom generally have been more successful because the organizational members immediately affected by the proposed projects collaborate in designing them. Pilot experiments often encounter resistance because others whose cooperation is required do not regard the changes as being in their interest. When they are involved as full participants and have the opporunity to contribute to developing new designs to improve their own situations as well, there is a greater likelihood that tension and conflict will give way to mutual cooperation. Similarly, supervisors and middle managers will have less reason to fear the introduction of new work designs that they, in collaboration with their subordinates, have determined than designs proposed by outside researchers and approved by senior management with little involvement of middle managers and supervisors themselves.

Third, the strategy of transforming organizations through the learning of their members opens up new possibilities for the diffusion of innovative redesign throughout the organization. In the pilot project approach, unless the initial experiment is successful, diffusion probably will not occur. Even if it is successful, the experiment may lack credibility because others in the organization do not have adequate information about the redesign or doubt if it would work as well under different conditions. They may also become anxious about being put under pressure to implement similar redesigns in their own areas.

Conversely, when opportunities for learning and innovation are, at the outset, extended more widely to members of the organization, the success or failure of early redesign attempts is not as critical. Obviously the more initiatives that succeed, the greater the prospect of continued innovation. However, new attempts at redesign can be undertaken that do not depend on the outcomes of previous ones. Likewise, the visibility and credibility of particular redesign attempts is not a major issue because other organizational members do not have to be convinced by these innovations. The question is whether they can convince themselves of the need for change in their own areas and plan and implement their own innovations. Information about the various initiatives being taken can contribute to the process of organizational transformation, but the main stimulus to change in any given area occurs through the learning of those involved. Managers in particular may still feel under pressure to introduce design innovations in their areas of responsibility, and some may react defensively. There is no clear way of overcoming this problem. Organizations cannot be transformed unless their managers are prepared to attempt active adaptive innovation. However, when compared with demands on them of the pilot experiment strategy, managers are not asked to emulate previous successful redesigns but rather to identify and implement changes demonstrably workable under the conditions they face. If some managers are unwilling to do this while others proceed to introduce new work designs and are successful in doing so, those who persist with traditional designs must accept that their career prospects could be adversely affected. More managers are likely to undertake innovations if it is clearly understood that as managers they are expected to find new adaptive designs and will be rewarded for their efforts.

Fourth, the attempt to diffuse innovation throughout an organization by means of demonstration pilot experiments often founders on the loss of top management commitment after the initial enthusiasm and approval. If this decline in support is perceived by other members, they will probably quickly withdraw from serious redesign efforts. A major limitation of the pilot experiment strategy is that top management involvement tends to be passive, in that it is restricted to approving experimental redesigns without playing an active and continuing role in organizational innovation. In such circumstances, it is to be expected that members at lower levels will doubt the extent of top management commitment and that senior managers themselves will tend to give priority to more immediate problems within the established bureaucratic framework. The strategy of designing for active adaptive organizational learning depends on the providing by senior management of positive ongoing leadership in the progressive transformation of the enterprise into a democratized learning organization. This process requires mechanisms through which the organization's leaders interact with one another and with the rest of the organization to give overall direction to innovative efforts, to support redesigns that have genuine active adaptive potential, and to take responsibility for their part in transforming the organization. The successful continuation and diffusion of active adaptive innovation in Telecom Western Australia and the American corporation to date are owing in large part to the active continuing leadership role management has been prepared to play in cooperation with the rest of the organization. Through this direct involvement, senior management not only demonstrates the extent of its commitment to active adaptive learning and innovation by the organization's members, but it is better informed by its own experience to determine its willingness to continue with the strategy in the future.

The strategy of democratizing organizations through the attempted diffusion of innovation from pilot experiments is not the only approach to sociotechnical redesign that has been taken. In Shell UK Limited, for example, the process began at the senior management level with the development of a draft statement of philosophy and objectives for the company in its changing environment. The statement was submitted for debate "down the line" with the intention that, as department heads and successively lower echelons explored the statement's meaning for themselves, they would initiate their own innovations to improve organizational performance and the quality of work life of employees. A parallel process of union–management discussions on productivity and gain sharing was commenced at the same time. The approach did stimulate constructive innovation in several locations (Hill, 1972). In Volvo, the initial broad management commitment to sociotechnical redesign also led to a growing number of innovations throughout the organization. Even so, the danger in the downward transmission of change is that employees at lower levels will perceive the proposals for change as being imposed upon them. Their own direct involvement seems to come rather late in the process of downward transmission, and conflict and resistance have arisen because individual and group interests within the traditional structure have been threatened (Herbst, 1976).

The strategy of transforming organizations through the active adaptive learning of their members does not offer a panacea for overcoming the difficulties associated with other approaches. It does, however, increase the likelihood that the forces of resistance to the democratization of organizations eventually can be overcome. The many sociotechnical redesign experiments conducted since the 1950s have provided essential knowledge and experience of democratic alternatives to bureaucratic organization. The strategy for transforming organizations reported here builds on this knowledge and experience by recognizing that organizations are more likely to be transformed through the conscious and collaborative efforts of their members than through demonstration experiments designed by outside experts. The immediate task is not to find ways to redesign organizations but to design the conditions that promote the effort by organizational members to undertake this challenge themselves through their own learning. Not all the members of an organization will respond, and many who do will produce proposals for redesign that fall short of what is theoretically possible. Others will rise to the challenge. Because they have played the leading part in discovering how the organization can be transformed, there is a greater prospect that it will be.

CONCLUSIONS

This and the preceding two chapters have attempted to explain the basic strategy of designing for active adaptive organizational learning. The experiences with Telecom Western Australia and the American corporation provide concrete examples of the strategy in action under different conditions. So far, experience suggests that organizations can be transformed into democratized vehicles for active adaptation to turbulent environments through progressively evolutionary processes. It also suggests that such processes are difficult and continuous, but this should come as no surprise. Given the pervasiveness of bureaucracy as the dominant organizational model of western industrial societies, it is vital to the prospects of organizations and their societies that they be debureaucratized and democratized. However difficult the task of transforming them may be, it will not be accomplished at all unless their members, through their own learning, develop the understanding and commitment necessary for pursuing democratic alternatives.

Even as the need to transform organizations has become critical, the challenge of managing the future has shifted to a higher level. Organizations are limited by their particular historicogeographic settings, and the crises that now confront societies are far more transcendcent. The emerging systems of interrelated problems are too large and complex to be dealt with at the level of single organizations alone. Accordingly, the strategy of learning and active adaptation must be extended to the larger system levels at which emergent crises are occurring. The prospects for doing this are discussed in Chapter 6.

6

Learning and Active Adaptation in Extended Social Fields

Democratizing single organizations in all sectors of society is necessary but not sufficient for active adaptation to turbulent environments. The major sources of uncertainty about the future no longer lie in the familiar task environments of established organizations. The threats and challenges that confront organizations as they attempt to pursue their own objectives are particular manifestations of more fundamental and universal changes affecting the future of entire societies. Figure 17 shows this basic change in the scale of change and uncertainty. The more immediate task environments of organizations are being subjected to a contextual invasion by change forces that now arise from much farther afield. Through the processes of learning and redesign discussed in the foregoing chapters single organizations can develop greater capabilities for responding to the changes that immediately affect them. Single organizations should become more able to contribute also to dealing with the larger interrelated problems and crises occurring at the level of society as a whole. The democratization of organizations that results in their members becoming self-managing in the pursuit of agreed-on directions provides their leaders with greater freedom to concentrate on external relations. In consequence, the leaders are better placed to play their part in helping to reduce the larger malaises of society—such as economic stagnation, inflation, deterioration in the physical habitat, energy crises, and so on. Nevertheless, even assuming the greatest active adaptive capability and the best intentions, single organizations (including the multinationals) do not possess the ability to contain and control the

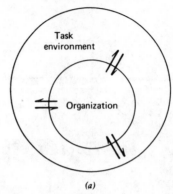

Figure 17a.   Organization–environment relations in the industrial age.

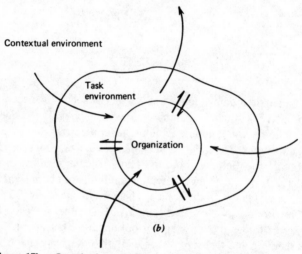

Figure 17b.   Organization–environment relations in turbulent transition.

trends that are exerting the most critical influences on societal directions in the future.

Governments, through their existing policy formation and administrative structures, are not able to regulate and direct these trends, either. Political systems based on elected representation and administrative hierarchies evolved during the industrial era and embody the logic of bureaucratic organization. Executive bodies and representative assemblies are limited in their policy making and planning by the short time lapse between elections. Political parties and pressure groups express established sectional interests and conflicts. Administrative agencies operate through centralized but segmented control hierarchies, they are oriented to specific functions and objectives, and there is little effective coordination among them. Despite their vast resources, bureaucratically organized governmental systems hinder rather than facilitate active adaptation to turbulence at the societal level (see Chapter 1).

New social designs are required at levels intermediate between the single stakeholders and the government to enable societies' members to become actively involved in managing the changes affecting them. Developing such designs entails both the decentralization of national crises so that they can be managed locally and the integration of single stakeholders at higher levels in the systems so that they can work together effectively in the pursuit of mutually desirable directions. Some initiatives have been taken in this direction, and Trist's work (as summarized in Chapter 1) points to certain essential features of adaptive social redesign at the socioecological level. To recapitulate briefly, sets of interdependences among stakeholders are identified as *domains* on the basis of functional or geographic linkages or both. Because the structures and boundaries of domains do not coincide with those of existing organizations and groupings, one or another kind of referent organization is needed to make the domain cohesive by providing a mechanism for interactive and collaborative planning. Referent organizations do not exercise hierarchical domination over the domain's members but facilitate negotiation and cooperation among them on issues of mutual concern. Several innovations in socioecological design have occurred, including the Craigmillar Festival Society and the Jamestown Area Labor–Management Committee discussed in Chapter 1. They are responses in localized settings to more widespread crises, such as economic decline, that have concrete meaning and can be acted on at the local level. The innovating organizations have broadly based local support and are outside of official administrative hierarchies. They seek to cooperate with government agencies, but they attempt to deal with the issues affecting their futures holistically rather than in piecemeal fashion according to fragmented functional responsibilities as defined by government bureaucracies. They establish the possibility, at the local level, of active adaptation through participation and collaboration.

These innovations demonstrate that the same choice of basic social designs—between bureaucracy and participative democracy—is as possible at the socioecological level as at the single organizational level. It is the choice between reducing people's active adaptive potential through continued strengthening of externally imposed controls or increasing that potential through social designs that provide for local collaborative self-management. However, single organizations and domains are qualitatively different kinds of systems, and the implications for developing new social designs are also different. Democratizing single organizations entails changing the existing relationships among their members from those of dominance–dependence to mutual interdependence. In principle, the same change is required at the level of extended social fields, but transforming existing bureaucratic administrative hierarchies is only part of the problem. Effective collaboration among members of a domain depends also on their willingness to effect a "figure–ground reversal" in their perspectives on relationships between themselves and their environments (Emery, 1977; Trist, 1977). Instead of looking at the environment from the standpoint of their own interests, they must be prepared to take the environment as their central concern—that is, the figure—and relegate their own particular groups and organizations to the ground. Only when this reversal occurs is it possible for them to plan collaboratively for the future of the domain itself. In a community such as Jamestown, for example, the difference is between each stakeholder group seeking to improve its future prospects *in* Jamestown or seeking to improve the prospects *of* Jamestown. In a domain such as health care, the figure–ground reversal would be from attempting to maximize one's own advantage in the system to seeking to improve the system's contribution to community well-being.

In turbulent environments it would seem only sensible for the stakeholders in any given domain to make this figure–ground reversal. They are not required to surrender their freedom of action completely, but effective collaboration depends on their recognizing their mutual interests and acting in this context. It seems equally obvious that stakeholders will not reverse their perspectives easily or willingly. Crises at the domain level may leave them with no viable alternative other than developing new collaborative relationships, but the instances in which this is happening are far outweighed by the persistence of competitive self-interest as the dominant preoccupation—even though the consequences are maladaptive. As with the redesign of single organizations, there is a growing body of knowledge and experience concerning the development of participative democratic alternatives to bureaucracy. Again, however, rational analysis and empirical demonstration evidently are not sufficient to stimulate the diffusion of innovative redesigns. For example, with the Jamestown experience under its very nose, the United States Congress had great difficulty in passing the Lundine Bill, which provided for relatively modest federal assistance to encourage similar local initiatives throughout the country. Implementation still remains unlikely. In Scotland economically disadvantaged communities literally adjacent to Craigmillar have been unable or unwilling to recognize the relevance of that innovation to them, and Craigmillar itself has had to struggle constantly against governmental attempts to impose bureaucratic controls on its local initiatives. With such resistance to the idea of democratic redesign at these localized levels, it is small wonder that the more far-reaching visions of societal transformation, such as Emery's concept of "adaptive systems for our future governance," Friedman's proposals for "societal guidance systems," Husen's exploration of "the learning society," and Schon's idea of "public learning" should appear to be still further out of reach (Emery, 1976; Friedman, 1973; Husen, 1974; Schon, 1971).

Resistance to participative democratic redesign in extended social fields occurs for similar reasons to those encountered in single organizations, but they are compounded by the even greater novelty and scale of the challenge. Previous innovations in social redesign are distrusted because they occurred elsewhere. Proposed innovations will be perceived as threatening entrenched interests and disrupting established power and bargaining relationships. The tradition of dependence on regulation through bureaucratic government is so strong that, despite its increasing failure, alternatives are almost unthinkable. The learning habits of the stakeholders in extended social fields are just as bureaucratized as they are in single organizations. To the difficulty of breaking with traditional dominance–dependence relationships, in this case between citizenry and government, is added the further challenge of creating new collaborative relationships among interdependent stakeholders where previously only independence or competition prevailed.

Single stakeholders in extended social fields that have become turbulent cannot, by their independent efforts, control change and uncertainty. To continue with the pursuit of narrow self-interest and reliance on bureaucratic government would leave the direction and outcomes of these change forces very much to chance. Recent experience and emergent trends indicate that if this course is chosen prospects will get worse. The alternative is for stakeholders to find new ways of acting in concert on the wider changes affecting them. To embark on the alternative course entails, first, recognizing that the futures of stakeholders in any given field are "directively correlated" (Somerhoff, 1969; Emery, 1977). Their prospects are affected by wider change in similar ways, and the actions of any stakeholder group can affect the situations of the others. Second, they must be prepared to plan on the basis of the actual and potential directive correlations between them. If they can recognize that their futures are directively correlated, then they should be able also to regard each other as potential coproducers of desirable changes in their shared environments, both now and in the future. They should be able not only to develop collaborative planned responses to the changes immediately affecting them, but they should plan to increase their potential for doing so over time.

The basic strategy of active adaptation in extended social fields is shown in Figure 18. Given a change in the environment (t_0), the most probable response by stakeholders is to change their behavior independently of one another in the pursuit of their various goals and objectives. In doing so, they help to produce a new environmental state that is more threatening than the initial change (t_1). If they recognize this, it is possible for them to collaborate in their responses to change with the intention of producing a future state favorable to attaining the goals of two or more stakeholders (t_2). In turn, it is possible to enlarge the basis of collaboration to coproduce desired future states by identifying still other stakeholders with whom the initial partners are potentially directively correlated (t_3). By such a process, it is possible for the field itself to be transformed into a social environ-

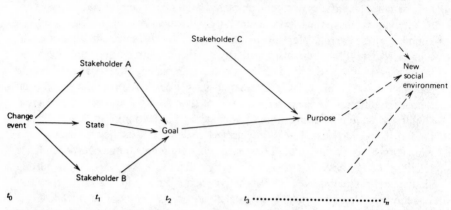

Figure 18. Strategy of active adaptation in extended social fields based on directive correlations and collaboration. As the set of directive correlations is increased, it is possible for the partners to pursue larger purposes than the goals attainable through a more limited set. By this process they can eventually transform the environment itself in pursuit of the ideals discussed in Chapter One.

ment that is more manageable and conducive to the survival and development of all (t_n).

How are interdependent stakeholders to accomplish this transformation of their shared environments? Since abstract knowledge of the requirements for active adaptation and empirical demonstration are not sufficient to move them in new directions, once more the answer is that they must learn to do it for themselves. New social designs are unlikely to work if they are imposed, and therefore a process of learning and planning is needed by which the stakeholders create the designs that are appropriate for active adaptive collaboration among them. Although, as discussed in Chapters 3 and 4, search conferences have been used to stimulate and guide active adaptation in single organizations, they can also provide the starting conditions for active adaptive learning and planning in extended social fields.

DESIGNING FOR PUBLIC LEARNING

The Search Conference in Active Adaptive Planning

Active adaptation in extended social fields entails, first, identifying potential domains linking interdependent stakeholders. Second, opportunities must be provided for them to inquire into the wider changes affecting them and to develop new collaborative strategies. Third, implementation of agreed-on strategies and continuous active adaptation at the domain level requires new structures. The purpose of the search conference is to provide a setting in which the process of planning and design can commence and develop.

Search Conference Purpose and Participation

Search conferences usually have brought together 30 to 40 individuals representing the range of interests in a geographical or functional domain, although
some recent conferences have involved approximately 100 participants. Search
conferences have been conducted over at least two continuous evenings and days.
The general purpose is to engage participants in exploring how wider change is affecting them all, developing shared images of a desirable future, examining present resources and constraints with respect to pursuing desired directions, and planning innovative strategies to enhance mutual prospects. Definition of the more
concrete task of each conference depends on the nature of the issues in question.
Table 5 indicates the range of planning tasks that have been undertaken through
search conferences.

The circumstances emerging in domains vary considerably. In Fremantle, for
example, it became apparent to the municipal authority that major inner urban re-
development was imminent. The main task of the search conference was to establish what kind of development would be desirable from the perspectives of the numerous stakeholders. Fort McMurray was going through a profound transition
from a small trading community to becoming the center of the Alberta oil sands region. Successive expansions had brought severe disruptions and given rise to social problems and conflicts. The search conference sought to identify the direc-

TABLE 5.
A Sample of Search Conference Tasks at the Domain Level

Domain	Search conference Task
Gungahlin	Value criteria for designing a new town
Geelong	Reduction of traffic congestion in a regional center linking a major city with tourist resorts
Fremantle	Future inner urban planning in a major port city
Department of Urban and Regional Development, Region 12	Future recreational planning requirements for 10 local government areas
Darling Ranges	Desirable futures for a physical region threatened by diverse, conflicting, and excessive uses
Fort McMurray (Canada)	The future development of community life in a rapidly expanding center for new resource indus-tries
The American Jail of the Future (USA)	National value criteria for guiding the future plan-ning of city and county jails
The New South Wales fruit-growing industry	The future of the industry in the region and the wider society

tions in which the people of Fort McMurray wanted it to develop as a place to live. Gungahlin was being planned as the fourth satellite town of Canberra in the Australian Capital Territory, and the task was to determine what attributes people would value as desirable in a new town. The Darling Ranges in Western Australia were threatened by a wide diversity of uses, and the varied and often conflicting needs of users made coordinated planning difficult. The search conference undertook the task of developing shared values among users concerning the future of the Ranges as a whole to provide a normative framework for planning.

The commitment to searching arises from a belief held by one or more stakeholders that change in the wider environment cannot be responded to adaptively through conventional structures and processes. In the Fremantle case the initiative was taken by the municipal authority on the advice of a consulting firm retained to develop proposals for inner urban planning. In Fort McMurray, traditional research and planning methods had produced a great deal of useful information, but this in itself did not provide adequate guidance about the ends planning should serve or the directions it should take. A planning officer of the Alberta Provincial Government became aware of the search conference as a participative planning methodology and discussed it with members of the Fort McMurray municipal administration, resulting in the decision to search. The sources of such initiatives vary as to the changes and crises that give rise to the need for active adaptation. In many cases, existing governmental authorities have been closely involved, either in taking the initiative themselves or in supporting participative planning through search conferences proposed by other stakeholder groups. The stimulus to engage in new collaborative inquiry and planning can come from anywhere in the domain, however.

Given this recognition by one or more stakeholders of the need for active adaptation through collaborative and participative planning, the next step is to determine the set of interdependent stakeholders comprising the domain and the participants who should be involved in the search conference. The participants may include voluntary organizations, employers, members of various age and sex groups, government officials, and so on. Established single organizations generally have relatively clearly defined purposes, boundaries, structures, and memberships whereas domains do not. The *domain* to start with may be no more than a vague concept referring to possible interdependences and opportunities to create new planning strategies and social designs. In some cases, domains can be defined fairly easily in terms that are valid and relevant from the perspectives of their members, but often the initial definition must be tentative and will be revised after subsequent experience. For example, in 1975 the Australian government sponsored a study of future recreational planning requirements in the municipalities that were considered to comprise a region. Search conferences were conducted in all the municipalities, and it became evident that only some had strong links. Others were weakly related, and each municipality had important interdependences with areas not included in the region as originally defined. As these realities emerged, the concept of the region underwent considerable redefinition.

Nevertheless, a start has to be made somewhere. Prior research and consultation can produce a tentative mapping of stakeholder groups that encompasses the probable range of perspectives on the planning issue or issues in question. From these groups, individuals should be sought who have demonstrated active concern for the future of their social environments rather than being active in promoting only their own interests. The stakeholder groups from which they are drawn should include perspectives that have no formal institutionalized expression as well as those that do. For example, in the recreational planning study, prior research by Glenn Watkins on a large national sample revealed conclusively that the great majority of Australians did not belong to formally organized groups for the purpose of recreation. Their involvement in recreational activity was casual and informal. Therefore, in the search conferences, it was important to incorporate their perspectives as well as drawing from the clubs and societies active and visible in organized recreation. Search conferences do not seek to be "representative" in the same sense that sample surveys do. They do seek interaction among many different views on planning issues because these views reflect the probable range of such views in the domain itself.

Similarly, search conferences are not intended to be vehicles for the political expression of personal or group interest in the manner of assemblies and public inquiries. When search conference participants come together, their purpose should be to discover new integrative strategies for pursuing interdependent ends. Search conference participants comprise a group engaged in explorations, learning, and planning on behalf of the entire domain. Without denying that conflicts of interest exist, the search conference is concerned with the common interests that stakeholders have in the future survival and development of the domain they all share. Participants should be invited on this basis; they should not be involved unless they agree to this basis for participation.

Search Conference Design

The emergence of trends affecting many different groups, the recognition by one or more stakeholders that these trends require new collaborative responses, the tentative definitions of the domain, and the selection of individuals who reflect a wide range of perspectives in the domain—all compose the essential background of a search conference at the domain level. Successful search conferences produce new shared understanding of change in the wider environment through interactive searching and learning, resulting in joint commitment to active adaptive strategies that enhance the prospects of the domain as a whole. The design of the search conference is important to achieving such outcomes. The underlying logic and structure of the conference task are the same as for single organizations. A typical task

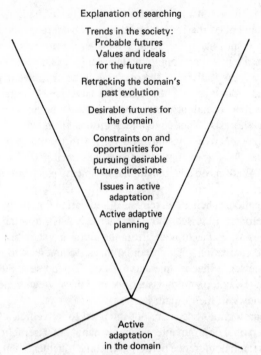

Figure 19.   Design of a search conference task at the domain level.

structure for a search conference at the domain level is shown in Figure 19. As with single organizations, the task of a domain search conference is designed around the logic of active adaptive inquiry, and the search conference is intended to provide a learning situation in which such inquiry can commence as well as enabling participants to learn the participative democratic alternative to bureaucracy through direct experience of the social organization and the processes of the search group.

Thus, the search conference begins with a brief explanation of conference objectives, the nature of searching, and the proposed stages that lead to the achievement of the objectives. This introduction leads directly into the first session where the focus is on trends in the society as a whole. Given that active adaptation in turbulent environments must be continuous and open-ended, the search conference initially seeks to identify shared values and ideals to guide future choices. Active adaptive values and ideals emphasize interdependence, cooperation, humanity, and the progressive enhancement of the social environment. Although ideals may be unattainable, they are endlessly approachable and therefore are fundamental points of reference of more limited goals, objectives, and purposes (see Chapter 1). Ideals are most likely to be expressed by search conference participants when they explore trends in the contextual environment that affect them all but are subject to no particular group's control. The further and more widely they search into their future, the more likely the participants are to express the hopes and fears shared by all. It is important that basic values and ideals be articulated at this stage to inform and guide choices of future directions during later stages of the search. The initial search into the wider environment also sets the pattern for the remainder of the conference. In introducing the session, conference managers should establish with the participants that the aim is to share ideas rather than debate them, that all contributions will receive equal recognition, and that there is room for everyone to contribute. The simple procedure of recording contributions on large sheets of paper and hanging them around the walls of the main room as the sheets are filled helps to confirm that there is room for all to participate, provides a sense of making progress toward the objectives, and allows conference managers to be perceived as resource people there to assist rather than to direct the conference activity.

Toward the end of the first session, the participants should reflect on the trends they have identified by evaluating them and becoming more conscious of their desires concerning the future. One way of creating this opportunity is for the participants to form smaller groups, placing positive or negative values on the trends in the wider environment detected by the conference during this session. An example of how the groups' task can be constructed is shown in Figure 20.

The groups should review the trends in the contextual environment as identified by the whole group. They then judge the trends from the extremes of good and improving through to bad and getting worse. From such an evaluation it should be-

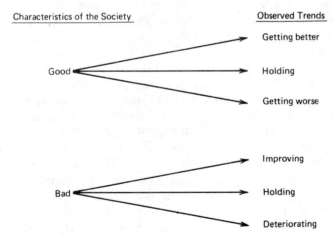

Figure 20. Framing the task of making value judgments about societal trends identified during the first session of a search conference.

come clear which values and ideals the participants hold with respect to the future. The first session of any search conference invariably concludes with the expression of shared values and ideals that do point to active adaptive rather than maladaptive future directions. This is not surprising because when individuals are asked to "dream" desirable futures at the level of the contextual environment, all but the most pathological will hope for the survival and development of the species as a whole. Moreover, they will recognize quite readily that desirable futures for themselves are inconceivable independently of this wider concern for the future of the world that they share with others. Hence, by the end of the first session on trends in the contextual environment, three things should already have been achieved. First, participants should have developed a shared understanding of what they think is happening in the contextual environment and how it affects them. Second, the session should have demonstrated the possibility of participative and collaborative planning among them. Third, the basic values and ideals to be served by their planned, collaborative actions should have emerged.

In the next session, attention turns to the evolution of the domain in question, asking what successive changes have brought the domain to its present state. The purpose is to develop shared awareness of the present structure and culture of the domain by reviewing previous developments. Out of the inquiry there should develop a general sense of both the service and disservice the domain's history can perform for its future. By retracking the domain's past, participants are better placed to identify what of that past should be retained, what should be done away with, and what is missing and must be created. When they have done so, they are in a position to relate the domain's evolution and present state to their basic ideals for the future. Invariably, there will be a mismatch. Turbulence in the contextual environment has thrown doubt on the future of the domain and its members. The past evolution of the domain is no sure or adequate guide for future planning.

Therefore, the third session is concerned with the directions the participants want the domain to take in the future. Given that their futures are directively correlated, the question is how they want those directive correlations to develop rather than leaving such development to chance. They now have two bodies of planning data—their judgments of trends in the contextual environment and ideals for the future of that environment and their assessment of their own domain in its present state. The task is to determine desirable future directions for the domain. These directions should be consistent with the values and ideals expressed about the future of the contextual environment in the first session. They usually are and for similar reasons. When allowed to search so widely, provided the participants can see and accept where they are supposed to be going with their learning and planning, they will identify desirable future directions that are desirable for all. Difficulties may arise later when it becomes apparent that seeking ideals entails the sacrifice of some short-term and short-sighted goals in order to create a new social environment conducive to the survival and development of all members of the domain. At this stage, the image of the domain's future is intended to be an idealized image consistent wth the participants' ideals with respect to the future in general.

Idealized images of domain futures provide overall direction for efforts at planned adaptation. In pursuing desired directions, however, domain members will encounter constraints. The task of the fourth session is to identify both the constraints that must be faced and the opportunities for active adaptation. Constraints may be owing to such factors as limited resources and the legacies of inadequate planning in the past. Existing relations between domain members are likely to be fragmented, entrenched interests may be in conflict, and present governmental structures and processes may present obstacles to pursuing desired directions through new initiatives. Conversely, in any domain there are factors that can increase the prospects for active adaptation. Resources can be shared and used in more creative and efficient ways. New collaborative relationships among domain members can be developed around mutual concerns. Efforts can be made to change the relationship of government to the domain—at least at the local level. By exploring existing constraints and potentialities in the domain and relating them to their desires for the future, participants develop a shared sense of purpose about the issues that warrant priority attention. They are asked to identify these issues as a prelude to selecting the most important ones for work in greater depth during subsequent sessions.

In deciding which issues are the most critical, the participants may be tempted to concern themselves with matters that are dominating their current debate about public policy. As Schon points out, however, by the time issues have gained currency in the public arena they have often already lost much of their salience. There is a time lag between the emergence of an issue and its widespread recognition as an important concern of public policy and planning (Schon, 1971). The attention of participants is better directed toward issues that are in the process of emerging. Figure 21 suggests that conference managers can help the participants to identify the issues likely to be important in the future in a way that challenges the participants to think about whether the critical issues are those that are already highly visible or those that are just emerging. Having made their judgments as to the increasing or declining salience of issues in their domain, the participants should then decide which issues to concentrate their efforts on in subsequent sessions. They can make their choice by marking on the already generated lists the three or so issues they would regard as the most important for them to do further work on during the remainder of the conference. Even when the lists of issues produced by the whole search groups are very long, participants making their own decisions about priorities usually tend to concentrate on only a few. In part, this occurs because various statements of issues refer to the same emergent phenomena. It also reflects, however, the participants' ability to discriminate between relatively peripheral concerns and those that are becoming of central importance.

Up to this stage, participants will have worked mainly as a whole group to es-

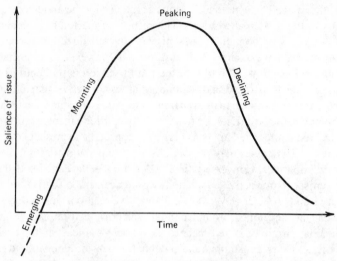

Figure 21. A framework for deciding priority issues in a search on the future of a domain.

tablish the value premises on which planned future strategies should be based. Now that they are clear about the major issues which they think should be addressed, it is appropriate for them to move into smaller groupings to explore the issues in depth and to develop proposals for active adaptation. Using the work done in the previous sessions as context, the task is to examine how wider trends are affecting particular issues, to evaluate current responses to those trends, and to produce new strategies that are more adaptive for pursuing desired directions. The small groups usually elect to concentrate on different issues and work in parallel. The structure of each group should be simple and should permit a wide sharing of leadership roles. Conference staff should remain available to all the groups but should avoid dominance–dependence relationships and the identification of individual staff with particular groups.

Toward the end of the search conference, the work of the small groups is presented and discussed in plenary. The two important questions are the adaptiveness of the aims and strategies they propose and the extent of support for the aims and strategies in the conference as a whole. Through periodic checking of the groups' progress, conference managers should have been able to ensure that they did not wander unchallenged into maladaptive paths. The extent of wider support for their proposals will depend on whether they have developed integrative strategies that promote the futures of the domain as a whole rather than pursuing narrower and conflicting interests. The structure and management of the search conference should have stimulated and supported learning that yields the wider understanding and commitment necessary for active adaptation. In a successful conference, participants will have worked through the logic of active adaptive inquiry and, given the participative democratic organization of the conference, developed relations of mutual concern and support based on new awareness of how their futures are directively correlated.

Search Conference Outcomes

Depending on the purpose for which the search conference is conducted, there are several outcomes. *First,* a report of the proceedings is prepared that should accurately convey the content and processes of the conference through its main stages. The report may be compiled by the conference staff in consultation with the participants or by the participants themselves. In many cases, the report is received by government bodies as a direct contribution to public policy and planning. In all cases the report should be made available to all stakeholders in the domain for their consideration. This leads to a *second* outcome—that search conference proposals invariably must be negotiated with domain members in order to gain broadly based support. The task of disseminating and discussing the proposals can be undertaken in a variety of ways. In one search conference on the future of a socioeconomically disadvantaged area, the participants decided that all interested groups should receive and discuss the report to test the adequacy and acceptability of the proposed planning directions. They took responsibility for contacting these groups and met again one month later to share the feedback they had obtained with one another and with representatives of local, state, and federal government. In Fort McMurray it was decided to make the final session of the conference open to all interested persons. In this session, participants not only reported on the work done by the groups, but they also explained to their fellow citizens the nature of searching as a means of participative planning. They proposed that a series of such conferences be conducted to involve increasing numbers of people in the community. *Third,* beyond obtaining wider commitment to search conference proposals, the participants should consider the further initiatives they can take in their own right. For example, in several of the 10 search conferences on future recreational planning requirements in Perth, referred to earlier, the participants decided to create new voluntary organizations linking the different stakeholders with one another and with local government. The purpose was to provide a mechanism for more effective communication, cooperation, and planning at the local level. Every search conference should close around this question because, whatever the other outcomes, there is always scope for participants to continue with the work they have commenced in the conference.

The Search Conference as a Design For Public Learning and Planning

The search conference has been developed in response to the emerging problem of active adaptation among interdependent stakeholders in extended social fields. At present, societies lack effective social designs and strategies for pursuing desirable future directions at this level. The independent promotion of self-interest by single stakeholders and reliance on bureaucratic government to regulate change and uncertainty affecting entire societies only increase the difficulty of developing new responses to influence future directions. Active adaptation in domains of interdependent stakeholders requires recognition of the directive correlations among them and collaboration to coproduce desired future states in the environments they share. Through its task structure, which follows the logic of active adaptation in turbulent environments, and its social organization, which embodies the design principle of participative democracy, the search conference provides an initial mechanism and conditions for new interactive learning and planning. Social designs for participative and collaborative planning at the domain level do not exist within the structures of bureaucratized industrial societies and therefore must be created. In Trist's terms, the search conference may be thought of as a temporary referent organization. Trist observes that referent organizations provide interactive settings for mutual planning, facilitate identification of domain boundaries and membership, act as a focus for establishing the ground rules of collaboration, stimulate the recognition of core values shared by domain members, and give support to information sharing and projects in the domain (Trist, 1979). Search conferences perform these functions but within a more explicit framework of ideals and values. They are designed to establish active adaptive ideals at the outset as the framework to which all subsequent planning and action can refer. We argued in Chapter 1 that consciously held ideals have the power to provide long-term direction by making it possible for more limited goals, objectives, and purposes to be evaluated according to whether they enhance the pursuit of ideals. When participants become collectively aware of the ideals and values on which their shared desires for the future are founded, collaboration should acquire deeper meaning and purpose than when participants are simply reacting to common external threats. Moreover, few widely legitimized bodies such as the Craigmillar Festival Society and the Jamestown Area Labor–Management Committee exist. The development of referent organizations that are able to cohere and mobilize diverse stakeholders in domains is extremely difficult. The search conference has the potential to increase the prospects for doing this by enabling representatives with many different perspectives to establish clear general agreement about their purpose in attempting to create new social designs and strategies for the future.

The search conference provides the starting conditions for learning and active adaptation at the domain level of societies. As with single organizations, designing for active adaptive learning among domain members has three essential dimensions: (1) framing the task in terms consistent with the logic of active adaptive inquiry, (2) creating and managing the opportunities for such inquiry, and (3) diffusing the learning experience and outcomes from the search conference so that progress can be made toward transforming the domain itself. Domain-based learning and active adaptation encounter difficulties similar to those that arise in the context of single organizations. The search conference confronts fundamental issues in the domain's future that are surrounded by increasing complexity and uncertainty. It is to be expected that at least some participants will draw back from the challenge of attempting to transform the conditions influencing their future prospects. They may remain obsessed with their own interests, indifferent to the circumstances and needs of others, and dependent on established bureaucracies to regulate their affairs. Search conference managers have the difficult task of helping participants to overcome these tendencies toward fight, flight, and dependence (cf. Bion, 1961). As the experiences reported in Chapter 4 demonstrate, the conference managers may not succeed in all cases. Similarly, there will be difficulties and obstacles involved in going beyond the search conference to achieve adaptive social redesign in the domain itself. These difficulties are compounded by the problem of defining the domain, the fragmentation of existing structures, and the dominating influence of interest group politics and government administration. The challenge is not only to transform existing structures but to activate new collaborative networks that must develop around referent organizations which often do not exist and must be created.

Despite such difficulties, search conferences increase the likelihood that the challenge of active adaptation at the domain level will be taken up by stakeholders and that initiatives toward developing new bases for participative and collaborative planning will emerge from the interactive learning process. At the very least, public policy and planning should be better informed about the futures desired by members of the domain and the strategies they are likely to support. Their desires for the future, their knowledge of the major planning issues in question, and their preferences for certain policies and planning strategies are based on deeper and broader understanding of change than is obtained, for example, by opinion surveys and public meetings. Surveys predetermine the items on which public opinion is to be sought. They focus respondents' attention on specific immediate issues. They present items as independent from one another. And individuals are able to respond only on the basis of their particular knowledge and perspectives at the time. Search conferences provide for important issues to be identified through participants' own inquiry. Commitment to specific choices is delayed until participants have developed appreciation of the wider changing environment in which such issues arise. Emphasis is on the interrelationships among issues. And participants have the opportunity to modify their views in the light of what they learn from one another. Public meetings do provide for some form of interaction between stakeholders, but again the focus is on immediate issues, and attention is directed mainly to confrontations between varied interests. Effort is devoted to winning support for particular viewpoints, and these meetings usually are dominated by the most aggressive, articulate, or politically skillful individuals and groups. Search conferences are designed on the premise that, although undoubtedly the interests of diverse stakeholders are varied and may be in conflict, single-minded pursuit of particular interests at the expense of others is self-defeating, given the trends toward increasing uncertainty that affect all members. Conflicts and differences over specific issues should be rationalized in the context of this wider understanding. Focusing immediately on particular issues and conflicts prevents learning and the discovery of alternative paths that can serve the long-term interests of all concerned. Search conferences are intended to stimulate creative thinking and planning around mutual concerns, leading to the joint pursuit of possibilities for active adaptation that previously had not been recognized or acted on. Public authorities generally appear to be disenchanted with traditional forms of "participative planning," such as opinion surveys and public meetings. This is not surprising because such processes accomplish little and may intensify existing conflicts. Search conferences, at the minimum, are likely to assist public authorities in identifying the common ground among various stakeholders and in alerting them to the future planning directions that would be widely supported because they increase the prospects for active adaptation.

However, search conferences have the potential for achieving more than this. They also increase the ability of stakeholders to reduce uncertainty and to pursue desired directions through their own pooled efforts. Participants at least become aware of the possibilities for assuming greater responsibility for managing their common affairs and taking new initiatives to promote their mutual well-being. Some participants will be prepared to continue beyond the conference by working to realize these possibilities in the domain itself. In many cases, search conferences have stimulated the development of new cooperative relationships among particular stakeholder groups, such as agreements to share resources and assist one another in various ways. The outcomes of some conferences have had more far-reaching effects, including the creation of new referent organizations and the development of ongoing planning efforts involving most or all of the domain members.

It should not be expected that all search conference participants will rise to the challenge of active adaptation or that any given domain will be transformed automatically as a consequence of searching. The search conference is only the beginning, but without the learning and discovery of new directions that it makes possible, societies will remain unable to manage change and reduce uncertainty at the domain level that is intermediate between single stakeholders and government. Craigmillar, Jamestown, and other ongoing attempts to develop new domain-based social designs provide encouraging demonstrations that active adaptation through participative democracy is feasible in extended social fields. Search conferences provide a means by which these kinds of initiatives can emerge and develop in domains that do not as yet possess referent organizations capable of cohering and mobilizing their members in the pursuit of agreed-on directions. They open up possibilities for new forms of cooperation among stakeholders and between them and government.

CONCLUSIONS

In turbulent environments, societies cannot achieve active adaptation through the redesign of single organizations alone. Neither are the traditional forms of government adequate. The policies and plans of governments are failing to deal effectively with issues that have become universally critical. Established political parties are losing credibility, as demonstrated by the vulnerability of their election candidates to the challenge of "single issue" groups and the upsurge of new parties. In many western countries, doubts about the future of existing representative systems already are emerging. New social designs are needed to enable interdependent stakeholders to participate and collaborate in developing strategies of active adaptation to the trends affecting their future prospects. The most appropriate unit of redesign appears to be the domain that is shared by organizations and groups, domains that are linked geographically and functionally. Initiatives such as Craigmillar and Jamestown provide examples of what can be achieved through domain-based collaboration, but the need for such designs and strategies emerged only recently. The familiar pattern of social organizations at the domain level has been that organizations and groups promote their own interests independently from, or in competition with, one another and that regulation has been imposed through government hierarchies. That system no longer works. Desired future states are more likely to be attained through the joint efforts of stakeholders to coproduce those states along the general lines depicted in Figure 18. Nevertheless, the most prevalent response has been for stakeholders and governments to persist with the old familiar pattern. As in single organizations, active adaptive innovations are resisted. Moreover, resistance is compounded because many stakeholders are likely to have difficulty in making the figure–ground reversal of perspectives that the act of transforming domains requires. Effective mechanisms for widespread participation and collaboration typically do not yet exist at the domain level.

The search conference is designed to provide the starting conditions for new learning and active adaptation in domains. It enables interdependent stakeholders to engage interactively in inquiry that produces new shared understanding of their environments and the trends affecting them. It enables them to identify the ideals and values that planned adaptation should serve and to develop cooperative strategies directed toward mutually desired future states. It also provides stakeholders with direct experience and knowledge of participative democratic social designs that can be used to develop more enduring bases for active adaptive planning in the domain itself. At the very least, search conferences produce knowledge and understanding that should enable public authorities to become better informed in their own planning efforts. They also, however, have the potential to enable domain members to move to a new level of shared responsibility for managing their own affairs and pursuing desirable future directions in a changing environment.

Although several hundred domain-based search conferences have been conducted to date, none has been traced through to the same extent as the organizational innovations reported in earlier chapters, with respect to their longer term consequences for learning and active adaptation. However, the continued survival and development of the Craigmillar initiative for more than 17 years and the achievements in Jamestown firmly establish the possibilities of ongoing active adaptation to reverse environmental threats such as economic decline and to enhance the future. Search conferences provide a means of stimulating active adaptation in many more domains. Not all will succeed, and the transformation of domains through participative redesign is a long and difficult process. They offer a viable alternative, however, to the maladaptive preoccupation with competitive self-interest and reliance on governmental control, which is taking societies deeper into uncontrollable turbulence.

If societies can move in these directions, they will gradually transform themselves into learning democracies. Instead of interfering more and more in the affairs of their constituents, governments will concentrate on providing overall national guidance, performing international and national functions that can be carried out only at governmental levels and providing resources when necessary to assist local domains in their efforts to create desirable futures for themselves. Governance will be shared on a very different basis from what it is today. With all the resources at their disposal, there are many things governments cannot do for people but that people are capable for doing for themselves. At present, societies are encumbered with ineffective governmental bureaucracies and are over-governed. They lack social designs through which people can contribute local initiative and leadership for managing the trends affecting their future. The search conference is such a design, and experiences with searching have provided the elementary foundations for a vision of a learning democracy as a future societal alternative.

Conclusions

Western societies are moving progressively deeper into turbulent transition. Mounting uncertainty about the future cannot be reduced through the structures and strategies of bureaucratic industrialism. Active adaptation to turbulence requires fundamental change in the dominant values and ideals, frameworks of understanding, and social designs of those societies. A basic alternative has been revealed in the form of participative democracy. If the social designs of western societies can be democratized, the prospects of acting in concert on wider change forces to influence future directions would be greatly enhanced. Thus, societies have a choice of futures, but the choice in favor of participative democracy is so fundamental that it will not be made easily, if at all. Certainly, experiences with resistance to many of the active adaptive innovations that have been initiated already (such as efforts to democratize work) suggest that the choice cannot be made *for* the people who would have to live with the consequences of that choice. It must be made *by* them, but they are unlikely to choose effectively within the confines of firmly established bureaucratic patterns and their prolonged experience of those patterns. Therefore, it has become necessary to create the conditions in which societies have opportunities to inquire into the trends affecting their futures, to question existing social designs and strategies, to identify desirable alternatives, and to plan to pursue those alternatives. Learning in industrial society has been bureaucratized, yet learning is central to active adaptation. The challenge of democratizing societies begins with democratizing learning.

Confronted with unprecedented turbulence in their social environments, human beings must recognize the radically different conditions affecting their prospects for survival and development. They must then proceed from that understanding, or at least awareness, to attempt to create the next age in their images of the desirable. Redesigning societies and their constituent organizations and communities entails new and continuous learning. There is a direct relationship between learning and participative democracy. A learning society must be a learning democracy. Without participative democratic social designs the new learning on which active adaptation depends cannot occur, and unless societies' members are actively involved in learning to manage their futures there can be no participative democracy.

The attempts at redesigning organizations and more extended social systems through the learning of their members reported in the foregoing chapters have been concerned with enabling people to gain both new understanding of their changing environments and personal experience of participative democracy. It is essential that this same learning process take place in education so that today's youth can enter adult life prepared for participation in making a new society beyond the industrial era. In the case of organizations, their members need to move outside the existing organizational settings to explore the possibilities for active adaptation through social redesign in learning environments such as those provided by the Telecom workshops. This is also necessary when the issues in question affect many different stakeholders whose future prospects are linked because they share a common domain. Because domains typically lack a mechanism of social design through which participative-collaborative learning and planning can occur, temporary designs such as the search conference are needed to stimulate joint active adaptation at the domain level. Democratized educational design can foster the development of individuals who are capable of learning and active adaptation in turbulent environments. In organizations and more extended social fields, designs for active adaptive learning increase the prospect that successful social redesign of work and community life will follow.

There is no shortage of knowledge about desirable alternatives to the present social designs and strategies of societies. The greatest task is to create them. Creation can be accomplished only by ordinary people in their ordinary yet threatened life circumstances. Planners, scientists, intellectuals, and others with specialized and more esoteric knowledge and skills can help, but people must make their own futures. The foregoing accounts of experience with designing for active adaptive learning are offered as demonstrations that, however difficult the undertaking, societies' members can learn to create, sustain, and adapt social designs that give them greater hope for desirable futures. If societies continue in their present directions, the 1980s and 1990s seem almost certain to be decades of crisis and conflict, with the probability of economic collapse and social and political upheaval looming ever larger. People clearly do not want this to happen, and there are desirable alternatives they are likely to choose if given the opportunity. Such opportunity is not provided by bureaucratic systems of education, production and government. It is present when people are allowed to discover and act on their human potential for learning and active adaptation.

F. E. Emery

Afterword

This Afterword is not my way of having the last word. It is simply the continuation of the countless exchanges of thought about these matters that began before Trevor Williams embarked on this remarkable series of adventures. I do not imagine that the series is ended, but it is timely to see where we are being led by his findings. It is his hope that I may be able to stand a little further back and take a broader view than he can at this point.

In an eminently practical and constructive way Williams has delved into the complex relation of democracy and education. It would appear that whenever industrial society is in one of its recurrent periods of economic downturn and social turmoil, as in the 1970s, the relationship of education and democracy becomes a leading question. Thus in the birthpangs of industrial civilisation Jean Jacques Rousseau gave us *Emile,* a plea for the humanization of education that would enable us to return to a true democracy based on peasant economy. Moved by the terrible years of the 1830s and the hungry 1840s John Stuart Mill again asserted the intimate interdependence of education and democracy, that participative democracy required an educated citizenery but that the requisite education could be gained only by participating in the governance of one's own affairs. Out of the Great Depression of the 1880s and the 1890s came Dewey with New Education, an education that was not to be simply a preparation for subsequent life in a democratic society but an apprenticeship in democratic living. In the economic, social, *and* political turmoil following World War I, G. D. H. Cole revived the broader emphases of Rousseau and Mill. The common core of these repeated attempts to introduce an alternative to the ruling paradigm of representative democracy has been identified by Carole Pateman (1970):

The major function of participation in the theory of participative democracy is therefore an educative one, educative in the very widest sense, including

195

both the psychological aspect and the gaining of practice in democratic skills and procedures. Thus there is no special problem about the stability of a participatory system; it is self-sustaining through the educative impact of the participatory process. (p. 42)

It is not surprising that this theme should arise in democratic societies when people's expectations have been crushed by economic disasters or world wars. Our faith in democratic forms of government is premised on the belief that the people know enough to contribute to their own governance. When the process of governance is failing to cope with economic and social change, there will be those who see this as proof that we must go back to rule by the few. There will be others, like Dewey, Cole, and Williams, who argue that what is called for are radical improvements in the ways in which people can know better what they want and have better ways of transforming that knowledge into control over their own affairs.

These are the two sides of the same penny. By the middle of the nineteenth century it was clear to Mill that more education would not be transformed into more control in a *representative* democracy. The relevant education could be gained only by directly participating in formulating and making the decisions by which one is to be governed. This can be made to seem a ridiculous proposition by proposing such a question as "How can the *vox populi* meaningfully participate in deciding between defense expenditure on supersonic interceptor aircraft or aircraft carriers?"

In the tradition of Dewey and Cole, Williams has directed his efforts to the prior and more fundamental question for our times: "How do we stop creating dumb oxen, of even our middle management, and create a general confidence in an ability to learn from personal experience?" If there is such a general ability and if people become confident in their possession of this ability, we can safely leave to the future the question of whether they can meaningfully participate in esoteric decisions about defense equipment. [Advances toward ways of participating in the higher order social decisions have already been made (Beer, in Emery, 1981)].

In keeping with the relatively nonideological character of our times, Williams has concentrated on the pragmatics (not the idea of pragmatism) to show what can be done in practice. As he ranges across the individual, organizational, and community levels on two continents, it must become obvious that the notion of "learning to learn" is central to any attempt to revitalize democracy.

Williams has clearly spelled out the further implication that the revitalization of democracy must entail debureaucratization of our administrative structures, both public and private. Beyond this he has stressed the need for a social change strategy that is very different from the top-down expert demonstrations that I was recommending in the hostile, unbelieving social climate of the early 1960s. I agree with this. It does in fact seem that the problem of debureaucratizing our societies is so huge that it can be accomplished only by a people who are confident in the validity of their own experiences. The prevailing lack of faith in the experts is matched only by the lack of faith in elected representatives. But at this point there is a very big BUT. By providing the forgoing account of his experiences with democratizing work situations, management education, and university education, Williams has disclosed in the strongest form I have yet encountered a persistent, and in the long run prevailing, lack in people of faith in the validity of their own experience.

Throughout his experiments Wiliams has dutifully noted the university students, managers, and others who responded negatively to the learning opportunities with which they were presented. Among the managers were those who were upset because there was not enough structured exposure to and drilling in the existent body of management theory. As far as I can gather, that criticism has not decreased since the end of the last series of workshops that are reported here. Neither has the success of the university experiments over many years brought about any decline in criticisms.

This phenomenon is common. For a great many years I thought it was probably a manifestation of what Erich Fromm termed "the fear of freedom"—something that was learned from growing up in an authoritarian climate and hence would be unlearned with the experience of successfully managing one's own activities. For the latter learning to take place we needed, I thought, only for the strong to carry the weak through the initial learning phase. From the time we did the follow-up study at the Hunsfoss Pulp and Paper Mill, I was uneasy and could not regard this hypothesis as other than just the best we had at the time. That follow-up indicated that some of the opposition to the democratization of the work was coming from very competent *workers* who dismissed the evidence of their eyes and insisted that the improved performance of their more lowly colleagues was a consequence of their increased motivation and had nothing to do with their brains. As far as they were concerned, it was only a matter of time before the Hunsfoss plant would have to recognize the intellectual incompetence of its workers and promote *them* to the level of foreman.

The work that Williams has done has brought us to where we are going beyond the point of simply challenging a traditional paradigm of organization. We effectively won that challenge by proving over and over again that better work could be done by groups that deposed first-line supervisors and managed their own productive activities. The role of the expert was relatively untouched by these developments. It seemed that self-managing groups of workers were as dependent on the experts as were the foremen. To go any further in the direction of self-management of one's own affairs, it has become necessary to ask why the knowledge of the experts is thought to be so much more valuable than the knowledge that the workers themselves bring to their task.

When managers are given a chance to learn from their own experience and complain that they have thereby been deprived of real learning, we have to reckon that we are up against something more than the paradigms of organization. I hesitate to suggest that we are brought up against a more fundamental paradigm than that which is challenged by the democratization of work. Nevertheless, I am inclined to think that we are.

It seemed that we were getting to the fundamentals when Douglas MacGregor proposed his Theory X and Theory Y. Over the following years there was much dispute about whether Theory Y could be achieved through individual job enrichment or autonomous work groups. That dispute has been more or less settled. We are still landed with the Williams problem: distrust of the expert but no way out of dependency on those experts.

This dilemma cannot be cracked unless we go beyond the challenge of the organizational paradigm to challenge the educational paradigm. It is education that sifts out and trains the expert.

It is not possible to challenge the prevailing educational paradigm by challenging the autocratic forms of delivering education. The problem is deeper than that. The only challenge that could possibly unseat the traditional paradigm of education is one that challenges the epistemology it takes for granted (Emery, 1981).

All of the education that results in a certificate of learning, in either the capitalist or Soviet world, is designed to overcome the "fact" that all human beings are basically incompetent to learn from any learning situation. They are basically incompetent, so these theories of education say, because they do not possess the sensory organisms that would be needed to extract information from those potential learning situations. It seems strange that the species that is the peak achievement of adaptive survival should be found to be fundamentally incompetent in learning about its environment. Strange, but that is precisely what was established by the British empiricists, Locke, Berkeley, and Hume. Kant did not refute this case but established that we gained less from direct personal experience than even *they* allowed. These gentlemen established the unchallengeable proposition that in the world described by Newton and Euclid, personal experience was limited to a kaleidoscopic inflow of sensations. In this inflow, they said, there is no direct evidence of the primary qualities of the things and events out there; no sensation can be seen to be determining any other; no ordering of sensations in space or time is directly perceivable. We can only infer these features from the shaky evidence of past associations.

Confronting this magisterial judgment was the fact that despite this formidable natural barrier mankind had attained such peaks of knowledge as those represented by Newton, Euclid, Copernicus, Aristotle, and Aquinas. Much of this was the inexplicable product of genius, but there was also the long cumulative development of Aristotelean logic and the massive upsurge of the sciences in the seventeenth century. This latter experience suggested how man might deliberately plan to advance knowledge. The weak, partial, and fallible experience of the individual might be surpassed by a collective process of recording and accumulating observations, by sifting, comparing, and classifying individual perceptions to yield concepts and hierarchies of conceptual structures, by purifying these by analysis, scholarly judgement, and the testing of logical implications. This was the work of committed scholars and scientists and only those who were suitably trained and certified had access to the bodies of specialized knowledge that were thus accumulated. Notice that "true kowledge" existed only in these accumulated stocks. Even the contributions of genius were unacceptable unless they could be seen as additions to those stocks. This knowledge was *not* an accumulation of common sense, aphorisms, and folk sayings but was in actively hostile competition with them.

From these insights Herbart created the bases for all modern education. He showed that by controlled exposure, assiduous drilling, and carefully planned exercises, associations could be formed in the mind of a pupil that would approximate parts of the conceptual structures established by scholarship. A so-called science of pedagogy was born to meet the emergency needs of industrial societies for mass education. The same principles carried over into the twentieth century expansion of secondary and tertiary education, training within industry, adult education and management education. New audiovisual technologies were assimilated to the old paradigm that had produced the class room, curricula, textbooks, chalk and talk, stick and carrot, and certificates of implantation.

When Einstein demonstrated that the universe was not in accord with the world of Newton and Euclid, people such as Dewey and A. N. Whitehead began to question whether human experience was as barren and fallible as deduced by the "Empiricists." These attacks on the dominant educational paradigm foundered on the demonstration that although Einstein had conquered the universe, the world of everyday objects and events to all intents and purposes still belonged to Newton and Euclid. Civil engineers and architects did not have to develop an Einsteinian mechanics, dynamics, or statics. The strong international movement for learning from experience (the New Education Fellowship) shrank into the box containing the only experience allowable as information in the Lockean paradigm—experience of one's own sensations and feelings as evidence of *subjective* states and changes. As embodied in recent fads for "experiential learning" and T-grouping, they constitute no challenge to the traditional educational program. Managers exposed to experiential learning are thereby no less in need of chalk and talk about well-established conceptual models of the *objective* world.

What Newton and Euclid set up, Heider and Gibson (1930-1980) have now knocked down (Emery, 1981). They have succeeded in demonstrating that although the space–time of activity may be Euclidean, the space–time of perception, and hence cognition, is *non*-Euclidean.

Veritable mountains of scientific data have been accumulated on how organisms perceive in a Euclidean world. The data have done no more than perplex us further as to how organisms ever managed to learn, adapt, and hence survive. By dropping the assumption of a Euclidian world, Heider and Gibson have been able to show that human beings are marvelously well adapted to learn from their individual experiences of the real non-Euclidean world. The world for each newborn member of the species is no "buzzing booming confusion" but a world for which they are predesigned by the successful evolution of their species to extract survival-relevant information. And this they in fact do, whether it is for finding the teat, avoiding cliffs when they start to crawl, or picking up the native tongue of their parents. By the same token, they are at a loss when confronted by technological extensions of the senses (e.g., TV) that are based on the assumption that the perceptual systems have evolved to cope with a Euclidean world. (Emery & Emery, 1980; Emery 1980).

With these findings the arguments of the Empiricists and Kant are demolished. This might seem to be a matter of concern only for epistemologists. Far from it. These findings have destroyed the hitherto unchallengeable justification for the traditional educational paradigm. That paradigm is now intellectually bankrupt and logically indefensible. This is "checkmate"; not Dewey's call of "mate."

These discoveries confront us with a revolution of knowledge with implications that far surpass those of the information revolution of the microprocessor. They challenge the very roots of western literate civilization, as epitomized in Plato's parable of the Cave. In particular, and of concern to us here, these discoveries transform our traditional notion of expertise. In the traditional paradigm the true expert could only be one who had undertaken the years of study necessary to absorb knowledge from the accumulated stock of his discipline. Anyone else who claimed such knowledge was a charlatan or, remotely possible, a genius.

Within the new paradigm everyone is expert to some degree from the moment their experiences allow them some direct perception of the invariants in the environment with which they were interacting. They would be less expert to the degree that they had been trained to look only at the "facts" (*not* their interrelatedness) and to the extent that they were inexperienced. *In this paradigm knowledge emerges as the individual perceives the world.* When two individuals share and reconcile their perceptions of the world, the process of accumulating social wisdom has already begun. In the old paradigm these two individuals could not be held to make any contribution to the knowledge unless they had both made reports about matters of fact that they had not consulted about to a trained enquirer. Even then such observations do not necessarily constitute a contribution to knowledge; they are only raw material. Only when they have been literally taken away and processed by a knowledge factory would we know whether they were "added value."

This contrast is brought into focus by the concept of a "search conference." I designed this kind of learning setting because, having left school at fourteen years of age, I could not deny the authority by which men extracted lumber from forests, coal from mines, and wheat from fields (and woman extracted meals from ovens) with no more than their perceptions and their shared experiences to go by. Even so I would not have ventured on this course without the moral support of such outstanding intellectual contemporaries as Heider, Asch, and Chein. They asserted with considerable intellectual force that if something was wrong it was in our basic assumptions about human nature—not in the obvious ability of individuals to learn, and learn to learn, from one another. I was more than pleased by the outcomes of the search conferences we conducted in the late 1950s and the early 1960s. With the revival of the concept of the search conference in Australia, Norway, and the United States in the 1970s, there was a backlash. The backlash was straight from the old educational paradigm, and it charged that "The search conferences were so designed that they excluded, or at least played down, the role of the expert. The participants were thereby restricted to playing around with unprocessed facts. Given the illusion that they were engaged in accummulating knowledge, they were in fact exposed to manipulation by conference managers who had equipped themselves beforehand with the processed facts."

Once the Heider–Gibson discoveries are understood, the search conference is a natural extension of the individual's power to explore and perceive how the world about him is structured and functioning. The real expert is then the one who has openly and widely experienced that particular world. The certified expert of the old educational paradigm will be one who has that world, and his knowledge of it, classified into compartments and organized around issues that serve the aggrandizement of his discipline, not such mundane purposes as living in the particular world with which a search conference is concerned. The certificates of this expert are not worth the paper on which they are written when people realize that they themselves are knowledgeable.

For more than 2000 years western civilization has been haunted by Plato's description of the ordinary human state of knowledge as being that of observing shadows in a cave. This picture of the human lot was profoundly reinforced by Locke and others in the birth stage of industrial civilization. As peasant people were forced into wage-slavery to power the industrial revolution, they pressed for democratic forms of government, if only to control the limits of their exploitation and their expected span of life. They managed to achieve the vote and representative forms of democracy. They were then led to believe that the shortcomings of representative democracy would be overcome when scholarships and free tertiary education enabled their sons and daughters to qualify as experts. This goal also was achieved. At this point, historically, we came to the point that Williams discovered in his studies: Education is itself the major block to further democratization of society. I do not think that John Stuart Mill, Dewey, or Cole could have conceived of such a fiendish contratemps in the affairs of people. I do not think that they could have predicted for one moment that educational institutions in the 1980s, could have taken over the role of the church in Aquinas' century, the thirteenth century.

What Williams reports is not a replay of history, a recycling of elites. Institutionalized education has lost its sole authority to certify experts—there are other ways to do that. Accepting that people can learn about the world "out there" from their individual perceptions, we can no longer find any contradiction between democracy and education.

The Japanese found that the presence of certified experts stymied the constructive work of their Quality Control Circles. In like manner so we will have to recognize the mind-deadening and confidence-eroding role that is still being played by the expert teachers supposedly preparing us for democratized work and life. This recognition should be possible now that we can clearly identify the assumptions that legitimated their past role.

References

Beer, Stafford "On heaping our sciences together." In F. E. Emery, Ed., *Systems thinking*, Vol. 2. London: Penguin, 1981.

Emery, F. E. "Adaptive systems for our future governance." In F. E. Emery, Ed. *Systems thinking*, Vol. 2. London: Penguin, 1981.

Emery, F. E. "Communications for a sustainable society, Year 2000." *Human Futures*, **3**, 1980, 202-8 (New Delhi).

Emery, F. E. "Educational paradigms." *Human Futures*, **4**, 1981, 3-20 (New Delhi).

Emery, M. and Emery, F. E. "A vacuous vision: The TV medium." *J. of the University Film Association*, **32**, 1980. 27-31.

Pateman, C. *Participation and democratic theory*. Cambridge: The University Press, 1970.

References

Ackoff, R. L. *Redesigning the future*. New York: Wiley, 1974.

Ackoff, R. L. and Emery, F. E. *On purposeful systems*. Chicago: Aldine Atherton, 1972.

Argyris C. and Schon, D. A. *Theory in practice*. Reading, MA Addison-Wesley, 1974.

Argyris, C. and Schon, D. A. *Organizational learning*. Reading, MA; Addison-Wesley, 1978.

Bell, D. *The coming of the postindustrial society*. Middlesex: Penguin, 1973.

Berry, D. F., Metcalfe, J. L., and McQuillan, W. F. "Neddy": An organizational metamorphosis. *Journal of management studies*, February 1974.

Bion, W. R. *Experiences in groups*. London: Tavistock, 1961.

Burns, T. and Stalker, G. S. *Management of innovation*. London: Tavistock, 1961.

Clarke, A. W., Ed. *Experimenting with organizational life*. New York: Plenum, 1976.

Craigmillar Festival Society. *People in partnership*. Craigmillar, 1978.

Crombie, A. *Postindustrialism and the world of work*. Canberra: Australian National University Center for Continuing Education, 1976.

Cummings, T. G. and Srivastva, S. *Management of work*. Kent, OH: Kent State University Press, 1977.

Davis, L. E. and Cherns, A. B. (eds.) *The quality of working life*. New York: Free Press, 1975.

Davis, L. E. and Taylor, J. C. (eds.) *Design of jobs*. Middlesex: Penguin, 1972.

Derber, M. Crosscurrents in workers' participation. *Industrial relations*, 1970, 9.

Emery, F. E. Adaptive systems for our future governance. *National labor institute bulletin*, 1976, 4.

Emery, F. E. *Futures we are in*. Leiden: Nijoff, 1977.

Emery, F. E. *Limits to choice*. Canberra: Australian National University Center for Continuing Education, 1978.

Emery, F. E. and Emery, M. Guts and guidelines for raising the quality of working life. In D. Gunzberg, Ed. *Bringing work to life*. Melbourne: Cheshire, 1975.

Emery, F. E. and Thorsrud, E. *Form and content in industrial democracy*. London: Tavistock, 1969.

Emery, F. E. and Thorsrud, E. *Democracy at work*. Leiden: Nijoff, 1976.

Emery, F. E. and Trist, E. L. *Towards a social ecology*. New York: Plenum, 1973.

Emery, M. *Searching: For new directions, in new ways, for new times*. Canberra: Australian National University Center for Continuing Education, 1976.

Emshoff, J. R. The Busch center: An organization designed to insure quality academic research on real world problems. *Interfaces,* 1977, 7.

Faure, E. *Learning to be.* Paris: UNESCO, 1972.

Friedman, J. *Retracking America.* New York: Anchor, 1973.

Hartman, G. W. The field theory of learning and its educational consequences. *National society for the study of education, forty-first yearbook, part 2,* 1942.

Hays, S. P. *The response to industrialism.* Chicago: University of Chicago Press, 1957.

Heller, F. A. Decision processes: An analysis of power sharing at senior organizational levels. In R. Dubin, Ed. *Handbook of work, organization and society.* Chicago: Rand McNally, 1976.

Herbst, P. G. *Sociotechnical design.* London: Tavistock, 1974.

Herbst, P. G. *Alternatives to hierarchies.* Leiden: Nijoff, 1976.

Hill, P. *Towards a new philosophy of management.* London: Gower, 1972.

Holly, D. *Beyond curriculum.* St. Albans: Paladin, 1974.

Hull, D. *Technology, change and democracy.* Industrial democracy papers 18. Adelaide: South Australian Government Department of Labor and Industry, 1980.

Husen, T. *The learning society.* London: Methuen, 1974.

Illich, I. *De-schooling society.* New York: Harper & Row, 1971.

Jamestown Area Labor–Management Committee. *Commitment at work.* Jamestown: 1977.

Jamieson, D. W. and Thomas, K. W. Power and conflict in the student–teacher relationship. *Journal of applied behavioral science,* 1974, 10.

Jenkins, D. *Job power.* Middlesex: Penguin, 1974.

Kingdon, D. R. *Matrix organization.* London: Tavistock, 1973.

Lewin, K. Field theory of learning. *National society for the study of education forty-first yearbook, part 2,* 1942.

Lewin, K. *Field theory in social science.* New York: Harper, 1951.

Likert, R. *The human organization.* New York: McGraw-Hill, 1967.

Lindblom, C. E. The science of muddling through. *Public Administration Review,* 1959, 19.

Lindstad, H. and Kvist, A. *The Volkswagen report.* Stockholm: Swedish Employers' Confederation, 1975.

Lindholm, R. and Norstedt, J. P. *The Volvo report.* Stockholm: Swedish Employers' Confederation, 1975.

Lorsch, J. W. and Lawrence, P. R. *Studies in organization design.* Homewood, IL: Richard D. Irwin, 1970.

Macoby, M. *The gamesman.* New York: Simon & Schuster, 1976.

Metcalfe, J. L. and McQuillan, W. F. *Managing turbulence: A design for economic development.* Berlin: Conference on interorganizational networks and public policy, June 1975.

Michael, D. N. *On learning to plan and planning to learn.* San Francisco: Jossey-Bass, 1973.

Miller, E. J. Technology, territory and time: The internal differentiation of production systems. *Human relations.* 1959. 12.

Noren, A. E. and Norstedt, J. P. *The Orrefors report.* Stockholm: Swedish Employers' Confederation, 1975.

Nokes, P. *The professional task in welfare practice.* London: Routledge & Kegan Paul, 1967.

Norstedt, J. P. and Aguren, S. *The Saab Scania report.* Stockholm: Swedish Employers' Confederation, 1973.

O'Toole, J. *Work in America*. Cambridge MA: MIT Press, 1973.

Ozbekhan, H. Planning and human action. In P. A. Weiss, ed., *Hierarchically organized systems in theory and practice*. New York: Hafner, 1971.

Paskow, A. Are college students educable? *Journal of Higher Education*, 1974, xlv.

Pellegrin, R. J. Schools as work settings. In R. Dubin, ed., *Handbook of work, organization and society*. Chicago, Rand McNally, 1976.

Piaget, J. *To understand is to invent*. Middlesex: Penguin, 1976.

Reimer, E. *School is dead*. Middlesex: Penguin, 1971.

Robertson, J. *The sane alternative*. London: James Robertson, 1978.

Schon, D. A. *Beyond the stable state*. London: Temple Smith, 1971.

Schutz, A. *Collected works*. Leiden: Nijoff, 1964.

Selznick, P. *Leadership in administration*. Evanston, IL: Row Peterson, 1957.

Slater, P. *The pursuit of loneliness*. Boston: Beacon, 1970.

Somerhoff, G. The abstract characteristics of living systems. In F. E. Emery, ed. *Systems thinking*. Middlesex: Penguin, 1969.

Susman, G. I. *Autonomy at work*. New York: Praeger, 1976.

Thomas, J. E. *The English prison officer since 1750: A study in conflict*. London: Routldge & Kegan Paul, 1972.

Thomas, J. E. and Williams, T. A. Change and conflict in the evolution of prison systems. *International Journal of Criminology and Penology*, 1977, 5.

Thompson, J. D. *Organizations in action*. New York: McGraw-Hill, 1967.

Thompson, W. I. *Passages about earth*. New York: Harper & Row, 1973.

Tocher, K. D. Planning systems. *Philosophical Transactions of the Royal Society*. 1977, 287.

Torner, P. *The Matfors report*. Stockholm: Swedish Employers' Confederation, 1975.

Trist, E. L., A concept of organizational ecology. *Australian Journal of Management*, 1977, 2.

Trist, E. L. *A new approach to economic development: An American experience*. Tavistock Institute for Operational Research, Linkage three, July 1978. (a)

Trist, E. L. *The environment and system response capability*. Aachen: First European forum on organization development, October 1978. (b)

Trist, E. L. *New directions of hope*. Glasgow: University of Glasgow, John Madge Memorial lecture, October 1978. (c)

Trist, E. L. *Employment alternatives for the eighties*. Toronto: Urban seminar six, November 1978. (d)

Trist, E. L., *A new approach to economic development: An American experience*. Tavistock Institute for Operational Research, Linkage three, July 1978. (a)

Trist, E. L. and Burgess, S. *Multiple deprivation: A human and economic approach*. Tavistock Institute for Operational Research, Linkage three, 1978.

Trist, E. L. *Referent organizations and the development of interorganizational domains*. Distinguished address to the Academy of Management annual meeting. Atlanta: August 1979.

Vickers, G. *The art of judgment*. London: Chapman and Hall, 1965.

Vickers, G. *Making institutions work*. New York: Halstead, 1973.

Wall, T. D. and Lischeron, J. A. *Worker participation*. London: McGraw-Hill, 1977.

Walton, R. E. How to counter alienation in the plant. *Harvard Business Review*, November-December 1972.

Walton, R. E. Innovative restructuring of work organization: Explaining why diffusion didn't take. In P. Mirvis and D. Berg, eds., *Failures in organization development and change*. New York: Wiley, 1977.

Weick, K. E. Educational organizations as loosely coupled systems. *Administrative science quarterly*, 1976, 21.

Williams, T. A. The search conference in active adaptive planning. *Journal of applied behavioral science*, 1979, 15.

Woodward, J. *Industrial organization: theory and practice*. London: Oxford University Press, 1965.

Author Index

207

Subject Index